S0-AKF-486

DENNIS HOPELESS
SERG ACUÑA
KENDALL GOODE
DOUG GARBARK

ROSS RICHIE CEO & Founder
JOY HUFFMAN CFO
MATT GAGNON Editor-in-Chief
FILIP SABLIK President, Publishing & Marketing
STEPHEN CHRISTY President, Development
LANCE KREITER Vice President, Licensing & Merchandising
ARUNE SINGH Vice President, Marketing
BRYCE CARLSON Vice President, Editorial & Creative Strategy
SCOTT NEWMAN Manager, Production Design
KATE HENNING Manager, Operations
SPENCER SIMPSON Manager, Sales
SIERRA HAHN Executive Editor
JEANINE SCHAEFER Executive Editor
DAFNA PLEBAN Senior Editor
SHANNON WATTERS Senior Editor
ERIC HARBURN Senior Editor
CHRIS ROSA Editor
MATTHEW LEVINE Editor
SOPHIE PHILIPS-ROBERTS Associate Editor
GAVIN GRONENTHAL Assistant Editor
MICHAEL MOCCIO Assistant Editor
GWEN WALLER Assistant Editor
AMANDA LaFRANCO Executive Assistant
JILLIAN CRAB Design Coordinator
MICHELLE ANKLEY Design Coordinator
KARA LEOPARD Production Designer
MARIE KRUPINA Production Designer
GRACE PARK Production Designer
CHELSEA ROBERTS Production Design Assistant
SAMANTHA KNAPP Production Design Assistant
JOSÉ MEZA Live Events Lead
STEPHANIE HOCUTT Digital Marketing Lead
ESTHER KIM Marketing Coordinator
CAT O'GRADY Digital Marketing Coordinator
AMANDA LAWSON Marketing Assistant
HOLLY AITCHISON Digital Sales Coordinator
MORGAN PERRY Retail Sales Coordinator
MEGAN CHRISTOPHER Operations Coordinator
RODRIGO HERNANDEZ Mailroom Assistant
ZIPPORAH SMITH Operations Assistant
BREANNA SARPY Executive Assistant

BOOM! STUDIOS   WWE   WWE BOOKS

Relive
Explore
Adventure
Discover

WWE Volume Six, July 2019. Published by BOOM! Studios, a division of Boom Entertainment, Inc. WWE is ™ & © 2019 WWE. All WWE programming, talent names, images, likenesses, slogans, wrestling moves, trademarks, logos and copyrights are the exclusive property of WWE and its subsidiaries. All other trademarks, logos and copyrights are the property of their respective owners. © 2019 WWE. All rights reserved. Originally published in single magazine form as WWE #21-25. ™ & © 2018, 2019 WWE. All rights reserved. BOOM! Studios™ and the BOOM! Studios logo are trademarks of Boom Entertainment, Inc., registered in various countries and categories. All characters, events, and institutions depicted herein are fictional. Any similarity between any of the names, characters, persons, events, and/or institutions in this publication to actual names, characters, and persons, whether living or dead, events, and/or institutions is unintended and purely coincidental. BOOM! Studios does not read or accept unsolicited submissions of ideas, stories, or artwork.

BOOM! Studios, 5670 Wilshire Boulevard, Suite 400, Los Angeles, CA 90036-5679. Printed in China. First Printing.

ISBN: 978-1-68415-389-3, eISBN: 978-1-64144-372-2

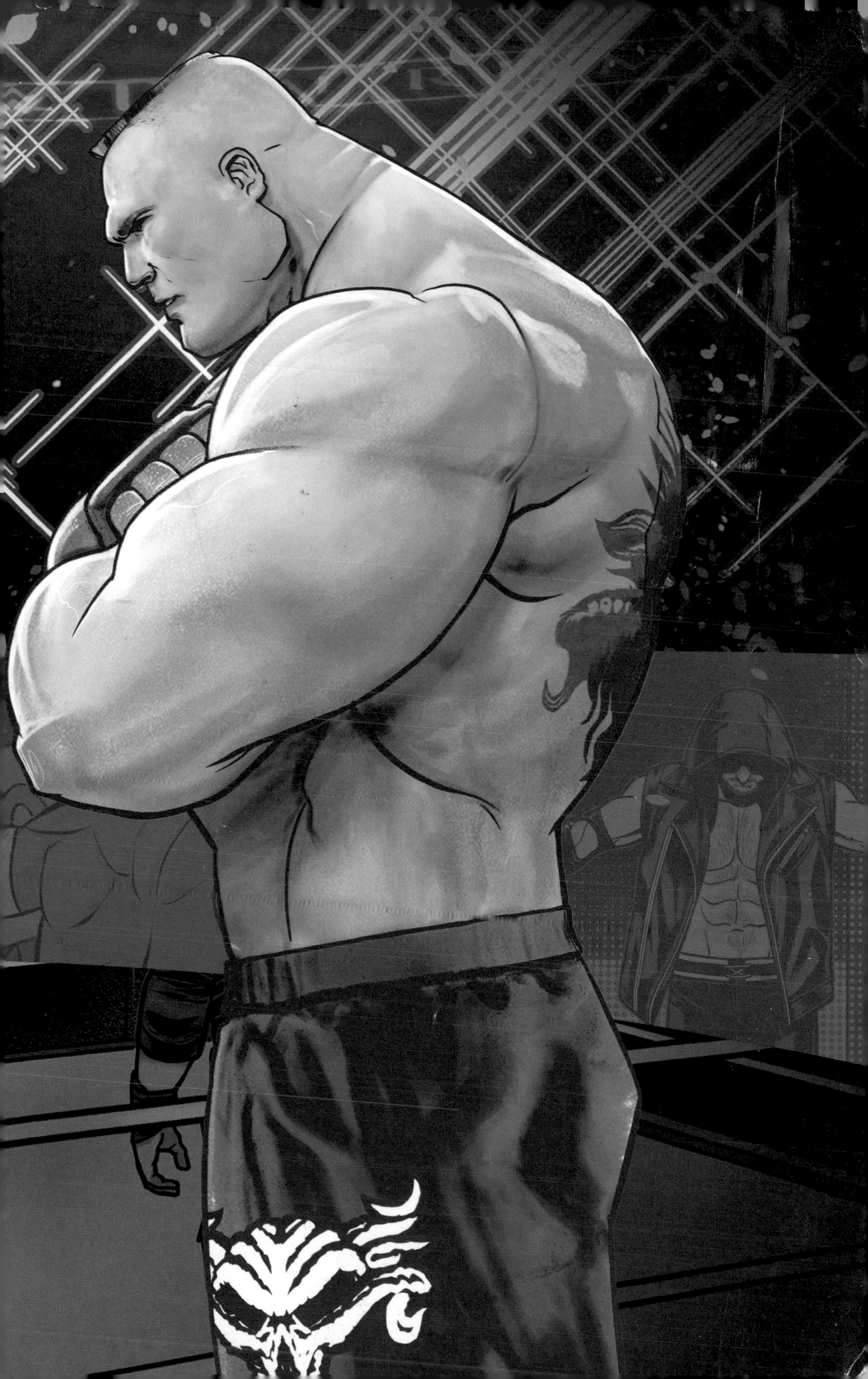

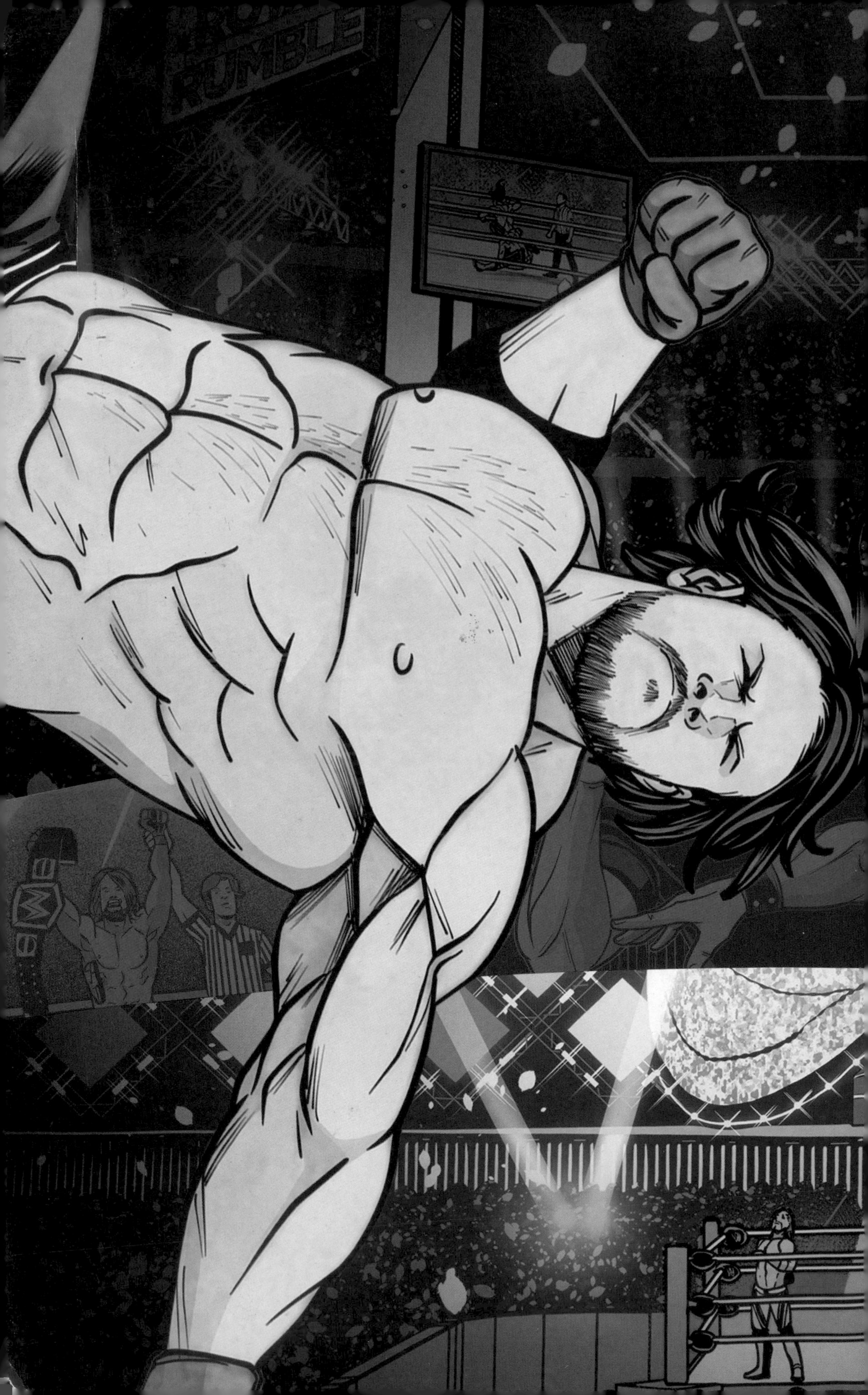
RUMBLE

THE
PHENOMENAL ONE

WRITTEN BY
DENNIS HOPELESS

ILLUSTRATED BY
SERG ACUÑA
KENDALL GOODE (CHAPTER 3)

COLORED BY
DOUG GARBARK

LETTERED BY
JIM CAMPBELL

COVER BY
MARCO D'ALFONSO

SERIES DESIGNER
GRACE PARK

COLLECTION DESIGNER
CHELSEA ROBERTS

EDITOR
CHRIS ROSA

SPECIAL THANKS TO
STEVE PANTALEO
CHAD BARBASH
BEN MAYER
JOHN JONES
STAN STANSKI
LAUREN DIENES-MIDDLEN
AND EVERYONE AT **WWE**

CHAPTER ONE

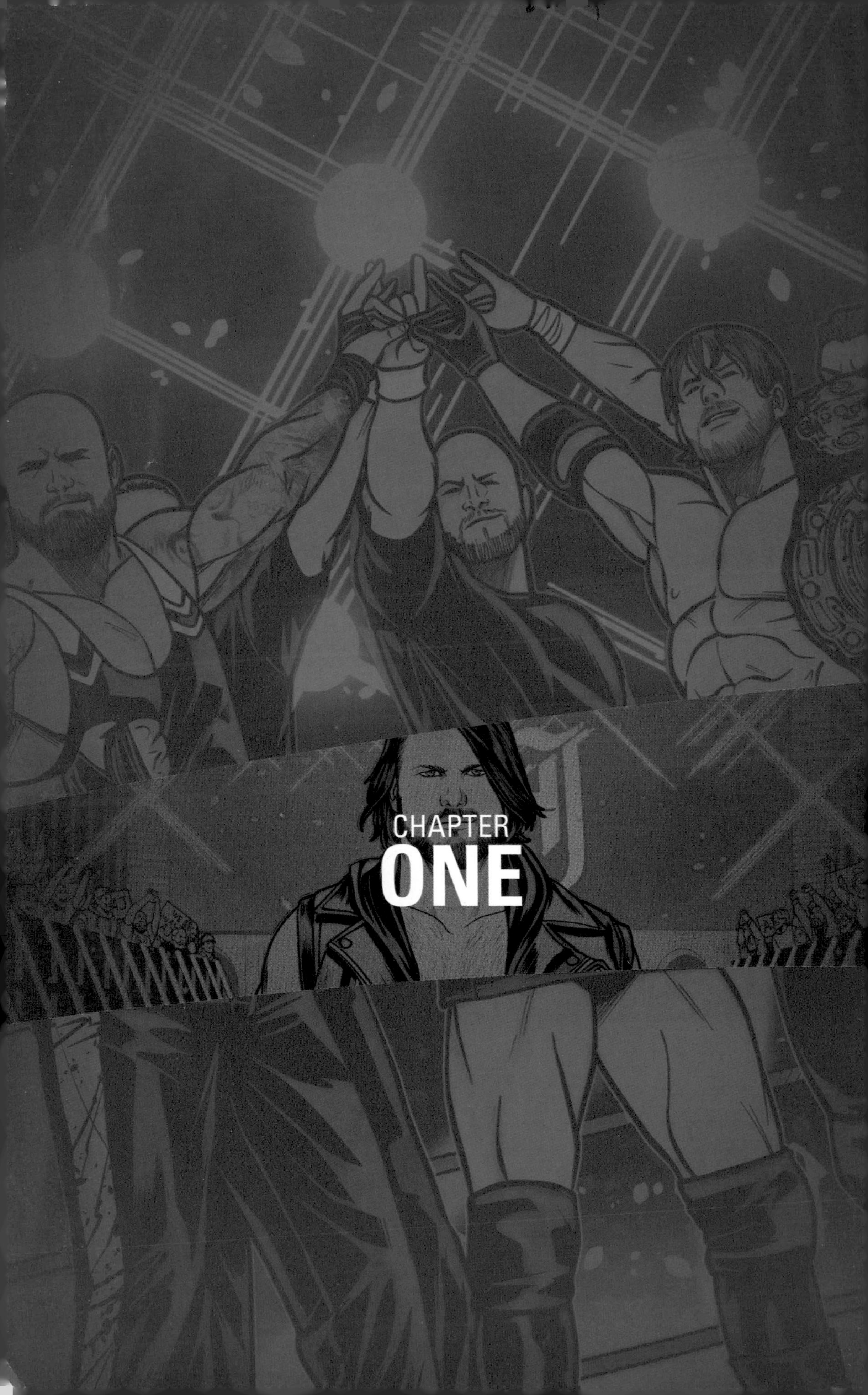

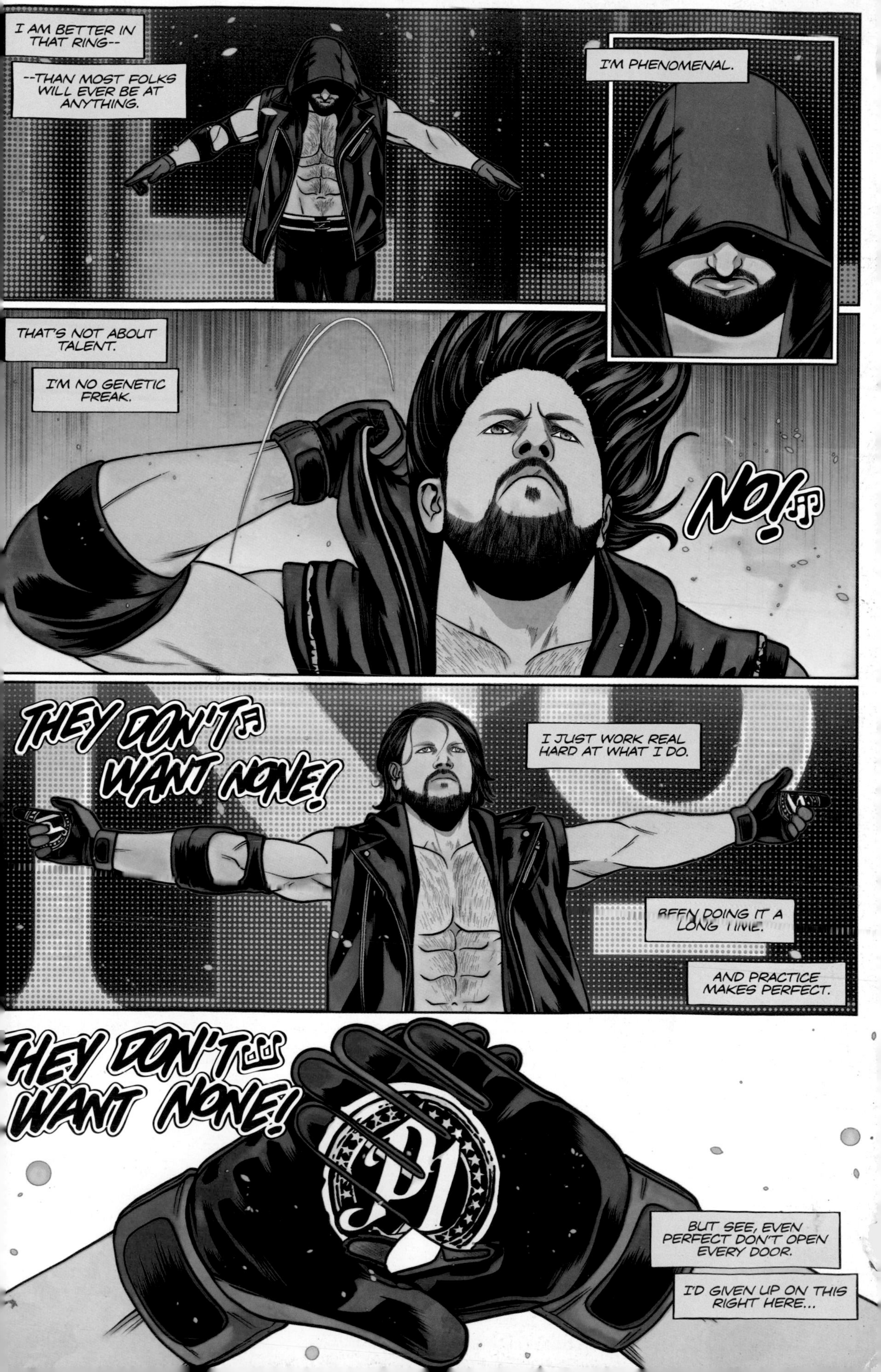

I AM BETTER IN THAT RING--
--THAN MOST FOLKS WILL EVER BE AT ANYTHING.
I'M PHENOMENAL.
THAT'S NOT ABOUT TALENT.
I'M NO GENETIC FREAK.
NO!
THEY DON'T WANT NONE!
I JUST WORK REAL HARD AT WHAT I DO.
BEEN DOING IT A LONG TIME.
AND PRACTICE MAKES PERFECT.
THEY DON'T WANT NONE!
BUT SEE, EVEN PERFECT DON'T OPEN EVERY DOOR.
I'D GIVEN UP ON THIS RIGHT HERE...

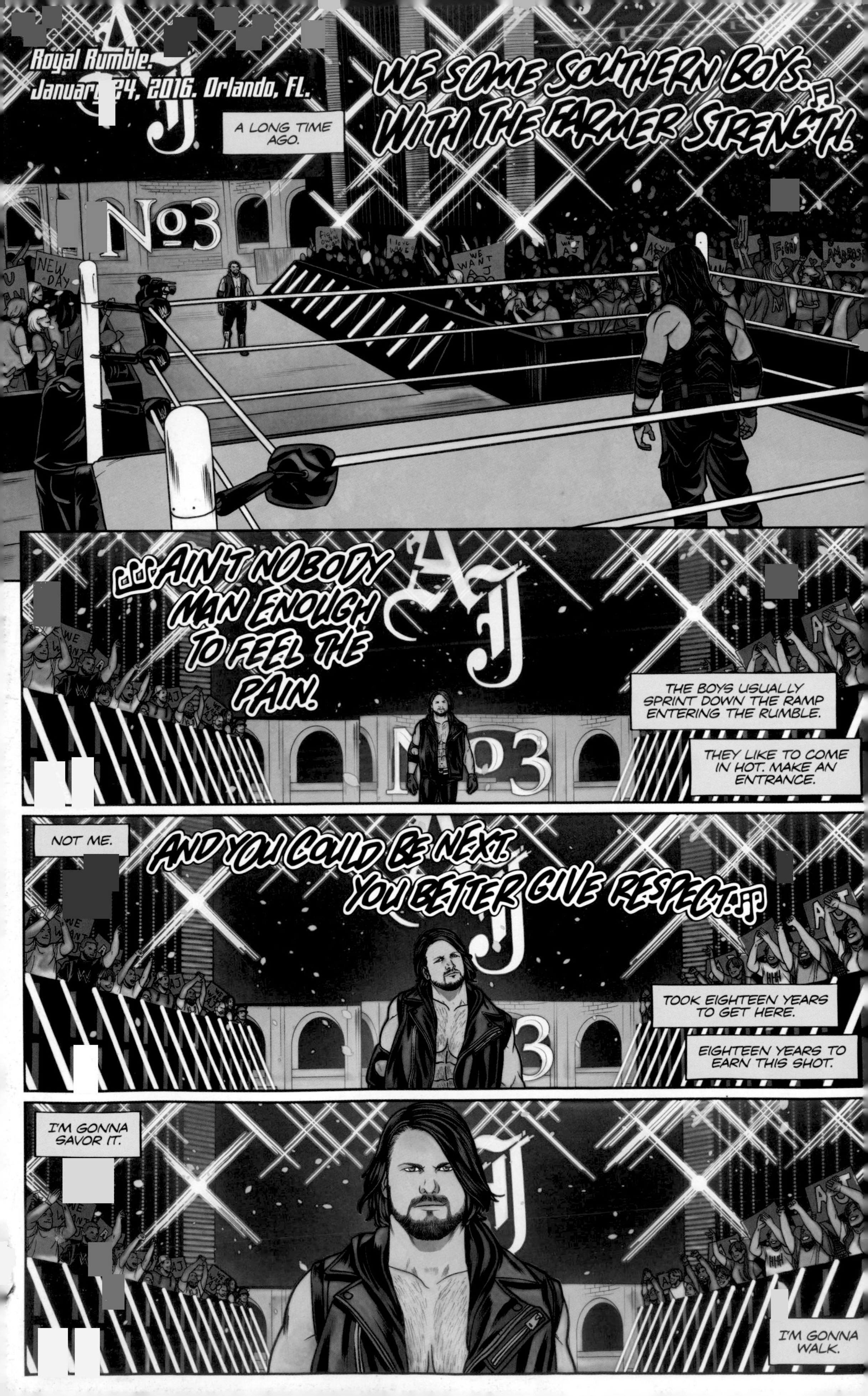

Royal Rumble.
January 24, 2016. Orlando, FL.
A LONG TIME AGO.
WE SOME SOUTHERN BOYS... WITH THE FARMER STRENGTH.
Nº3
AIN'T NOBODY MAN ENOUGH TO FEEL THE PAIN.
THE BOYS USUALLY SPRINT DOWN THE RAMP ENTERING THE RUMBLE.
THEY LIKE TO COME IN HOT. MAKE AN ENTRANCE.
NOT ME.
AND YOU COULD BE NEXT. YOU BETTER GIVE RESPECT...
TOOK EIGHTEEN YEARS TO GET HERE.
EIGHTEEN YEARS TO EARN THIS SHOT.
I'M GONNA SAVOR IT.
I'M GONNA WALK.

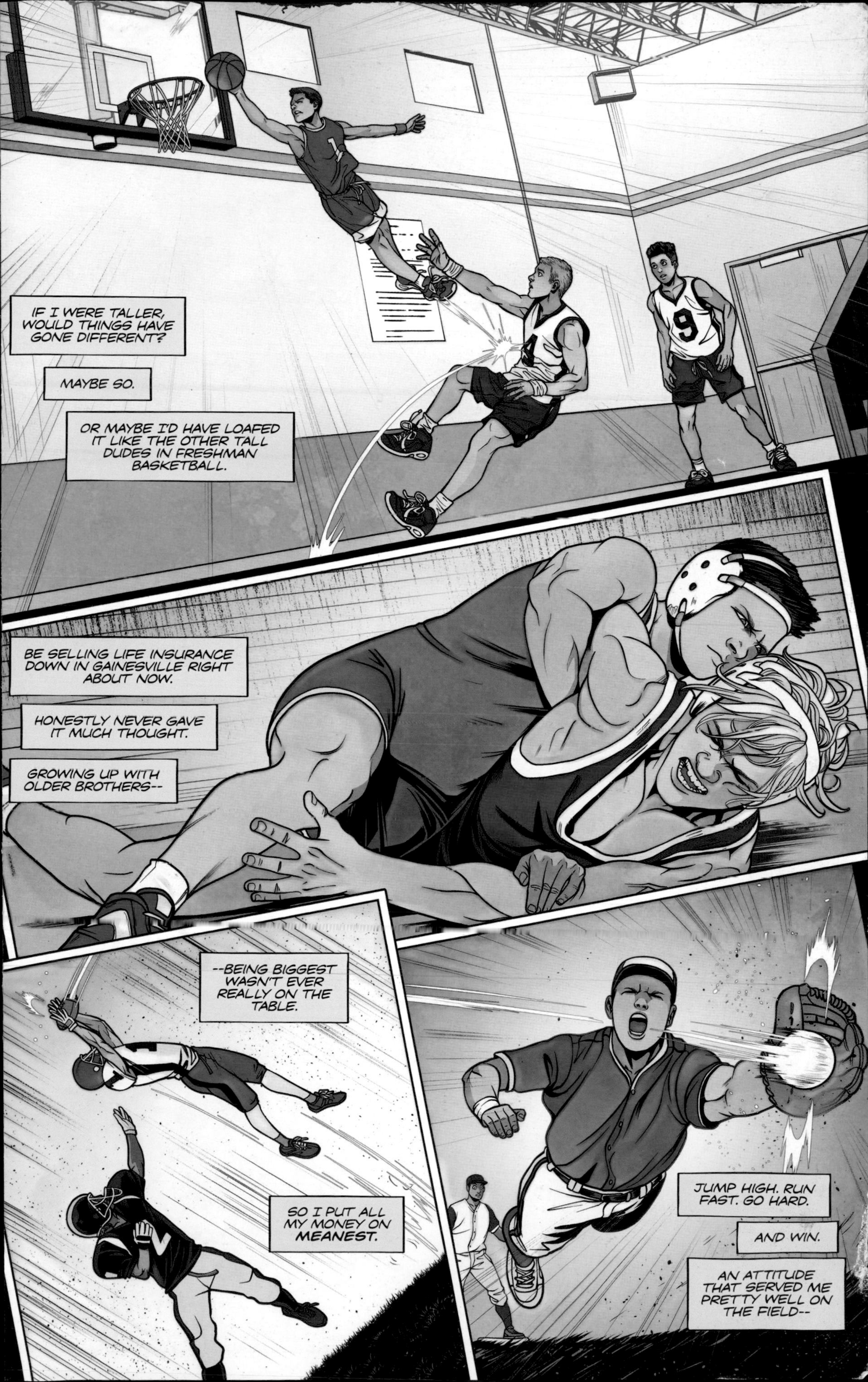
IF I WERE TALLER, WOULD THINGS HAVE GONE DIFFERENT?
MAYBE SO.
OR MAYBE I'D HAVE LOAFED IT LIKE THE OTHER TALL DUDES IN FRESHMAN BASKETBALL.
BE SELLING LIFE INSURANCE DOWN IN GAINESVILLE RIGHT ABOUT NOW.
HONESTLY NEVER GAVE IT MUCH THOUGHT.
GROWING UP WITH OLDER BROTHERS--
--BEING BIGGEST WASN'T EVER REALLY ON THE TABLE.
SO I PUT ALL MY MONEY ON MEANEST.
JUMP HIGH. RUN FAST. GO HARD.
AND WIN.
AN ATTITUDE THAT SERVED ME PRETTY WELL ON THE FIELD--

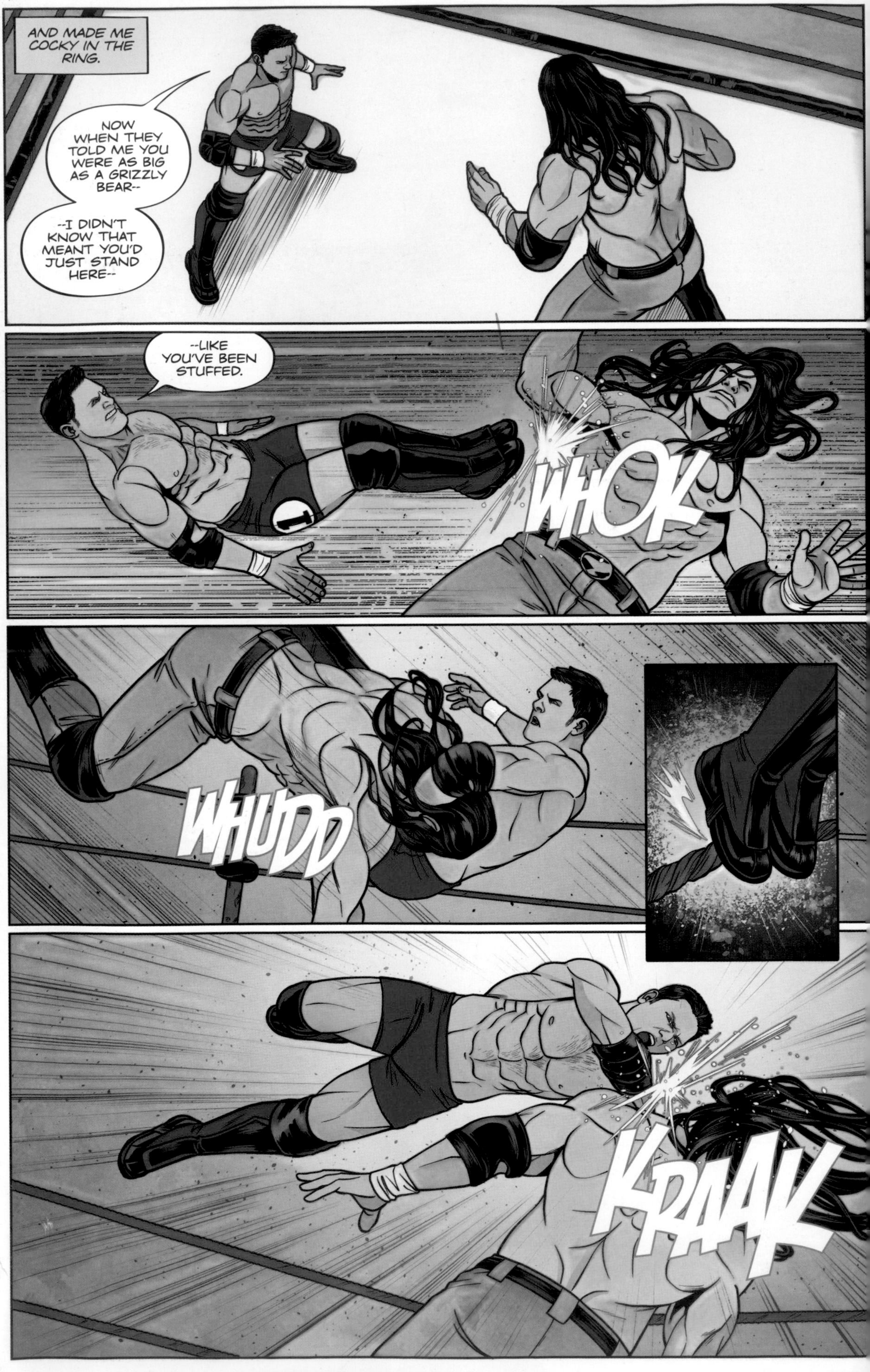
AND MADE ME COCKY IN THE RING.
NOW WHEN THEY TOLD ME YOU WERE AS BIG AS A GRIZZLY BEAR--
--I DIDN'T KNOW THAT MEANT YOU'D JUST STAND HERE--
--LIKE YOU'VE BEEN STUFFED.
WHOK
WHUDD
KRAAK

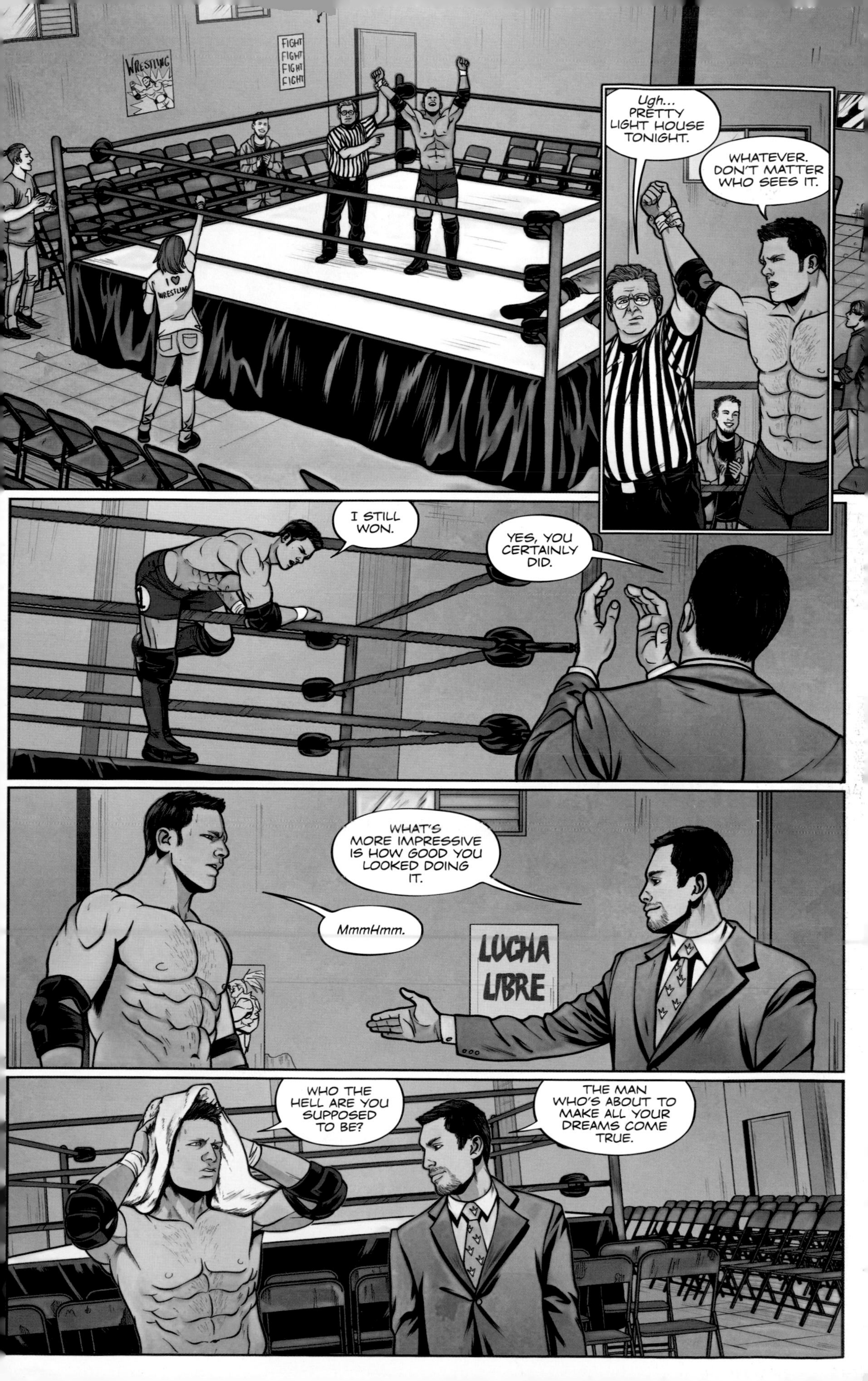
FIGHT FIGHT FIGHT FIGHT
WRESTLING
I ♥ WRESTLING
Ugh... PRETTY LIGHT HOUSE TONIGHT.
WHATEVER. DON'T MATTER WHO SEES IT.
I STILL WON.
YES, YOU CERTAINLY DID.
WHAT'S MORE IMPRESSIVE IS HOW GOOD YOU LOOKED DOING IT.
MmmHmm.
LUCHA LIBRE
WHO THE HELL ARE YOU SUPPOSED TO BE?
THE MAN WHO'S ABOUT TO MAKE ALL YOUR DREAMS COME TRUE.

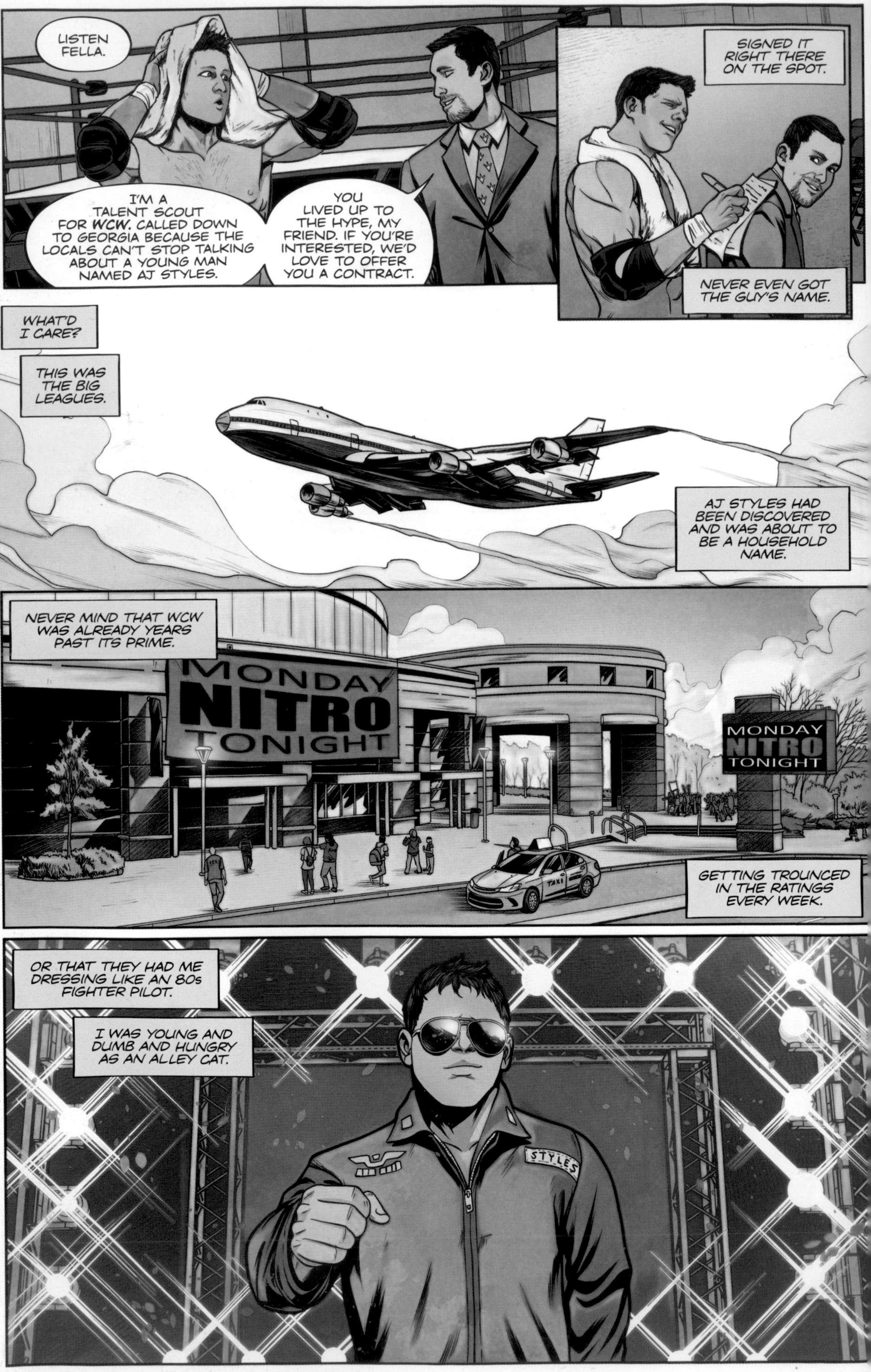
LISTEN FELLA.
I'M A TALENT SCOUT FOR WCW. CALLED DOWN TO GEORGIA BECAUSE THE LOCALS CAN'T STOP TALKING ABOUT A YOUNG MAN NAMED AJ STYLES.
YOU LIVED UP TO THE HYPE, MY FRIEND. IF YOU'RE INTERESTED, WE'D LOVE TO OFFER YOU A CONTRACT.
SIGNED IT RIGHT THERE ON THE SPOT.
NEVER EVEN GOT THE GUY'S NAME.
WHAT'D I CARE?
THIS WAS THE BIG LEAGUES.
AJ STYLES HAD BEEN DISCOVERED AND WAS ABOUT TO BE A HOUSEHOLD NAME.
NEVER MIND THAT WCW WAS ALREADY YEARS PAST ITS PRIME.
MONDAY NITRO TONIGHT
MONDAY NITRO TONIGHT
TAXI
GETTING TROUNCED IN THE RATINGS EVERY WEEK.
OR THAT THEY HAD ME DRESSING LIKE AN 80s FIGHTER PILOT.
I WAS YOUNG AND DUMB AND HUNGRY AS AN ALLEY CAT.
STYLES

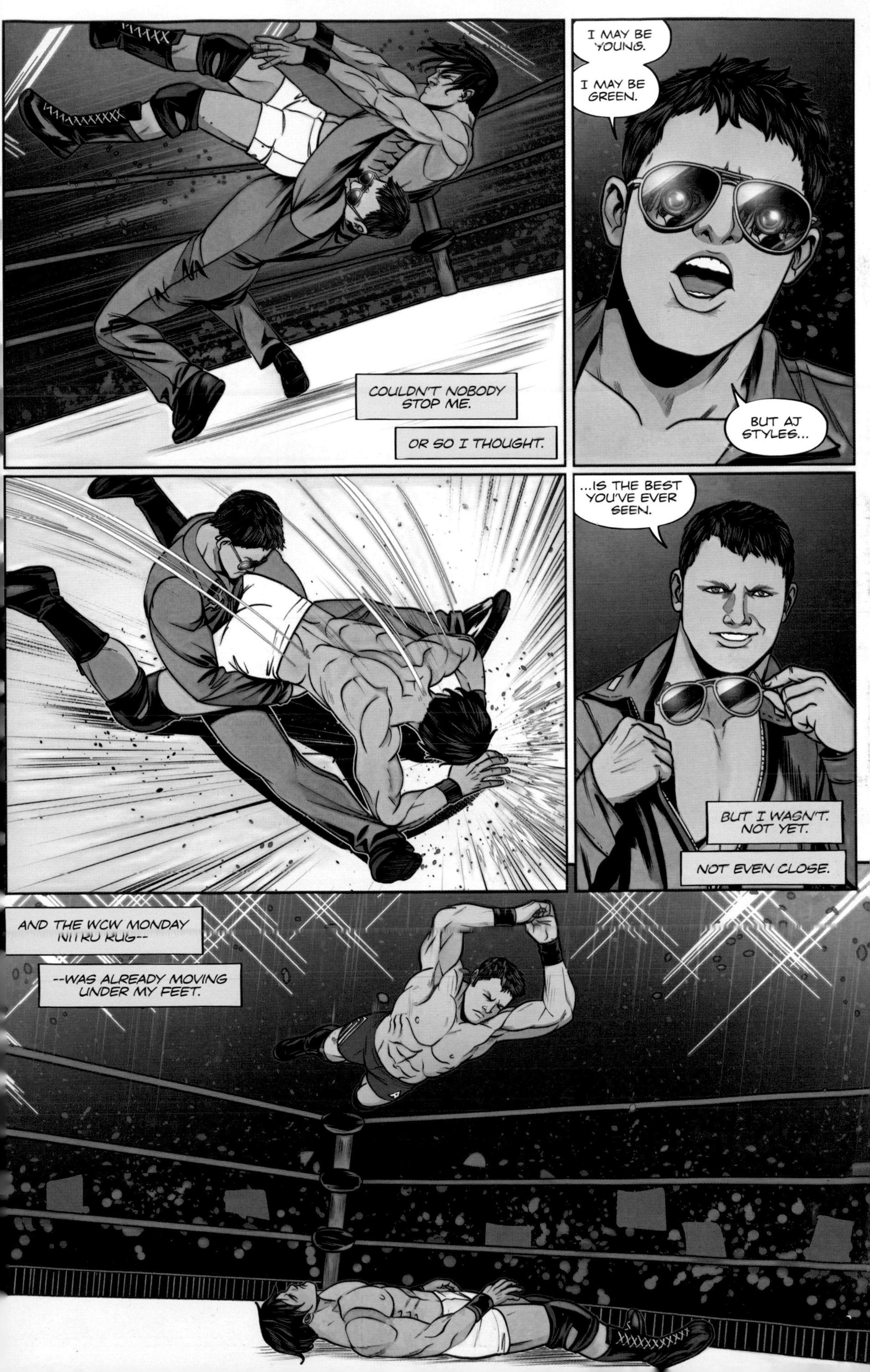
COULDN'T NOBODY STOP ME.
OR SO I THOUGHT.
I MAY BE YOUNG.
I MAY BE GREEN.
BUT AJ STYLES...
...IS THE BEST YOU'VE EVER SEEN.
BUT I WASN'T. NOT YET.
NOT EVEN CLOSE.
AND THE WCW MONDAY NITRO RUG--
--WAS ALREADY MOVING UNDER MY FEET.

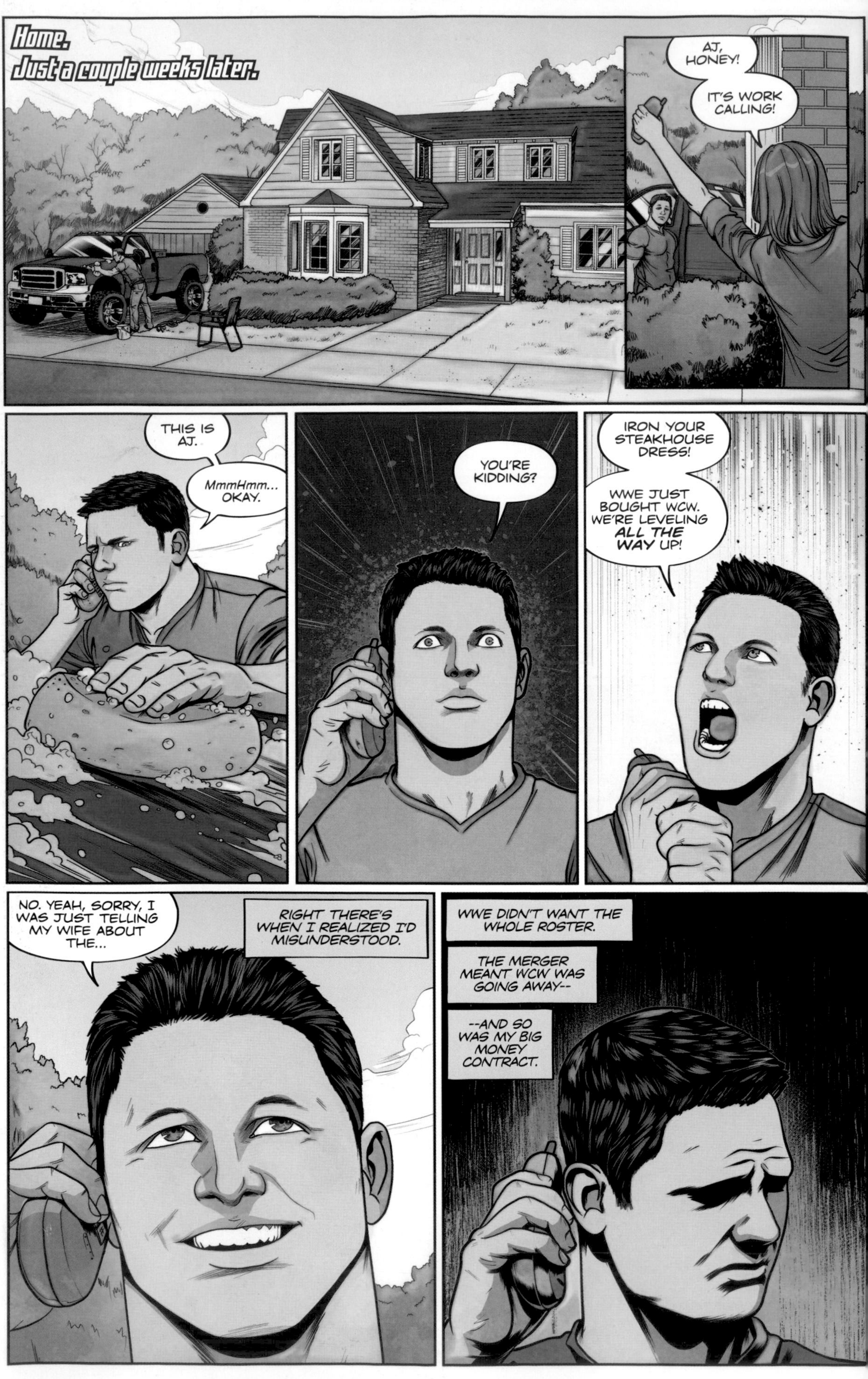
Home.
Just a couple weeks later.
AJ, HONEY!
IT'S WORK CALLING!
THIS IS AJ.
MmmHmm... OKAY.
YOU'RE KIDDING?
IRON YOUR STEAKHOUSE DRESS!
WWE JUST BOUGHT WCW. WE'RE LEVELING ALL THE WAY UP!
NO. YEAH, SORRY, I WAS JUST TELLING MY WIFE ABOUT THE...
RIGHT THERE'S WHEN I REALIZED I'D MISUNDERSTOOD.
WWE DIDN'T WANT THE WHOLE ROSTER.
THE MERGER MEANT WCW WAS GOING AWAY--
--AND SO WAS MY BIG MONEY CONTRACT.

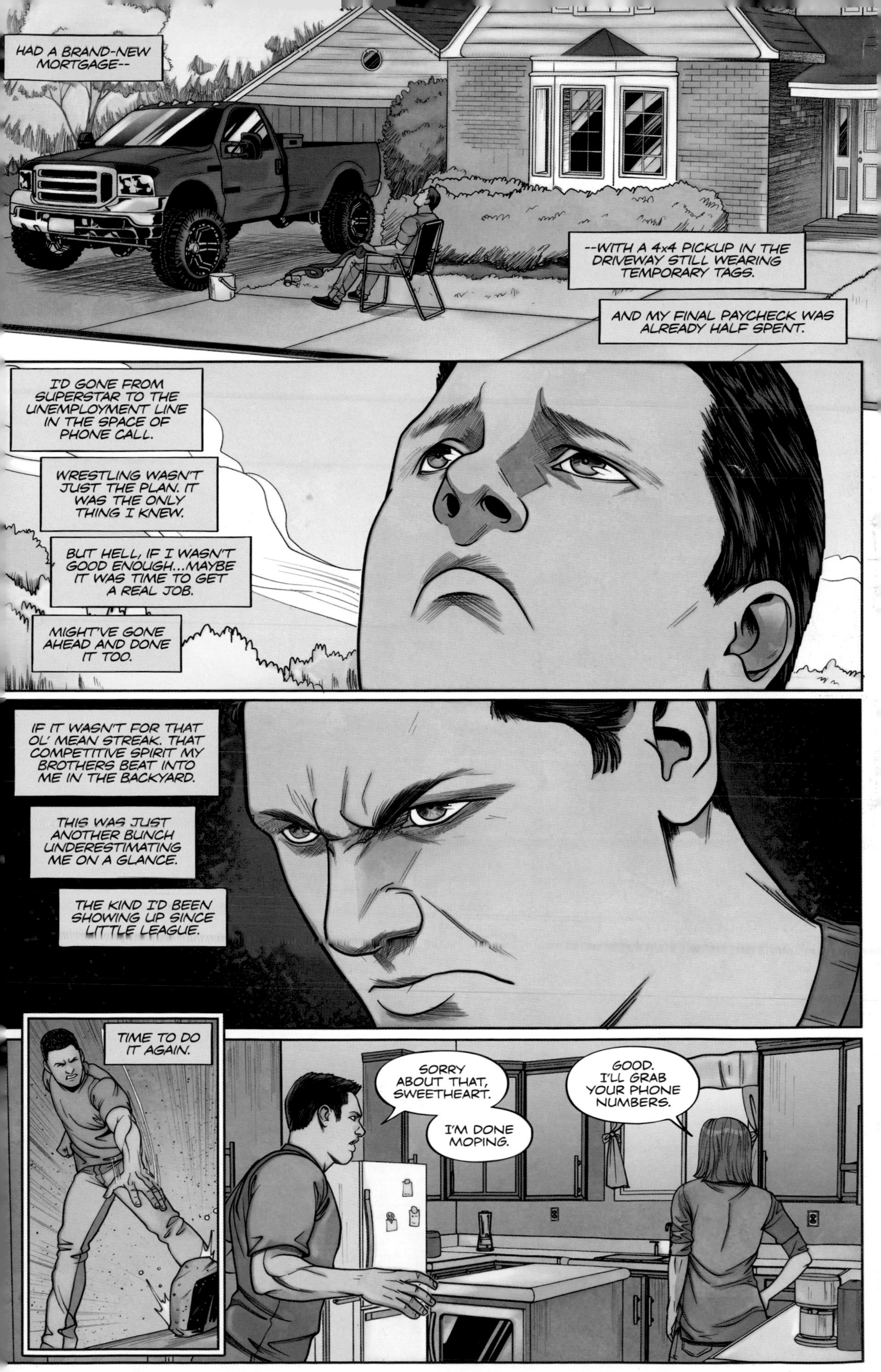
HAD A BRAND-NEW MORTGAGE--
--WITH A 4x4 PICKUP IN THE DRIVEWAY STILL WEARING TEMPORARY TAGS.
AND MY FINAL PAYCHECK WAS ALREADY HALF SPENT.
I'D GONE FROM SUPERSTAR TO THE UNEMPLOYMENT LINE IN THE SPACE OF PHONE CALL.
WRESTLING WASN'T JUST THE PLAN. IT WAS THE ONLY THING I KNEW.
BUT HELL, IF I WASN'T GOOD ENOUGH...MAYBE IT WAS TIME TO GET A REAL JOB.
MIGHT'VE GONE AHEAD AND DONE IT TOO.
IF IT WASN'T FOR THAT OL' MEAN STREAK. THAT COMPETITIVE SPIRIT MY BROTHERS BEAT INTO ME IN THE BACKYARD.
THIS WAS JUST ANOTHER BUNCH UNDERESTIMATING ME ON A GLANCE.
THE KIND I'D BEEN SHOWING UP SINCE LITTLE LEAGUE.
TIME TO DO IT AGAIN.
SORRY ABOUT THAT, SWEETHEART.
I'M DONE MOPING.
GOOD. I'LL GRAB YOUR PHONE NUMBERS.

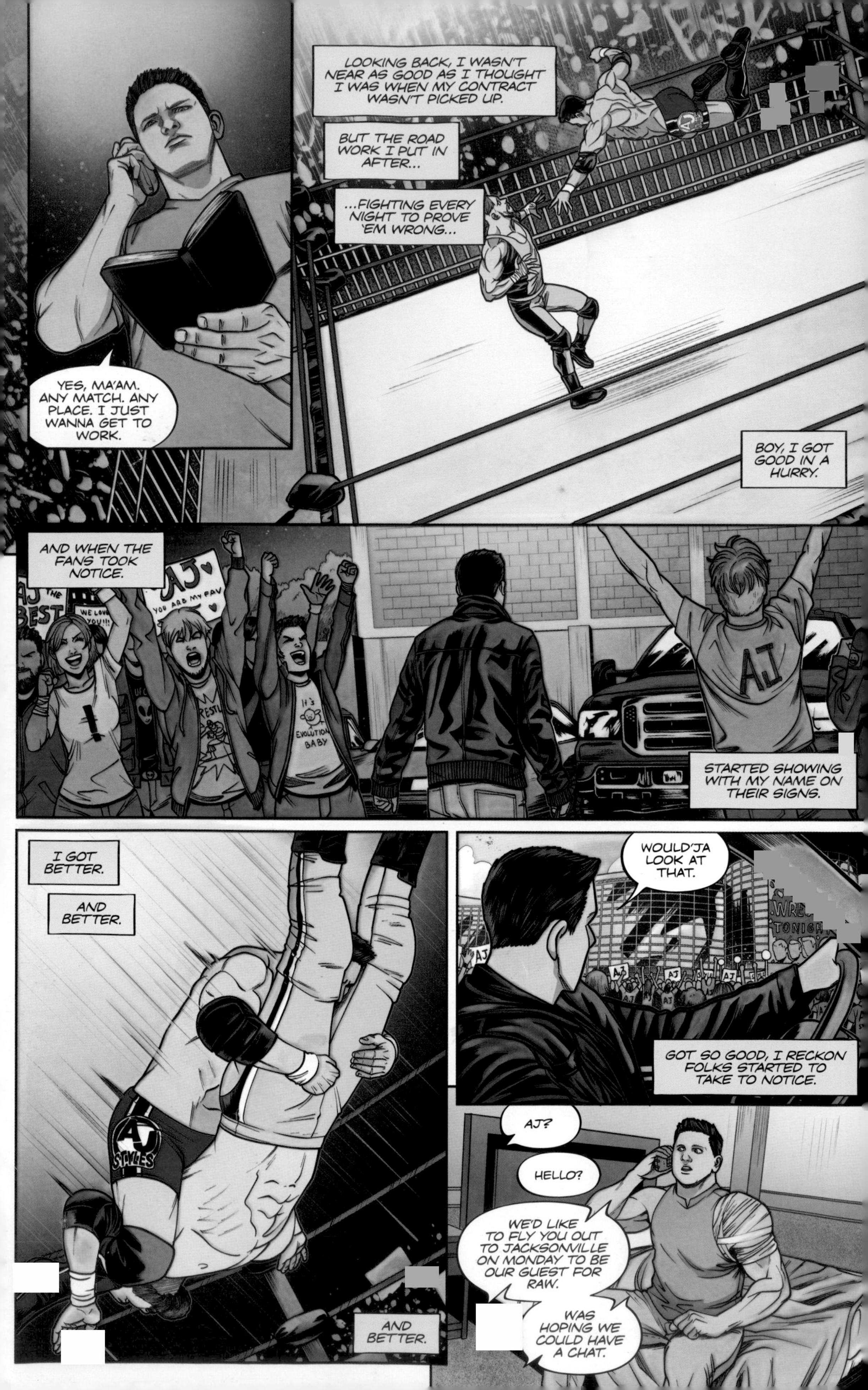
YES, MA'AM. ANY MATCH. ANY PLACE. I JUST WANNA GET TO WORK.
LOOKING BACK, I WASN'T NEAR AS GOOD AS I THOUGHT I WAS WHEN MY CONTRACT WASN'T PICKED UP.
BUT THE ROAD WORK I PUT IN AFTER...
...FIGHTING EVERY NIGHT TO PROVE 'EM WRONG...
BOY, I GOT GOOD IN A HURRY.
AND WHEN THE FANS TOOK NOTICE.
STARTED SHOWING WITH MY NAME ON THEIR SIGNS.
I GOT BETTER.
AND BETTER.
AND BETTER.
WOULD'JA LOOK AT THAT.
GOT SO GOOD, I RECKON FOLKS STARTED TO TAKE TO NOTICE.
AJ?
HELLO?
WE'D LIKE TO FLY YOU OUT TO JACKSONVILLE ON MONDAY TO BE OUR GUEST FOR RAW.
WAS HOPING WE COULD HAVE A CHAT.

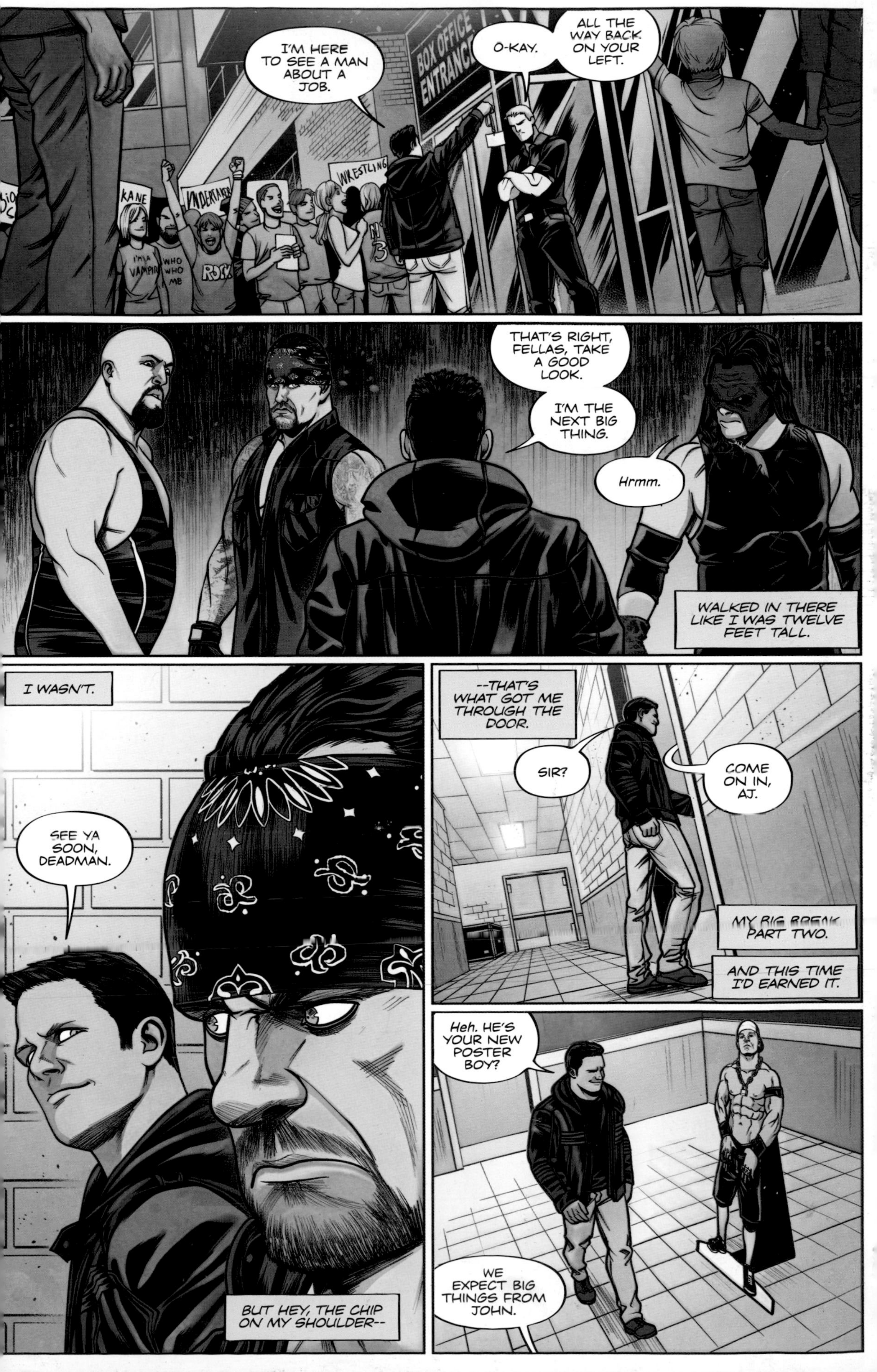

I'M HERE TO SEE A MAN ABOUT A JOB.
O-KAY.
ALL THE WAY BACK ON YOUR LEFT.
BOX OFFICE ENTRANCE
THAT'S RIGHT, FELLAS, TAKE A GOOD LOOK.
I'M THE NEXT BIG THING.
Hrmm.
WALKED IN THERE LIKE I WAS TWELVE FEET TALL.
I WASN'T.
SEE YA SOON, DEADMAN.
BUT HEY, THE CHIP ON MY SHOULDER--
--THAT'S WHAT GOT ME THROUGH THE DOOR.
SIR?
COME ON IN, AJ.
MY BIG BREAK PART TWO.
AND THIS TIME I'D EARNED IT.
Heh. HE'S YOUR NEW POSTER BOY?
WE EXPECT BIG THINGS FROM JOHN.

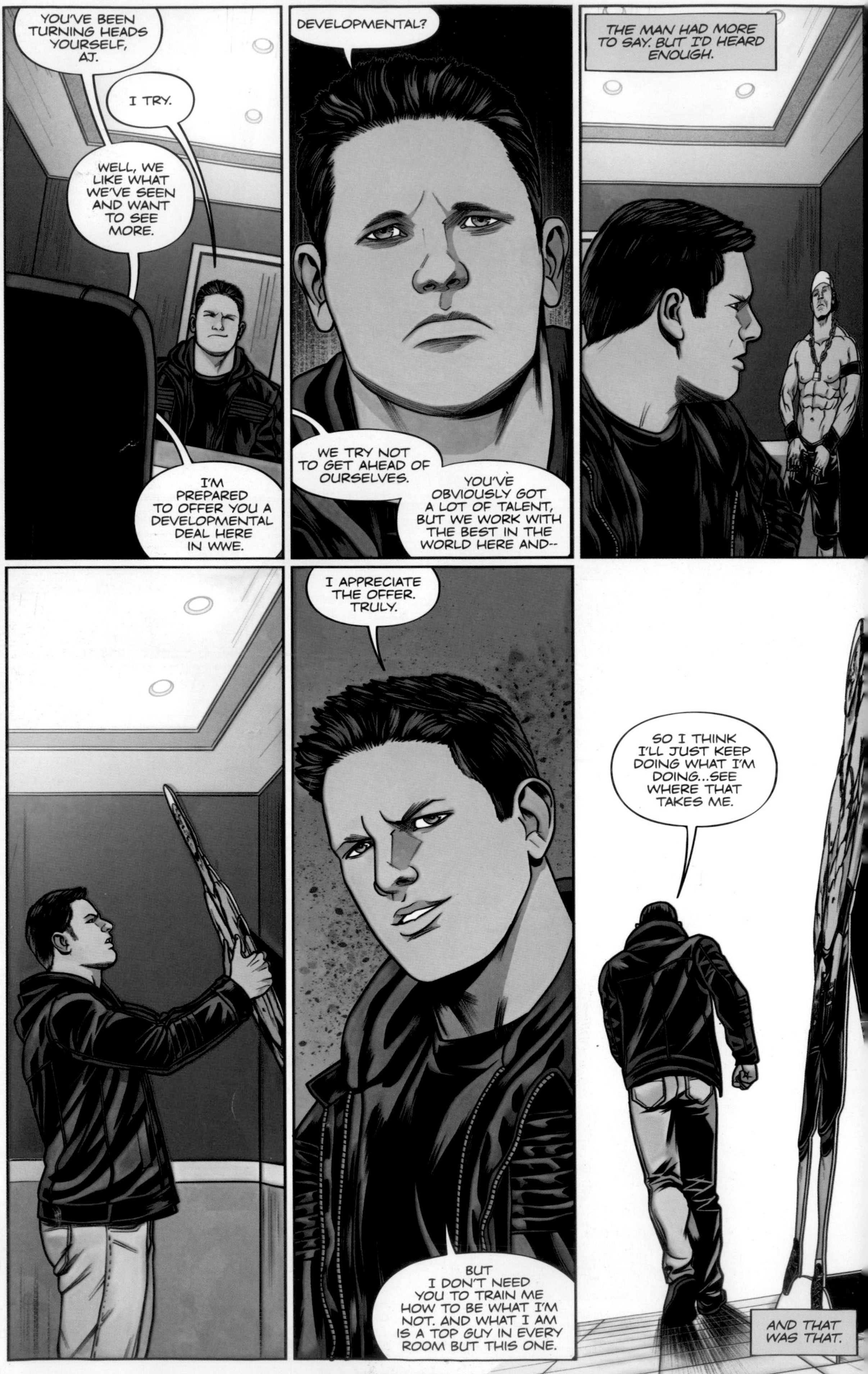
YOU'VE BEEN TURNING HEADS YOURSELF, AJ.
I TRY.
WELL, WE LIKE WHAT WE'VE SEEN AND WANT TO SEE MORE.
I'M PREPARED TO OFFER YOU A DEVELOPMENTAL DEAL HERE IN WWE.
DEVELOPMENTAL?
WE TRY NOT TO GET AHEAD OF OURSELVES.
YOU'VE OBVIOUSLY GOT A LOT OF TALENT, BUT WE WORK WITH THE BEST IN THE WORLD HERE AND--
THE MAN HAD MORE TO SAY. BUT I'D HEARD ENOUGH.
I APPRECIATE THE OFFER. TRULY.
BUT I DON'T NEED YOU TO TRAIN ME HOW TO BE WHAT I'M NOT. AND WHAT I AM IS A TOP GUY IN EVERY ROOM BUT THIS ONE.
SO I THINK I'LL JUST KEEP DOING WHAT I'M DOING...SEE WHERE THAT TAKES ME.
AND THAT WAS THAT.

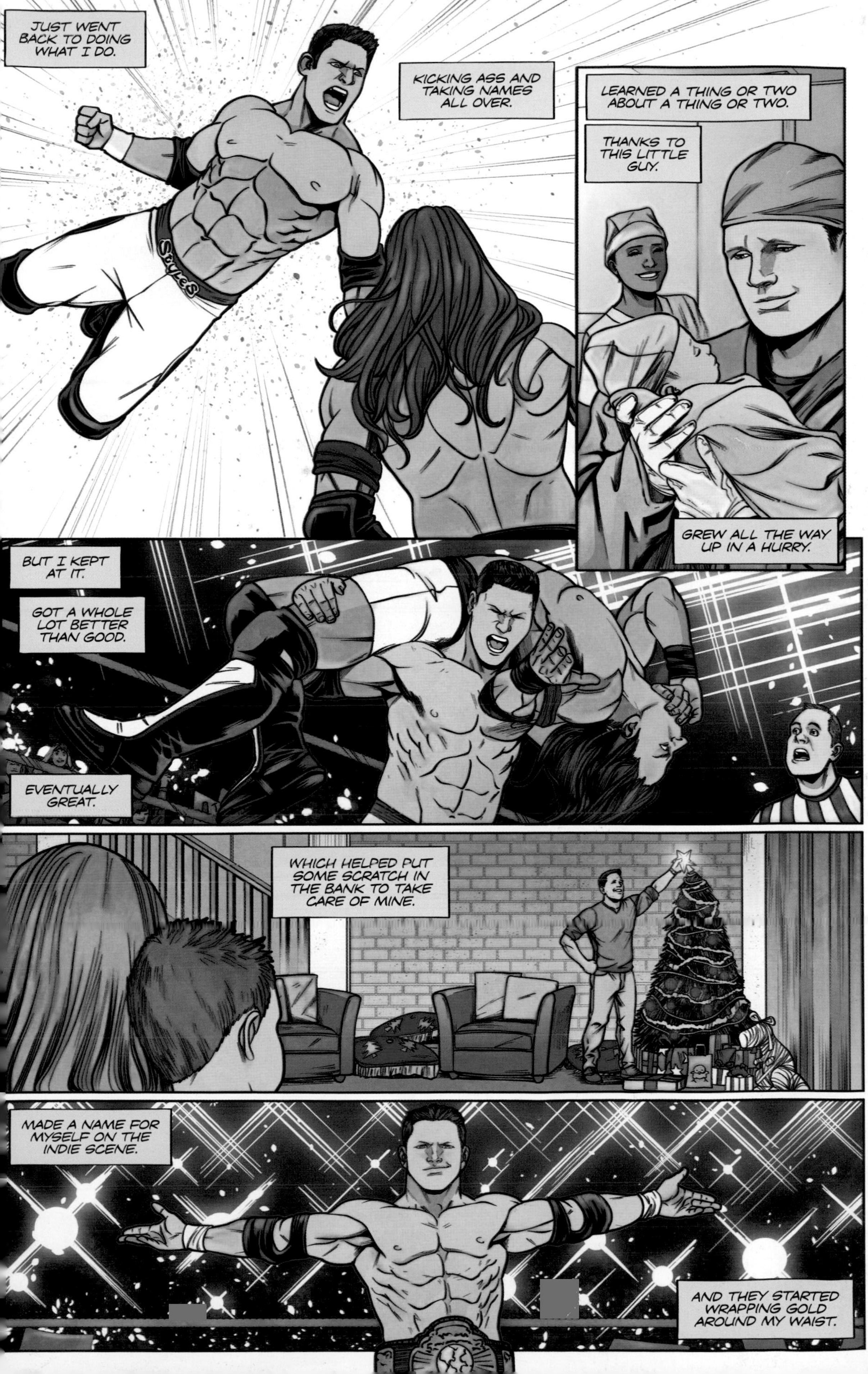
JUST WENT BACK TO DOING WHAT I DO.
KICKING ASS AND TAKING NAMES ALL OVER.
STYLES
LEARNED A THING OR TWO ABOUT A THING OR TWO.
THANKS TO THIS LITTLE GUY.
GREW ALL THE WAY UP IN A HURRY.
BUT I KEPT AT IT.
GOT A WHOLE LOT BETTER THAN GOOD.
EVENTUALLY GREAT.
WHICH HELPED PUT SOME SCRATCH IN THE BANK TO TAKE CARE OF MINE.
MADE A NAME FOR MYSELF ON THE INDIE SCENE.
AND THEY STARTED WRAPPING GOLD AROUND MY WAIST.

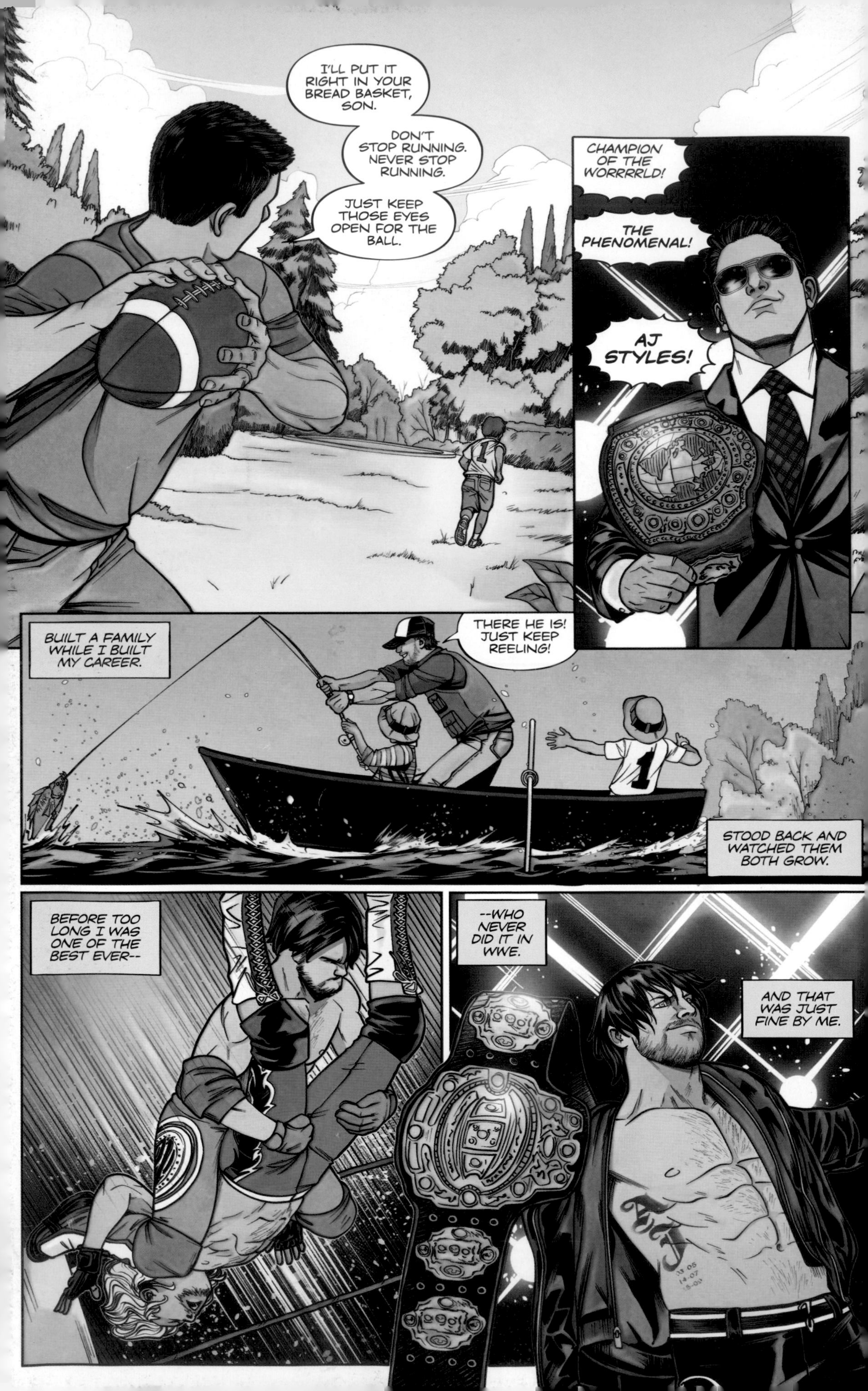
I'LL PUT IT RIGHT IN YOUR BREAD BASKET, SON.
DON'T STOP RUNNING. NEVER STOP RUNNING.
JUST KEEP THOSE EYES OPEN FOR THE BALL.
CHAMPION OF THE WORRRRLD!
THE PHENOMENAL!
AJ STYLES!
BUILT A FAMILY WHILE I BUILT MY CAREER.
THERE HE IS! JUST KEEP REELING!
STOOD BACK AND WATCHED THEM BOTH GROW.
BEFORE TOO LONG I WAS ONE OF THE BEST EVER--
--WHO NEVER DID IT IN WWE.
AND THAT WAS JUST FINE BY ME.

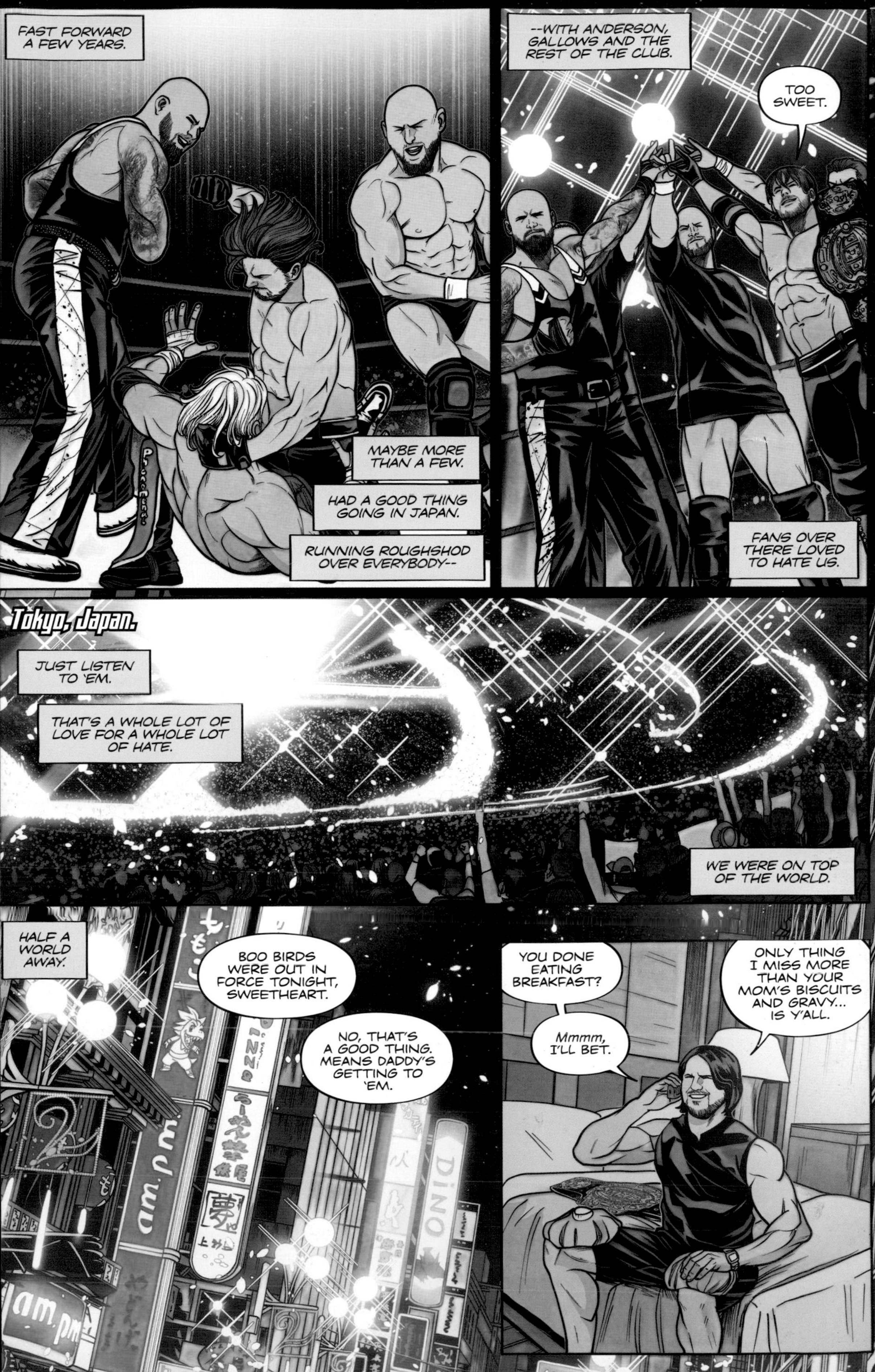

FAST FORWARD A FEW YEARS.
MAYBE MORE THAN A FEW.
HAD A GOOD THING GOING IN JAPAN.
RUNNING ROUGHSHOD OVER EVERYBODY--
--WITH ANDERSON, GALLOWS AND THE REST OF THE CLUB.
TOO SWEET.
FANS OVER THERE LOVED TO HATE US.
Tokyo, Japan.
JUST LISTEN TO 'EM.
THAT'S A WHOLE LOT OF LOVE FOR A WHOLE LOT OF HATE.
WE WERE ON TOP OF THE WORLD.
HALF A WORLD AWAY.
BOO BIRDS WERE OUT IN FORCE TONIGHT, SWEETHEART.
NO, THAT'S A GOOD THING. MEANS DADDY'S GETTING TO 'EM.
YOU DONE EATING BREAKFAST?
Mmmm, I'LL BET.
ONLY THING I MISS MORE THAN YOUR MOM'S BISCUITS AND GRAVY... IS Y'ALL.

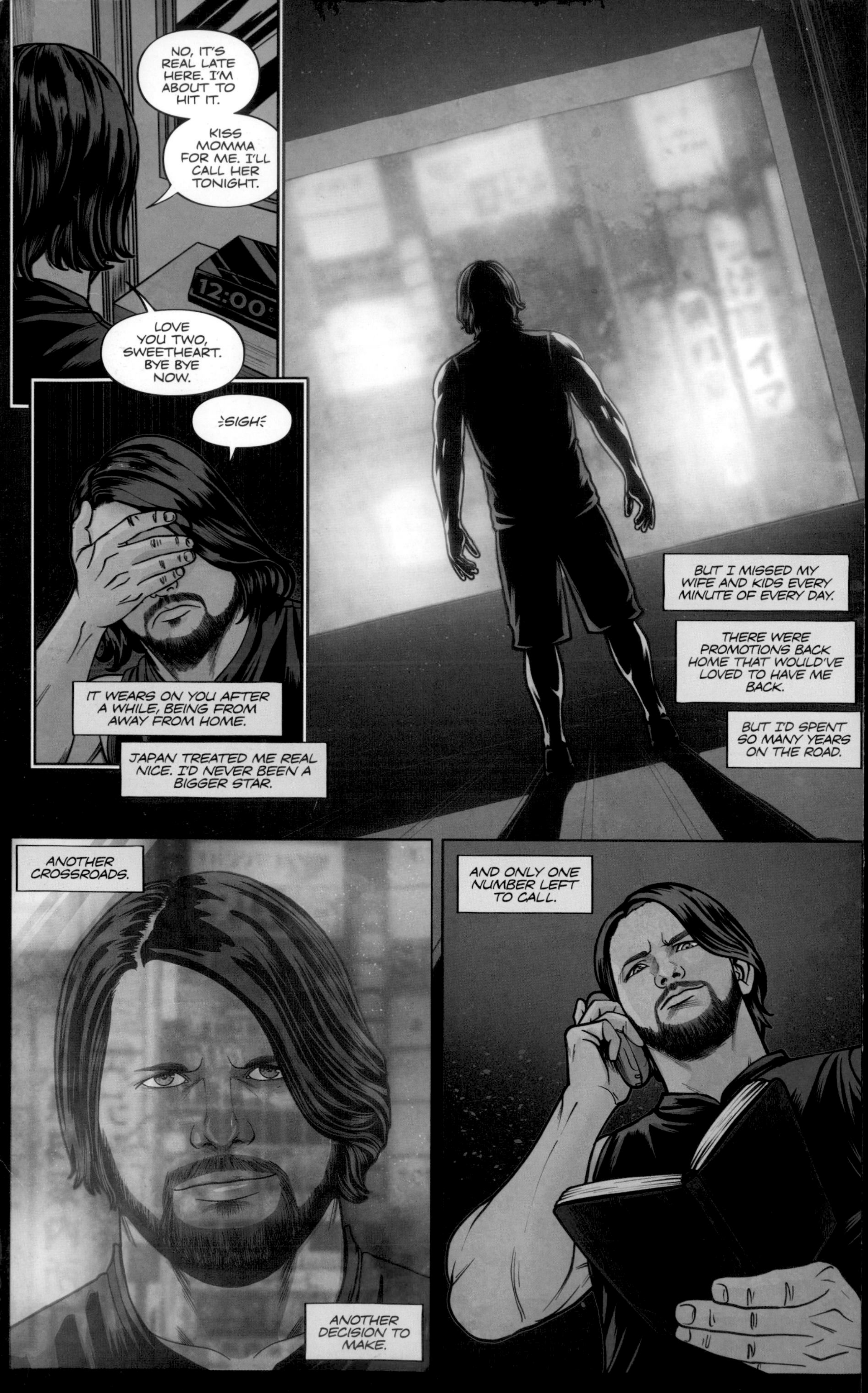
NO, IT'S REAL LATE HERE. I'M ABOUT TO HIT IT.
KISS MOMMA FOR ME. I'LL CALL HER TONIGHT.
12:00
LOVE YOU TWO, SWEETHEART. BYE BYE NOW.
SIGH
IT WEARS ON YOU AFTER A WHILE, BEING FROM AWAY FROM HOME.
JAPAN TREATED ME REAL NICE. I'D NEVER BEEN A BIGGER STAR.
BUT I MISSED MY WIFE AND KIDS EVERY MINUTE OF EVERY DAY.
THERE WERE PROMOTIONS BACK HOME THAT WOULD'VE LOVED TO HAVE ME BACK.
BUT I'D SPENT SO MANY YEARS ON THE ROAD.
ANOTHER CROSSROADS.
ANOTHER DECISION TO MAKE.
AND ONLY ONE NUMBER LEFT TO CALL.

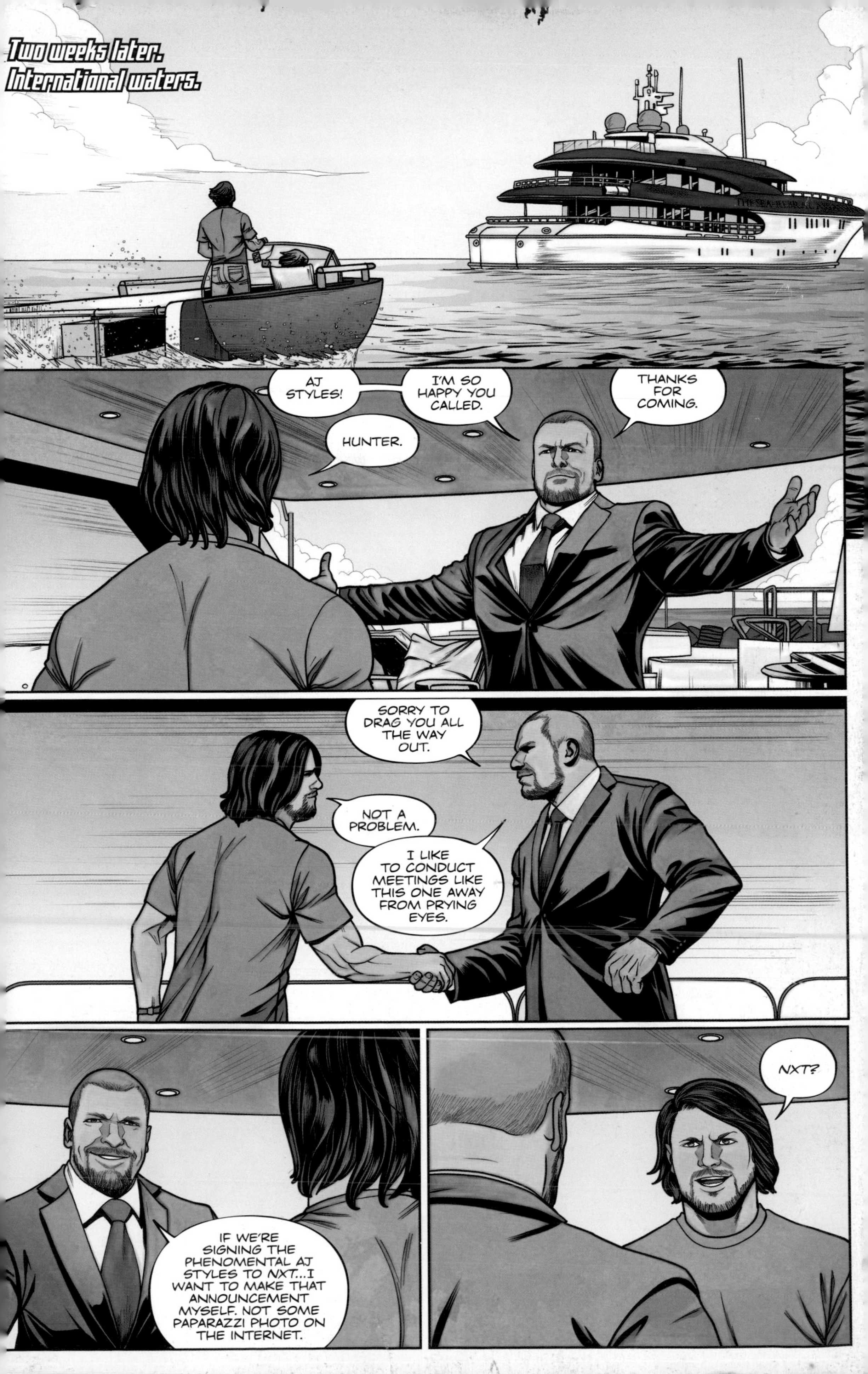
Two weeks later.
International waters.
AJ STYLES!
I'M SO HAPPY YOU CALLED.
HUNTER.
THANKS FOR COMING.
SORRY TO DRAG YOU ALL THE WAY OUT.
NOT A PROBLEM.
I LIKE TO CONDUCT MEETINGS LIKE THIS ONE AWAY FROM PRYING EYES.
IF WE'RE SIGNING THE PHENOMENAL AJ STYLES TO NXT...I WANT TO MAKE THAT ANNOUNCEMENT MYSELF. NOT SOME PAPARAZZI PHOTO ON THE INTERNET.
NXT?

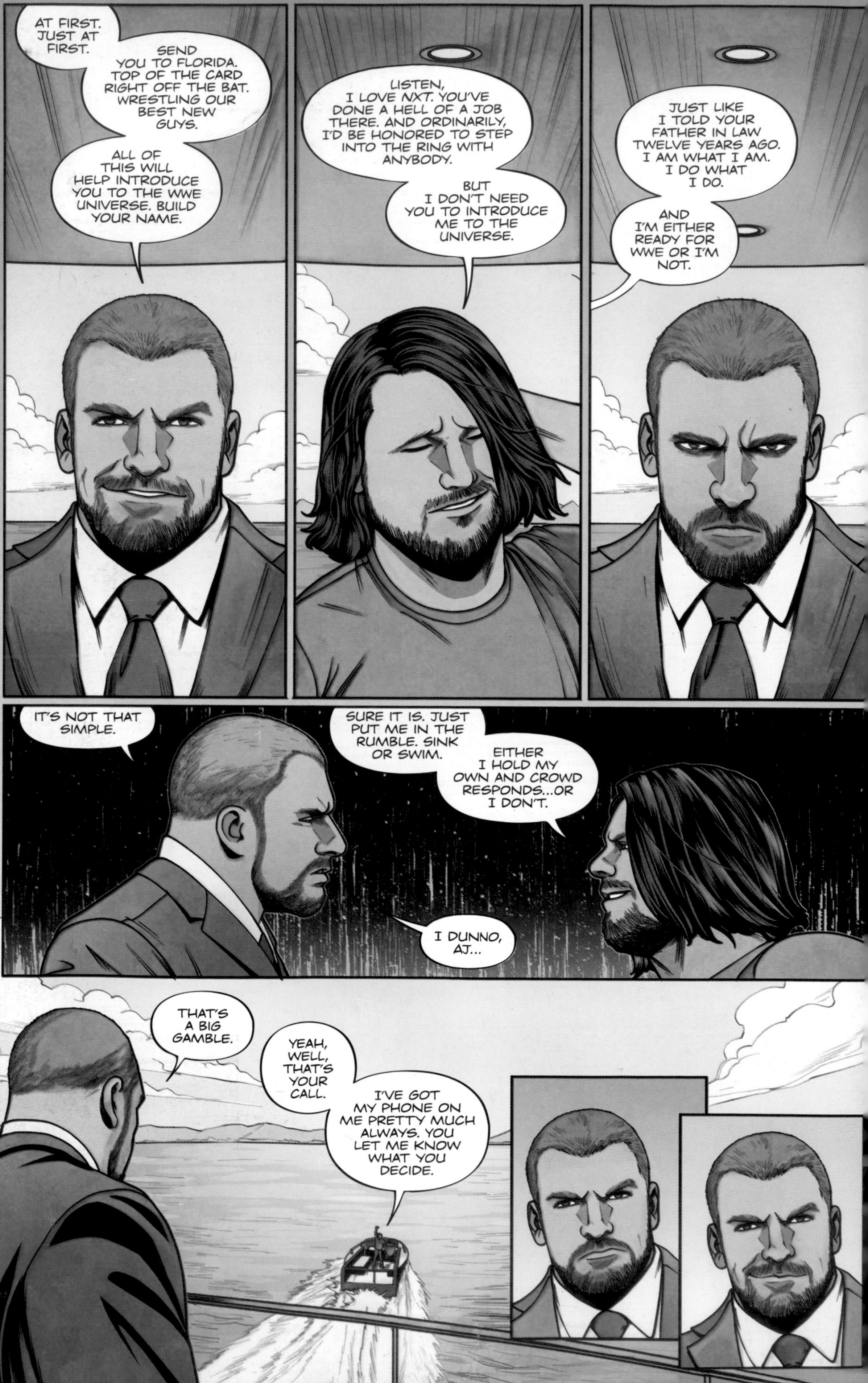
AT FIRST. JUST AT FIRST.
SEND YOU TO FLORIDA. TOP OF THE CARD RIGHT OFF THE BAT. WRESTLING OUR BEST NEW GUYS.
ALL OF THIS WILL HELP INTRODUCE YOU TO THE WWE UNIVERSE. BUILD YOUR NAME.
LISTEN, I LOVE NXT. YOU'VE DONE A HELL OF A JOB THERE. AND ORDINARILY, I'D BE HONORED TO STEP INTO THE RING WITH ANYBODY.
BUT I DON'T NEED YOU TO INTRODUCE ME TO THE UNIVERSE.
JUST LIKE I TOLD YOUR FATHER IN LAW TWELVE YEARS AGO. I AM WHAT I AM. I DO WHAT I DO.
AND I'M EITHER READY FOR WWE OR I'M NOT.
IT'S NOT THAT SIMPLE.
SURE IT IS. JUST PUT ME IN THE RUMBLE. SINK OR SWIM.
EITHER I HOLD MY OWN AND CROWD RESPONDS...OR I DON'T.
I DUNNO, AJ...
THAT'S A BIG GAMBLE.
YEAH, WELL, THAT'S YOUR CALL.
I'VE GOT MY PHONE ON ME PRETTY MUCH ALWAYS. YOU LET ME KNOW WHAT YOU DECIDE.

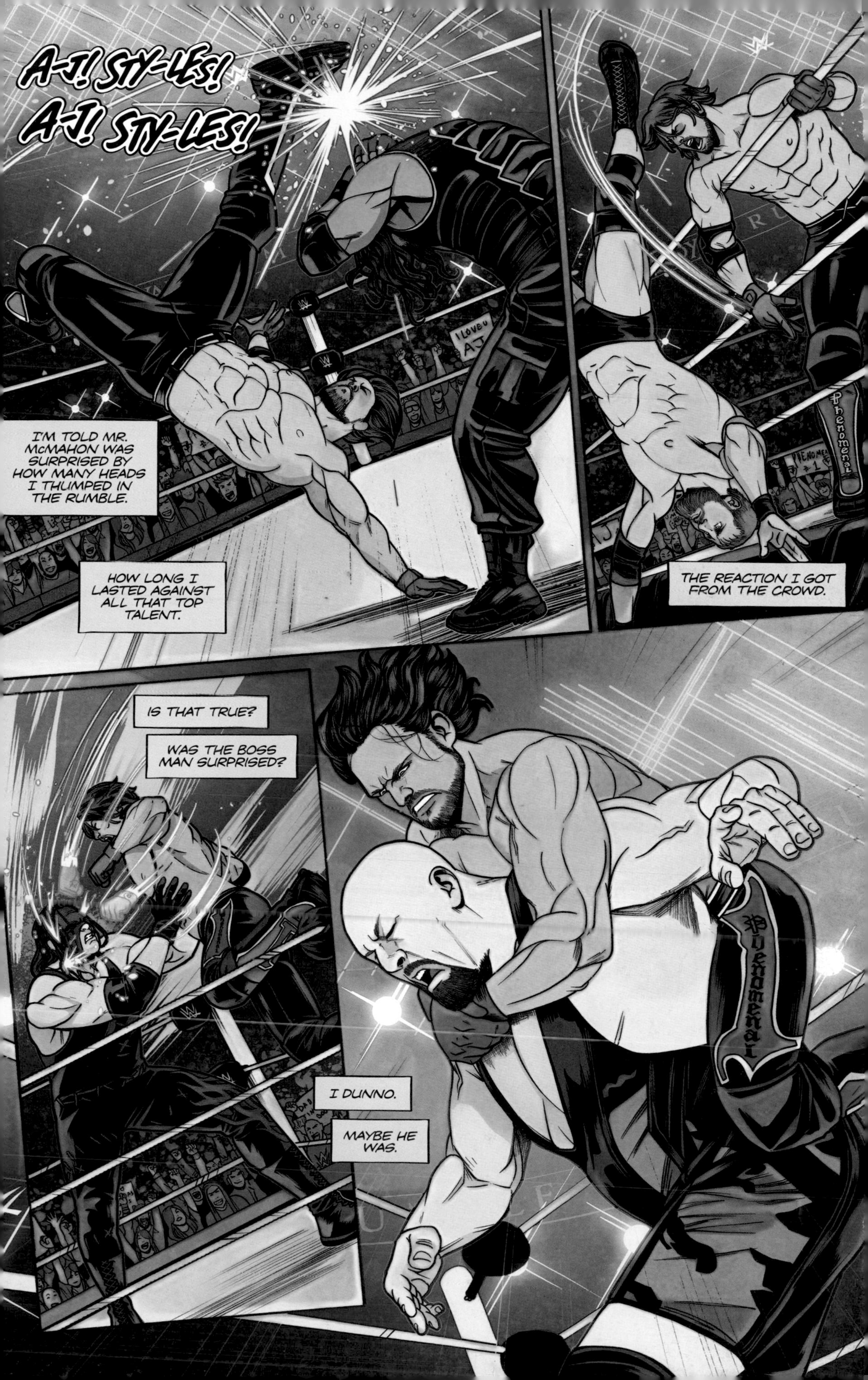
A-J! STY-LES!
A-J! STY-LES!
I'M TOLD MR. McMAHON WAS SURPRISED BY HOW MANY HEADS I THUMPED IN THE RUMBLE.
HOW LONG I LASTED AGAINST ALL THAT TOP TALENT.
THE REACTION I GOT FROM THE CROWD.
IS THAT TRUE?
WAS THE BOSS MAN SURPRISED?
I DUNNO.
MAYBE HE WAS.

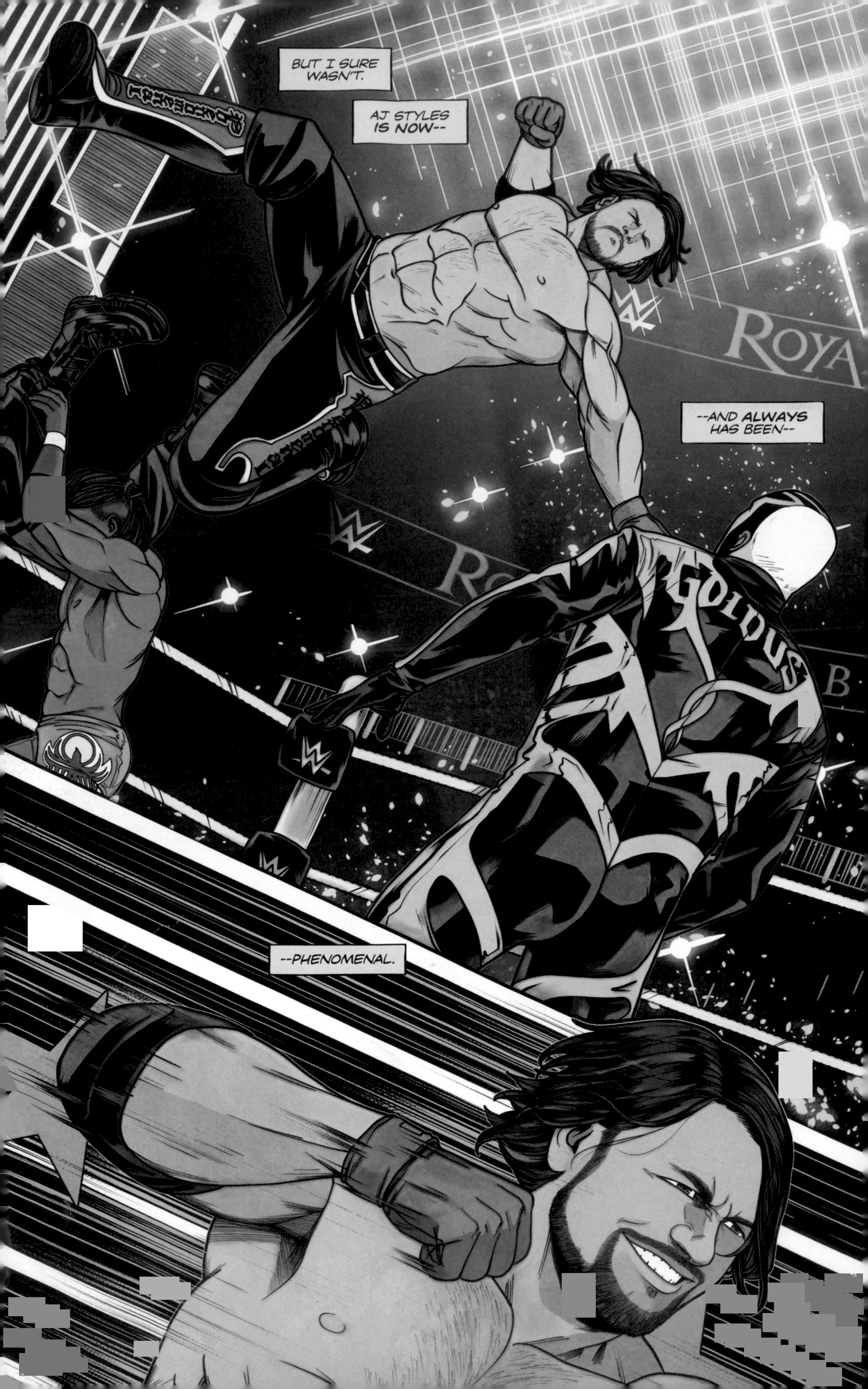
BUT I SURE WASN'T.
AJ STYLES IS NOW--
--AND ALWAYS HAS BEEN--
--PHENOMENAL.

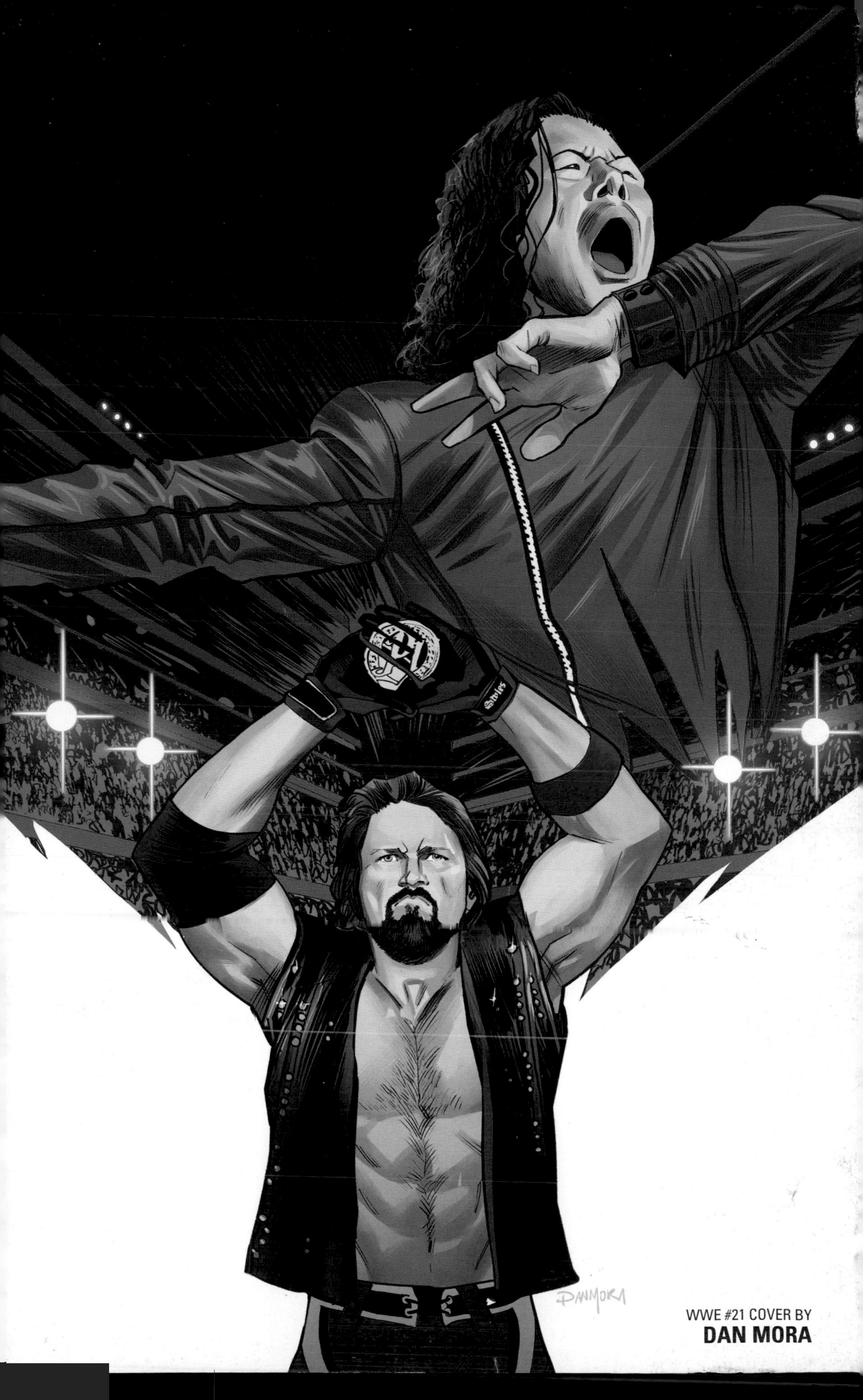
DANMORA

WWE #21 COVER BY
DAN MORA

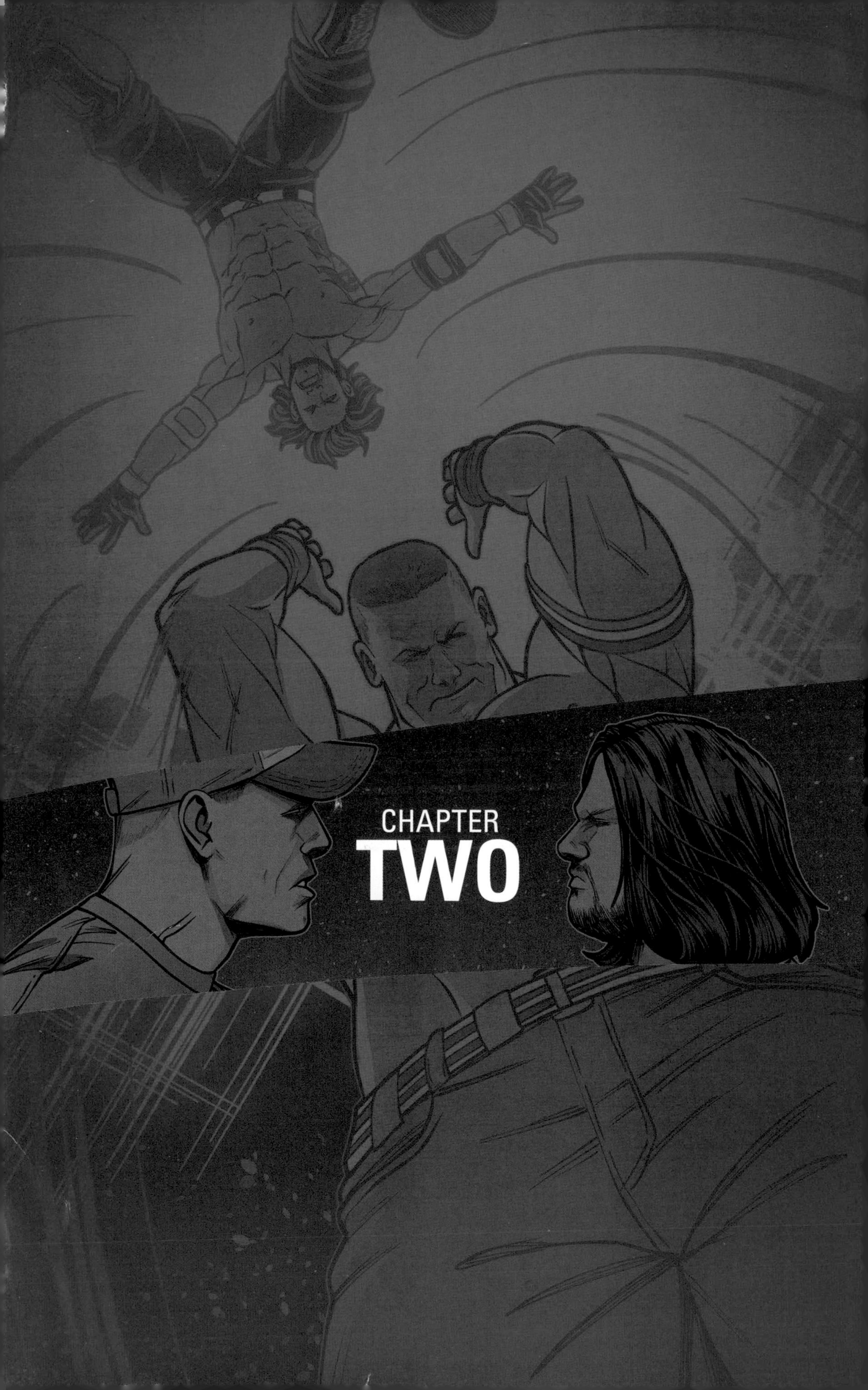
CHAPTER
TWO

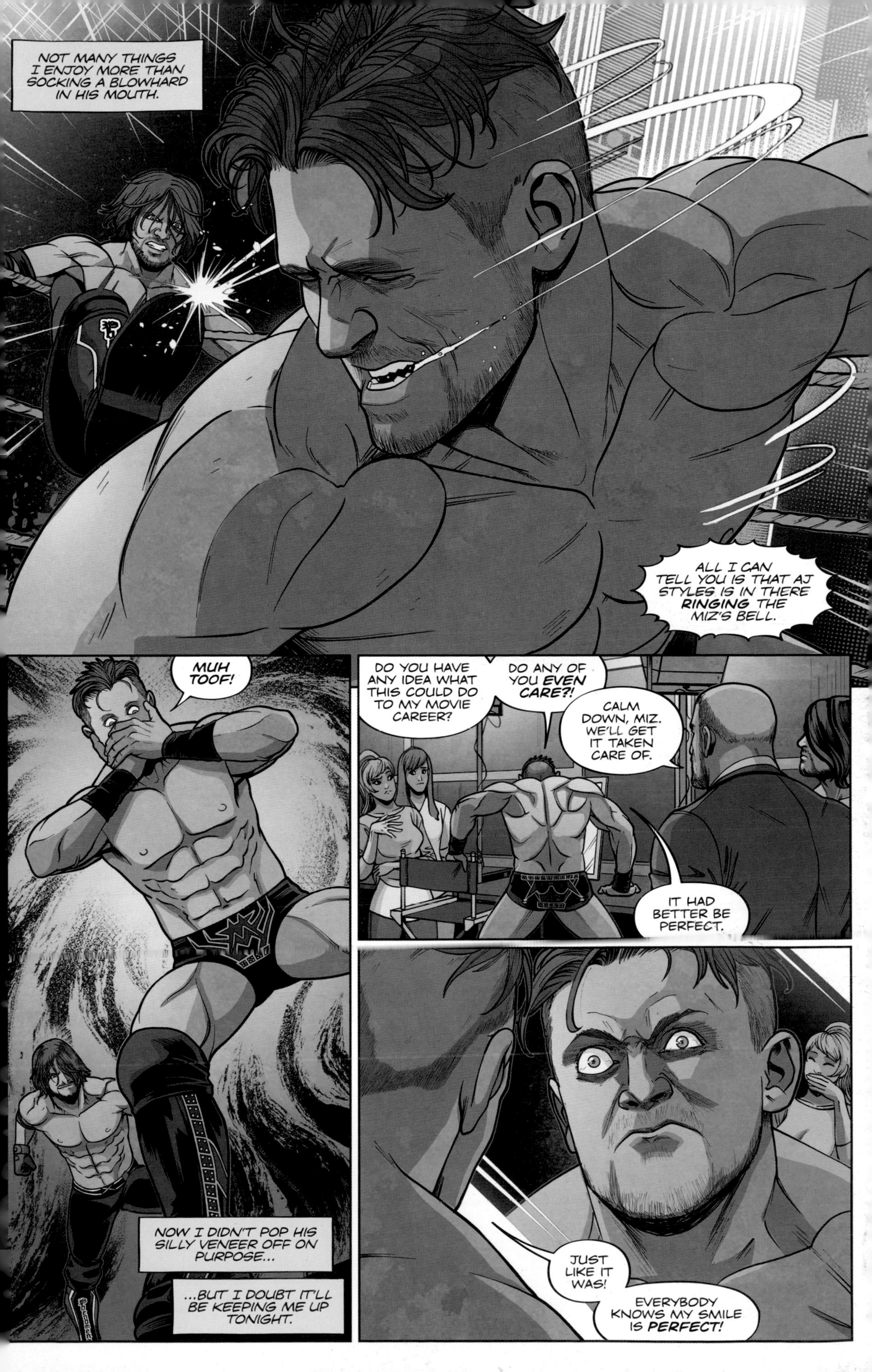
NOT MANY THINGS I ENJOY MORE THAN SOCKING A BLOWHARD IN HIS MOUTH.
ALL I CAN TELL YOU IS THAT AJ STYLES IS IN THERE RINGING THE MIZ'S BELL.
MUH TOOF!
NOW I DIDN'T POP HIS SILLY VENEER OFF ON PURPOSE...
...BUT I DOUBT IT'LL BE KEEPING ME UP TONIGHT.
DO YOU HAVE ANY IDEA WHAT THIS COULD DO TO MY MOVIE CAREER?
DO ANY OF YOU EVEN CARE?!
CALM DOWN, MIZ. WE'LL GET IT TAKEN CARE OF.
IT HAD BETTER BE PERFECT.
JUST LIKE IT WAS!
EVERYBODY KNOWS MY SMILE IS PERFECT!

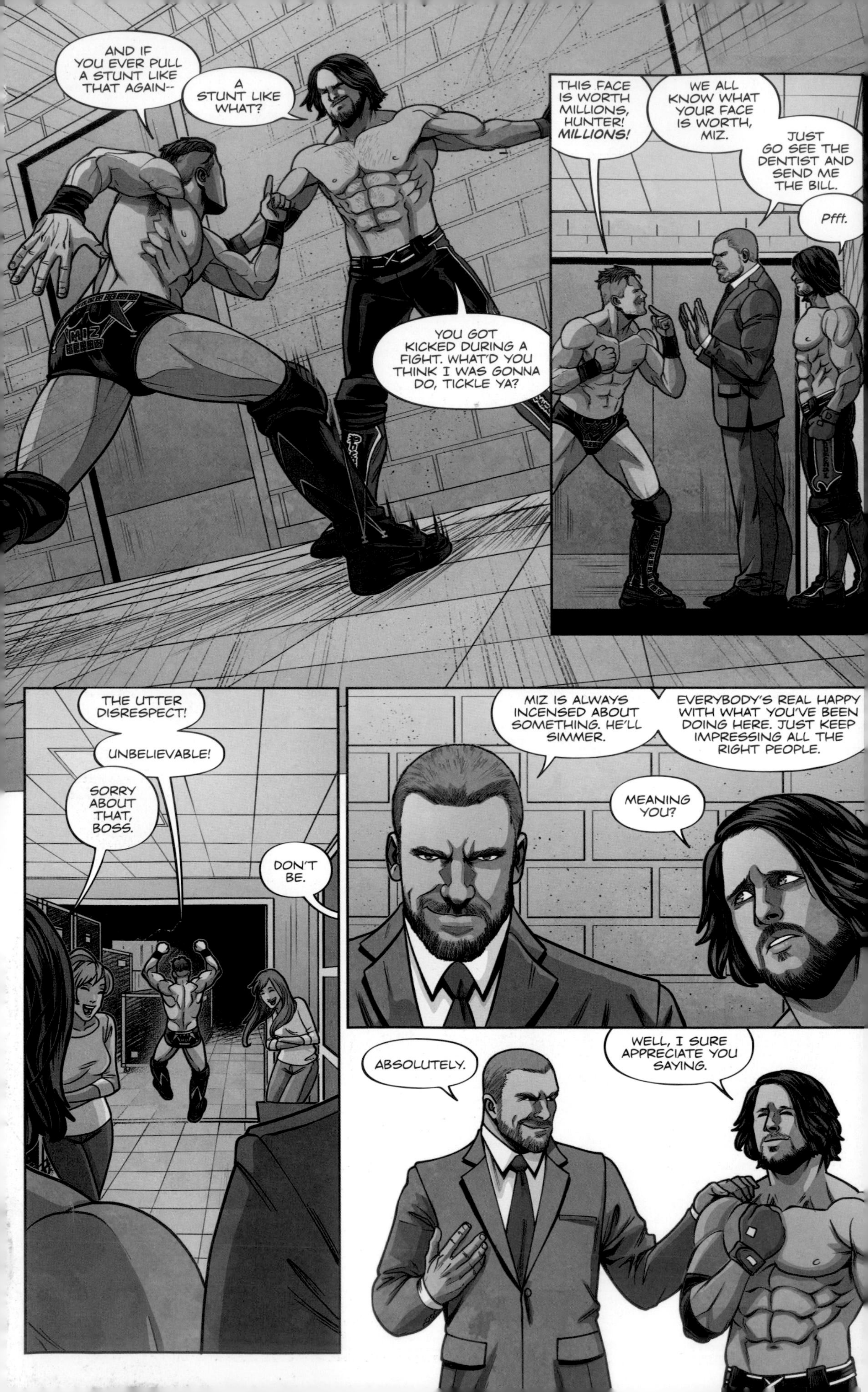
AND IF YOU EVER PULL A STUNT LIKE THAT AGAIN--
A STUNT LIKE WHAT?
YOU GOT KICKED DURING A FIGHT. WHAT'D YOU THINK I WAS GONNA DO, TICKLE YA?
THIS FACE IS WORTH MILLIONS, HUNTER! *MILLIONS!*
WE ALL KNOW WHAT YOUR FACE IS WORTH, MIZ.
JUST GO SEE THE DENTIST AND SEND ME THE BILL.
Pfft.
THE UTTER DISRESPECT!
UNBELIEVABLE!
SORRY ABOUT THAT, BOSS.
DON'T BE.
MIZ IS ALWAYS INCENSED ABOUT SOMETHING. HE'LL SIMMER.
EVERYBODY'S REAL HAPPY WITH WHAT YOU'VE BEEN DOING HERE. JUST KEEP IMPRESSING ALL THE RIGHT PEOPLE.
MEANING YOU?
ABSOLUTELY.
WELL, I SURE APPRECIATE YOU SAYING.

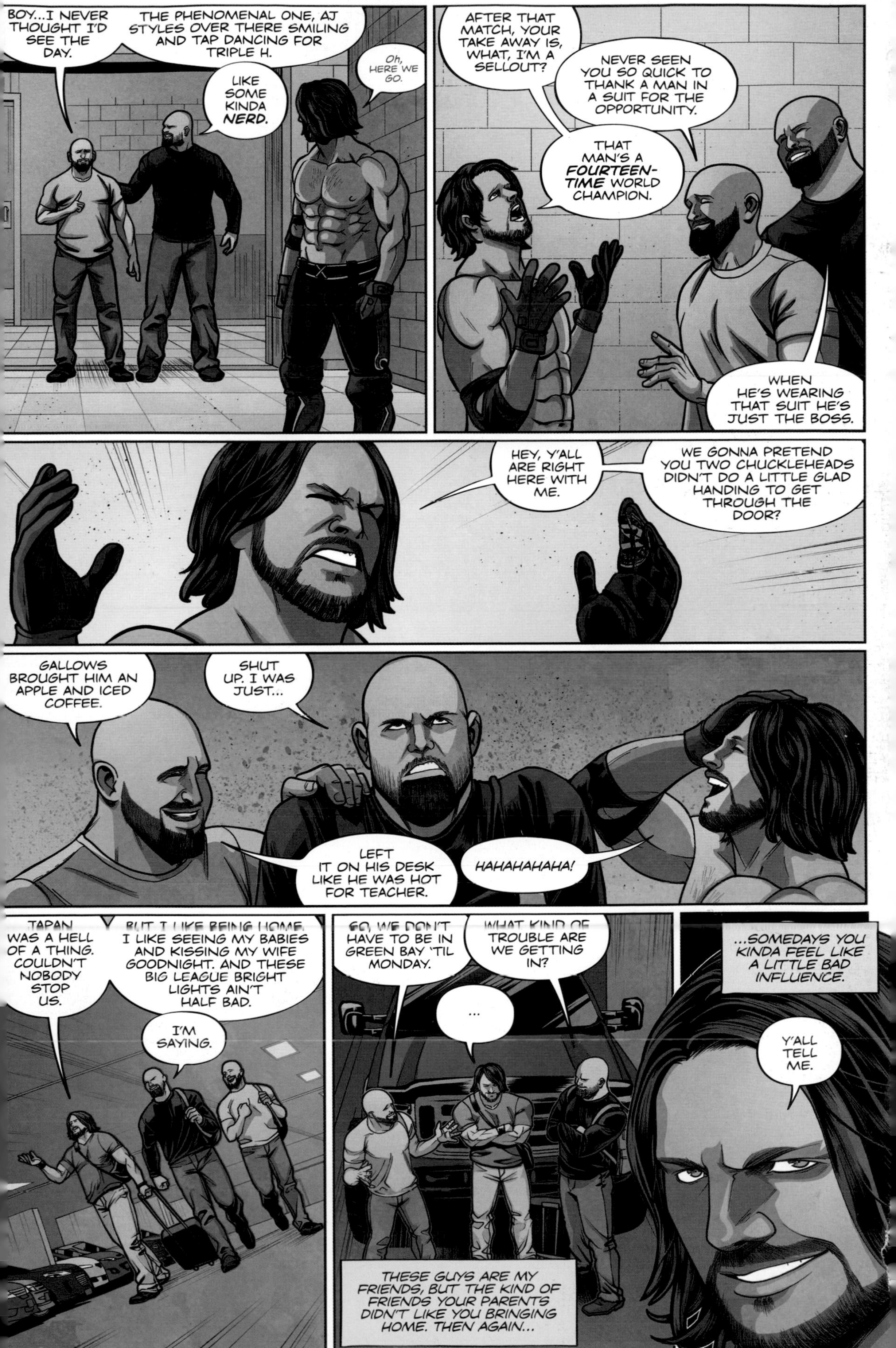

BOY...I NEVER THOUGHT I'D SEE THE DAY.
THE PHENOMENAL ONE, AJ STYLES OVER THERE SMILING AND TAP DANCING FOR TRIPLE H.
LIKE SOME KINDA **NERD.**
Oh, HERE WE GO.
AFTER THAT MATCH, YOUR TAKE AWAY IS, WHAT, I'M A SELLOUT?
NEVER SEEN YOU SO QUICK TO THANK A MAN IN A SUIT FOR THE OPPORTUNITY.
THAT MAN'S A ***FOURTEEN-TIME*** WORLD CHAMPION.
WHEN HE'S WEARING THAT SUIT HE'S JUST THE BOSS.
HEY, Y'ALL ARE RIGHT HERE WITH ME.
WE GONNA PRETEND YOU TWO CHUCKLEHEADS DIDN'T DO A LITTLE GLAD HANDING TO GET THROUGH THE DOOR?
GALLOWS BROUGHT HIM AN APPLE AND ICED COFFEE.
SHUT UP. I WAS JUST...
LEFT IT ON HIS DESK LIKE HE WAS HOT FOR TEACHER.
HAHAHAHAHA!
JAPAN WAS A HELL OF A THING. COULDN'T NOBODY STOP US.
BUT I LIKE BEING HOME. I LIKE SEEING MY BABIES AND KISSING MY WIFE GOODNIGHT. AND THESE BIG LEAGUE BRIGHT LIGHTS AIN'T HALF BAD.
I'M SAYING.
SO, WE DON'T HAVE TO BE IN GREEN BAY 'TIL MONDAY.
WHAT KIND OF TROUBLE ARE WE GETTING IN?
...
THESE GUYS ARE MY FRIENDS, BUT THE KIND OF FRIENDS YOUR PARENTS DIDN'T LIKE YOU BRINGING HOME. THEN AGAIN...
...SOMEDAYS YOU KINDA FEEL LIKE A LITTLE BAD INFLUENCE.
Y'ALL TELL ME.

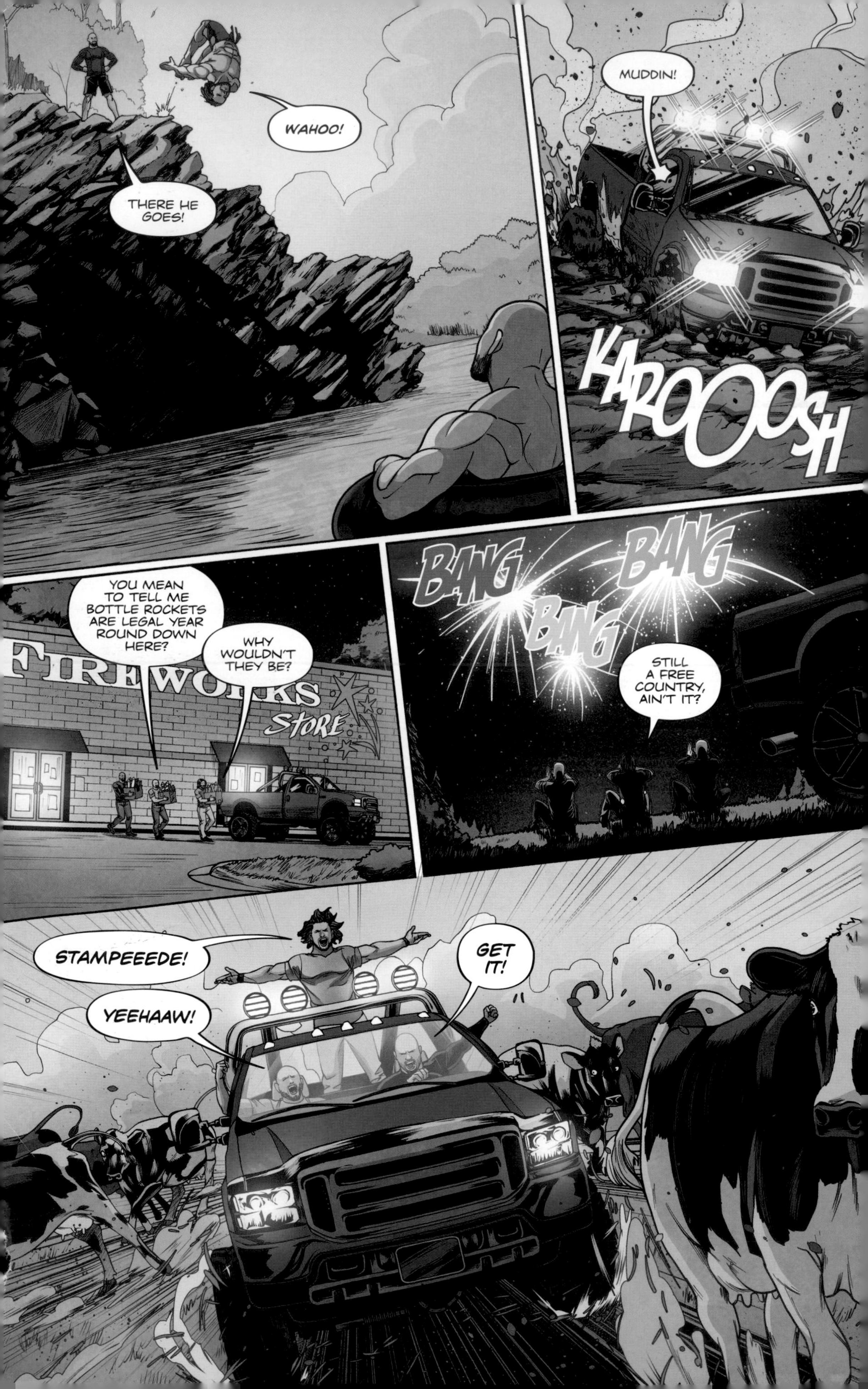
WAHOO!
THERE HE GOES!
MUDDIN!
KAROOOSH
YOU MEAN TO TELL ME BOTTLE ROCKETS ARE LEGAL YEAR ROUND DOWN HERE?
WHY WOULDN'T THEY BE?
FIREWORKS STORE
BANG
BANG
BANG
STILL A FREE COUNTRY, AIN'T IT?
STAMPEEEDE!
YEEHAAW!
GET IT!

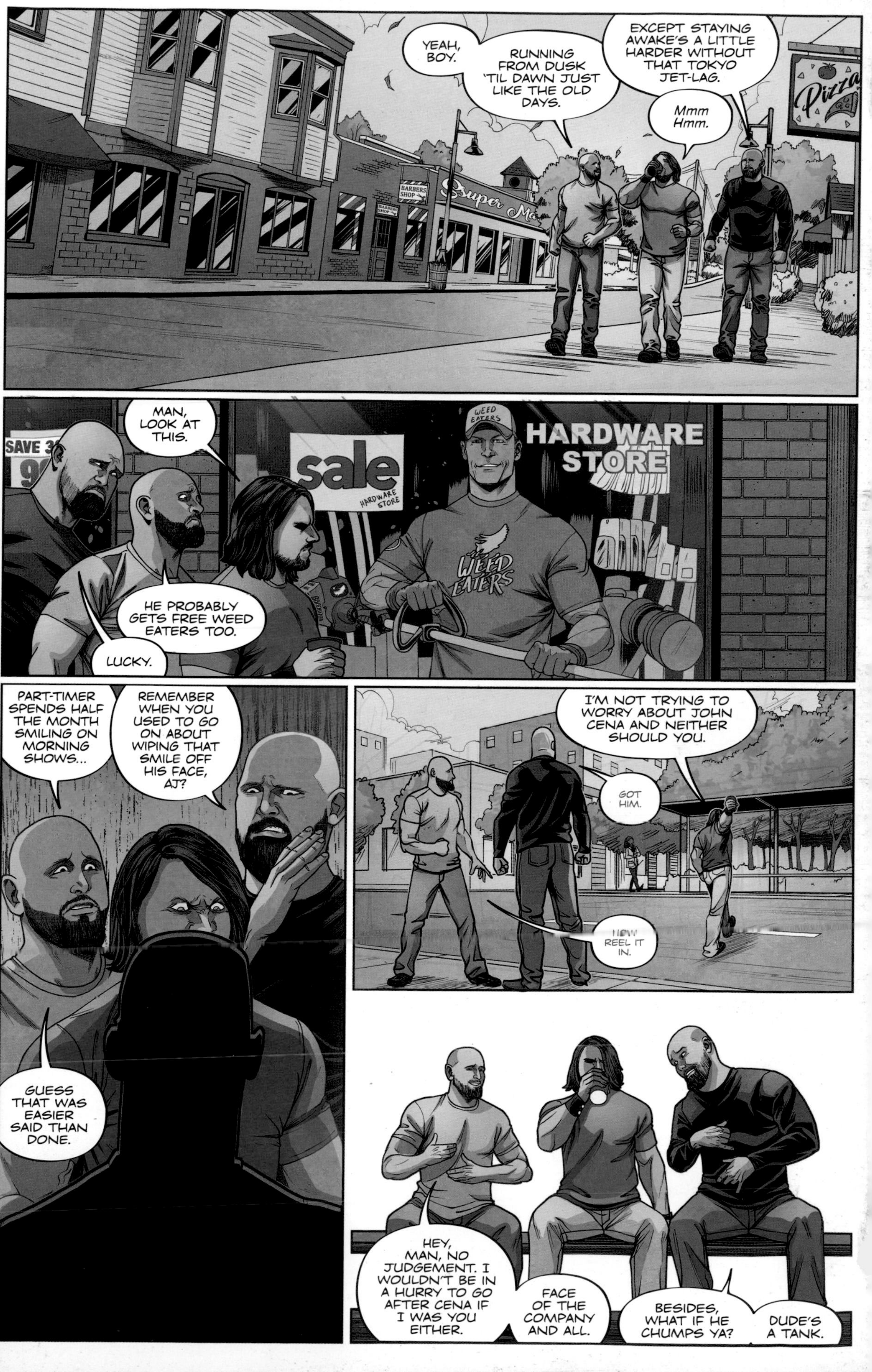

YEAH, BOY.
RUNNING FROM DUSK 'TIL DAWN JUST LIKE THE OLD DAYS.
EXCEPT STAYING AWAKE'S A LITTLE HARDER WITHOUT THAT TOKYO JET-LAG.
Mmm Hmm.
Pizza
BARBERS SHOP
Super Ma
MAN, LOOK AT THIS.
SAVE 3
sale
HARDWARE STORE
WEED EATERS
HARDWARE STORE
HE PROBABLY GETS FREE WEED EATERS TOO.
LUCKY.
PART-TIMER SPENDS HALF THE MONTH SMILING ON MORNING SHOWS...
REMEMBER WHEN YOU USED TO GO ON ABOUT WIPING THAT SMILE OFF HIS FACE, AJ?
GUESS THAT WAS EASIER SAID THAN DONE.
I'M NOT TRYING TO WORRY ABOUT JOHN CENA AND NEITHER SHOULD YOU.
GOT HIM.
REEL IT IN.
HEY, MAN, NO JUDGEMENT. I WOULDN'T BE IN A HURRY TO GO AFTER CENA IF I WAS YOU EITHER.
FACE OF THE COMPANY AND ALL.
BESIDES, WHAT IF HE CHUMPS YA?
DUDE'S A TANK.

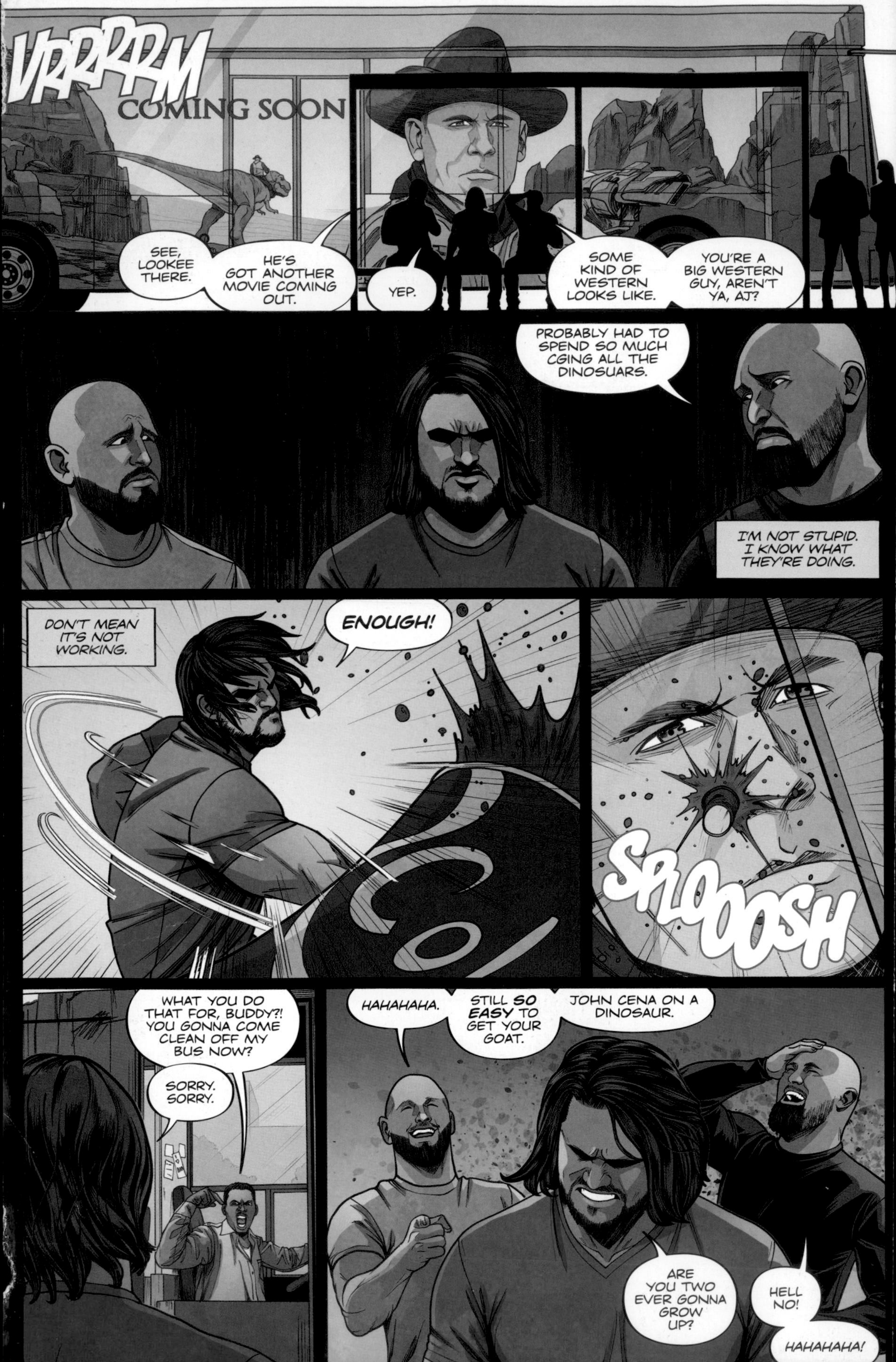
VRRRRRM
COMING SOON
SEE, LOOKEE THERE.
HE'S GOT ANOTHER MOVIE COMING OUT.
YEP.
SOME KIND OF WESTERN LOOKS LIKE.
YOU'RE A BIG WESTERN GUY, AREN'T YA, AJ?
PROBABLY HAD TO SPEND SO MUCH CGING ALL THE DINOSUARS.
I'M NOT STUPID. I KNOW WHAT THEY'RE DOING.
DON'T MEAN IT'S NOT WORKING.
ENOUGH!
SPLOOOSH
WHAT YOU DO THAT FOR, BUDDY?! YOU GONNA COME CLEAN OFF MY BUS NOW?
SORRY. SORRY.
HAHAHAHA.
STILL SO EASY TO GET YOUR GOAT.
JOHN CENA ON A DINOSAUR.
ARE YOU TWO EVER GONNA GROW UP?
HELL NO!
HAHAHAHA!

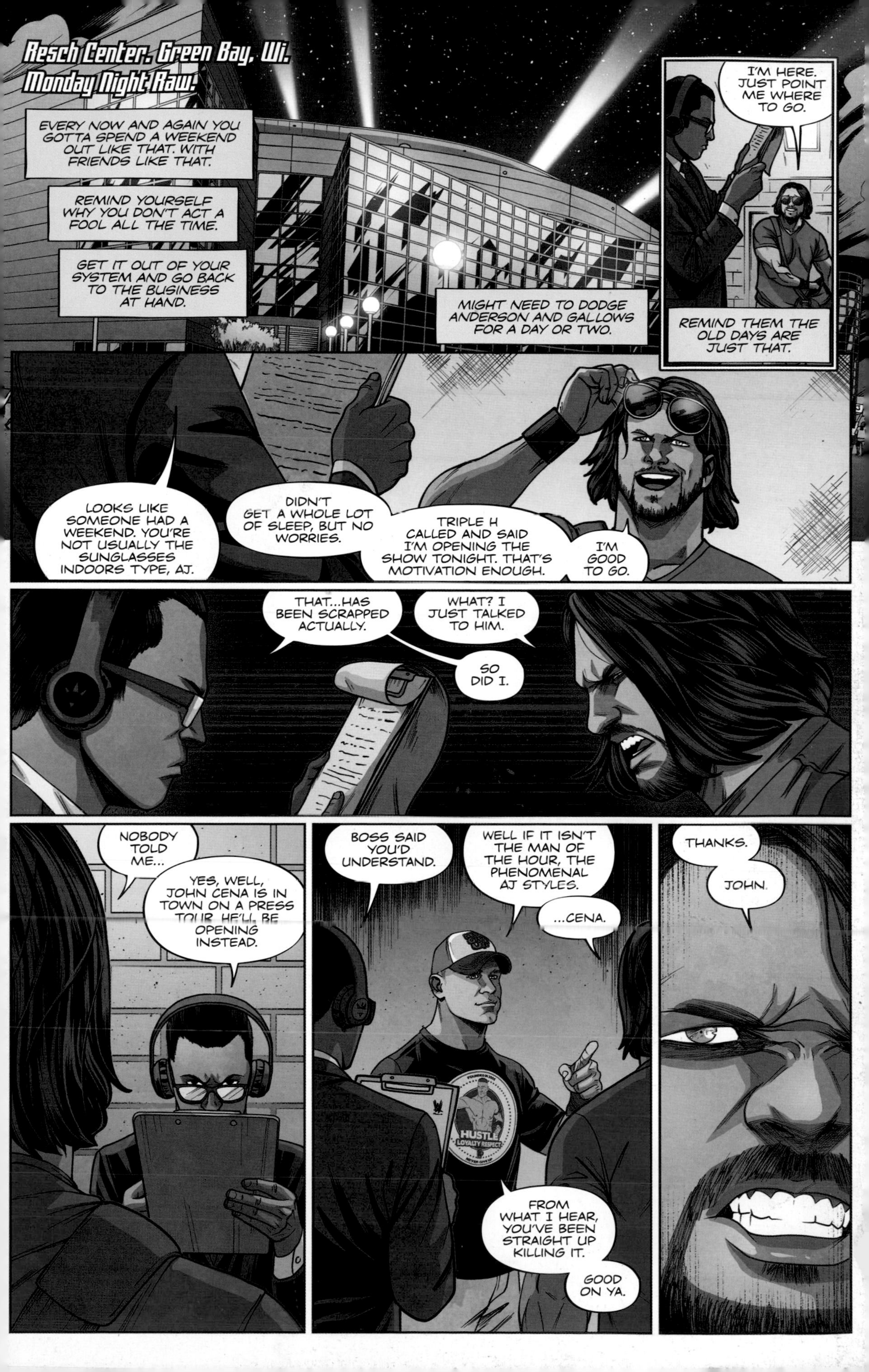
Resch Center. Green Bay, Wi.
Monday Night Raw.
EVERY NOW AND AGAIN YOU GOTTA SPEND A WEEKEND OUT LIKE THAT. WITH FRIENDS LIKE THAT.
REMIND YOURSELF WHY YOU DON'T ACT A FOOL ALL THE TIME.
GET IT OUT OF YOUR SYSTEM AND GO BACK TO THE BUSINESS AT HAND.
MIGHT NEED TO DODGE ANDERSON AND GALLOWS FOR A DAY OR TWO.
I'M HERE. JUST POINT ME WHERE TO GO.
REMIND THEM THE OLD DAYS ARE JUST THAT.
LOOKS LIKE SOMEONE HAD A WEEKEND. YOU'RE NOT USUALLY THE SUNGLASSES INDOORS TYPE, AJ.
DIDN'T GET A WHOLE LOT OF SLEEP, BUT NO WORRIES.
TRIPLE H CALLED AND SAID I'M OPENING THE SHOW TONIGHT. THAT'S MOTIVATION ENOUGH.
I'M GOOD TO GO.
THAT...HAS BEEN SCRAPPED ACTUALLY.
WHAT? I JUST TALKED TO HIM.
SO DID I.
NOBODY TOLD ME...
YES, WELL, JOHN CENA IS IN TOWN ON A PRESS TOUR. HE'LL BE OPENING INSTEAD.
BOSS SAID YOU'D UNDERSTAND.
WELL IF IT ISN'T THE MAN OF THE HOUR, THE PHENOMENAL AJ STYLES.
...CENA.
FROM WHAT I HEAR, YOU'VE BEEN STRAIGHT UP KILLING IT.
GOOD ON YA.
THANKS.
JOHN.

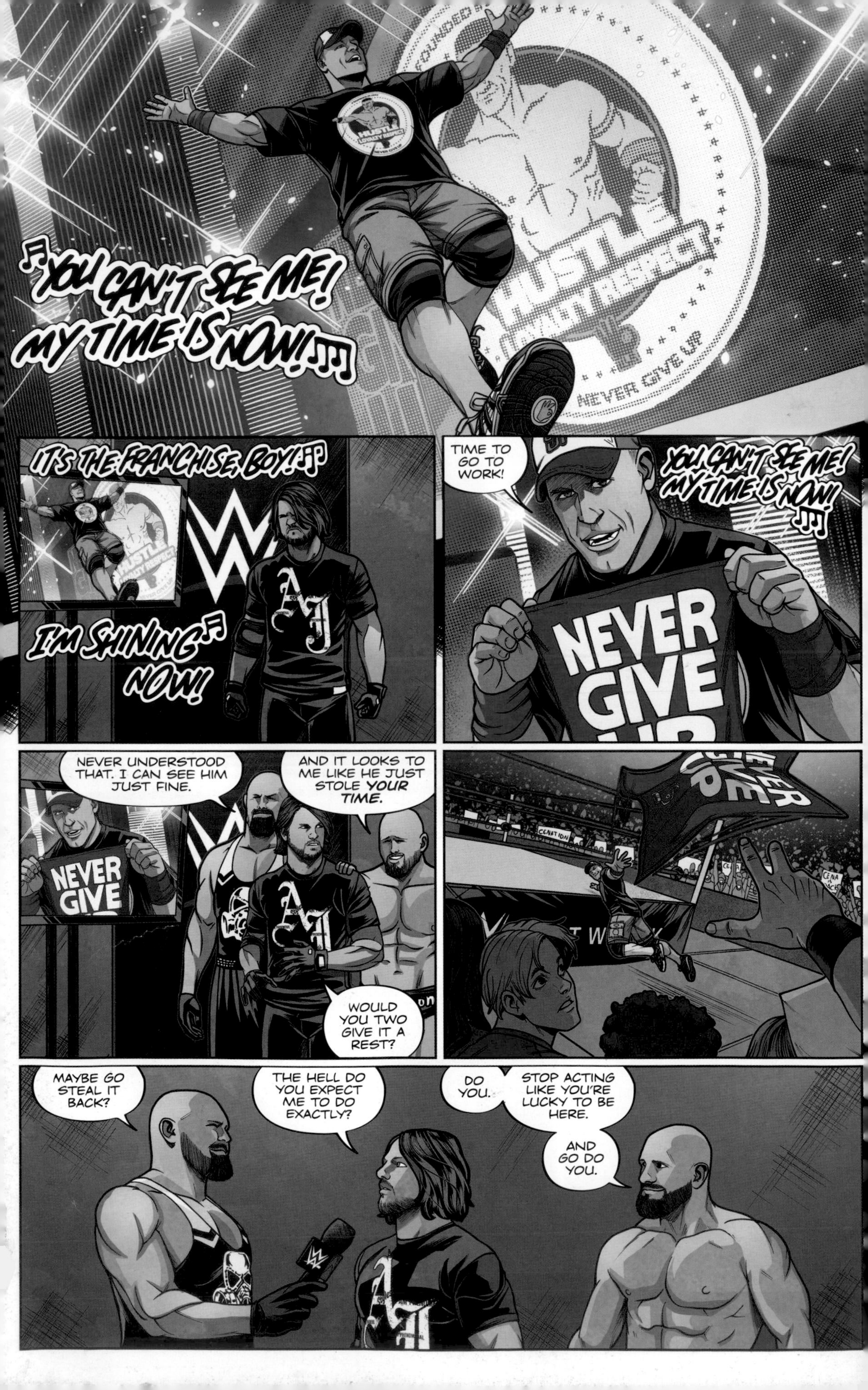

♬YOU CAN'T SEE ME! MY TIME IS NOW!♬
IT'S THE FRANCHISE, BOY!♬
I'M SHINING NOW!♬
TIME TO GO TO WORK!
YOU CAN'T SEE ME! MY TIME IS NOW!♬
NEVER GIVE UP
NEVER UNDERSTOOD THAT. I CAN SEE HIM JUST FINE.
AND IT LOOKS TO ME LIKE HE JUST STOLE *YOUR TIME.*
WOULD YOU TWO GIVE IT A REST?
MAYBE GO STEAL IT BACK?
THE HELL DO YOU EXPECT ME TO DO EXACTLY?
DO YOU.
STOP ACTING LIKE YOU'RE LUCKY TO BE HERE.
AND GO DO YOU.

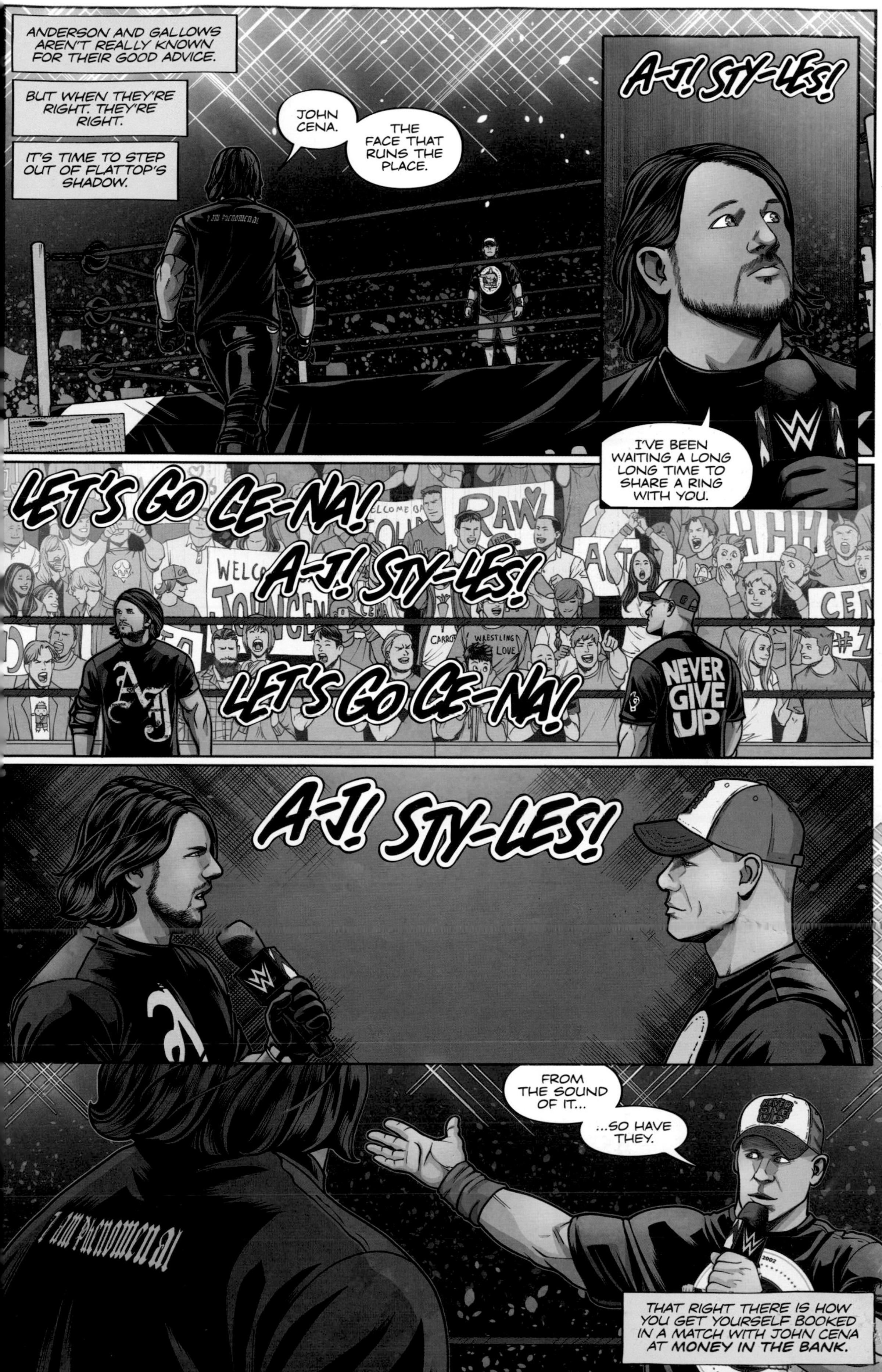

ANDERSON AND GALLOWS AREN'T REALLY KNOWN FOR THEIR GOOD ADVICE.
BUT WHEN THEY'RE RIGHT. THEY'RE RIGHT.
IT'S TIME TO STEP OUT OF FLATTOP'S SHADOW.
JOHN CENA.
THE FACE THAT RUNS THE PLACE.
I AM PHENOMENAL
A-J! STY-LES!
I'VE BEEN WAITING A LONG LONG TIME TO SHARE A RING WITH YOU.
LET'S GO CE-NA!
A-J! STY-LES!
LET'S GO CE-NA!
NEVER GIVE UP
A-J! STY-LES!
FROM THE SOUND OF IT...
...SO HAVE THEY.
I AM PHENOMENAL
THAT RIGHT THERE IS HOW YOU GET YOURSELF BOOKED IN A MATCH WITH JOHN CENA AT MONEY IN THE BANK.

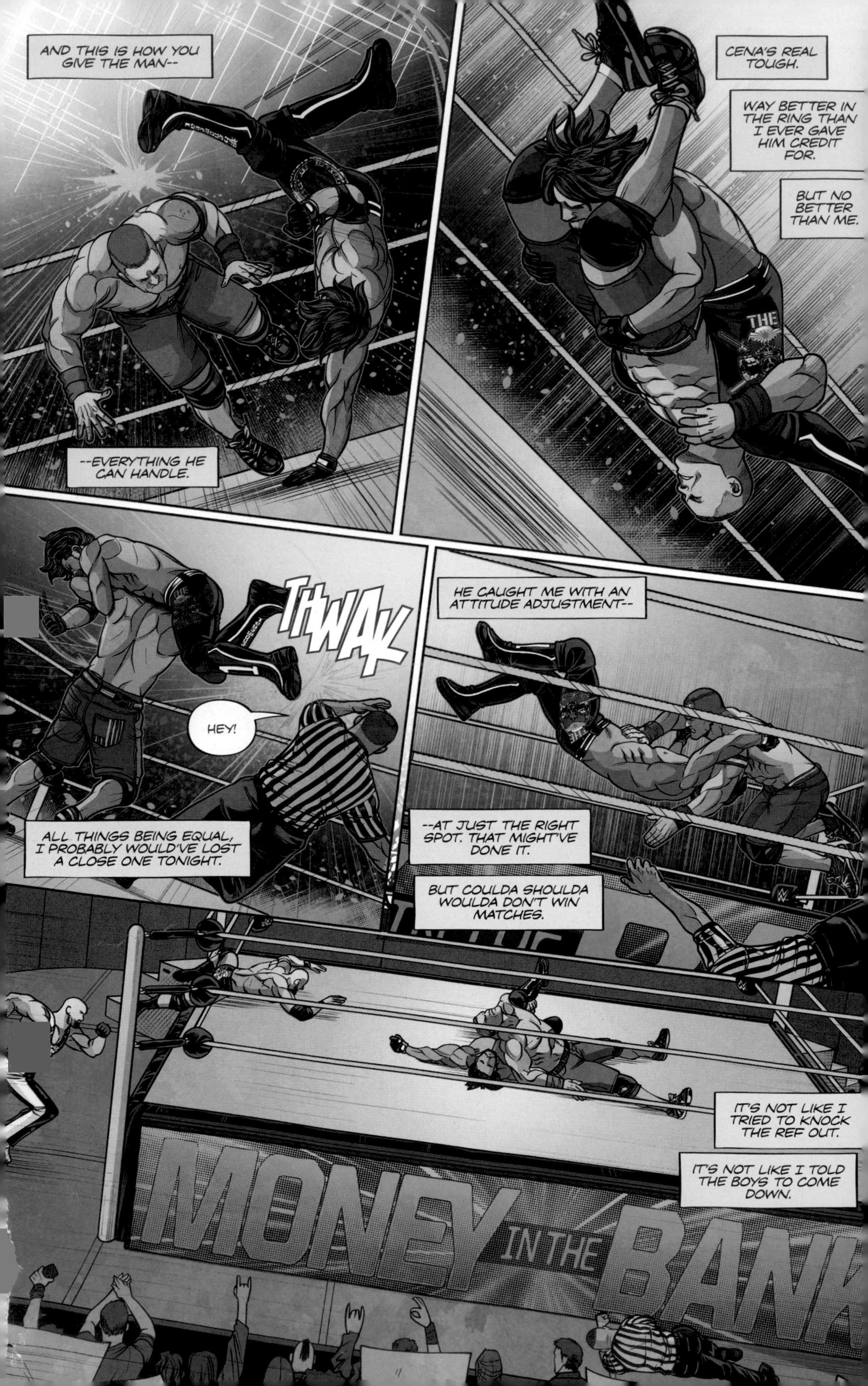
AND THIS IS HOW YOU GIVE THE MAN--
--EVERYTHING HE CAN HANDLE.
CENA'S REAL TOUGH.
WAY BETTER IN THE RING THAN I EVER GAVE HIM CREDIT FOR.
BUT NO BETTER THAN ME.
THWAK
HEY!
ALL THINGS BEING EQUAL, I PROBABLY WOULD'VE LOST A CLOSE ONE TONIGHT.
HE CAUGHT ME WITH AN ATTITUDE ADJUSTMENT--
--AT JUST THE RIGHT SPOT. THAT MIGHT'VE DONE IT.
BUT COULDA SHOULDA WOULDA DON'T WIN MATCHES.
IT'S NOT LIKE I TRIED TO KNOCK THE REF OUT.
IT'S NOT LIKE I TOLD THE BOYS TO COME DOWN.
MONEY IN THE BANK

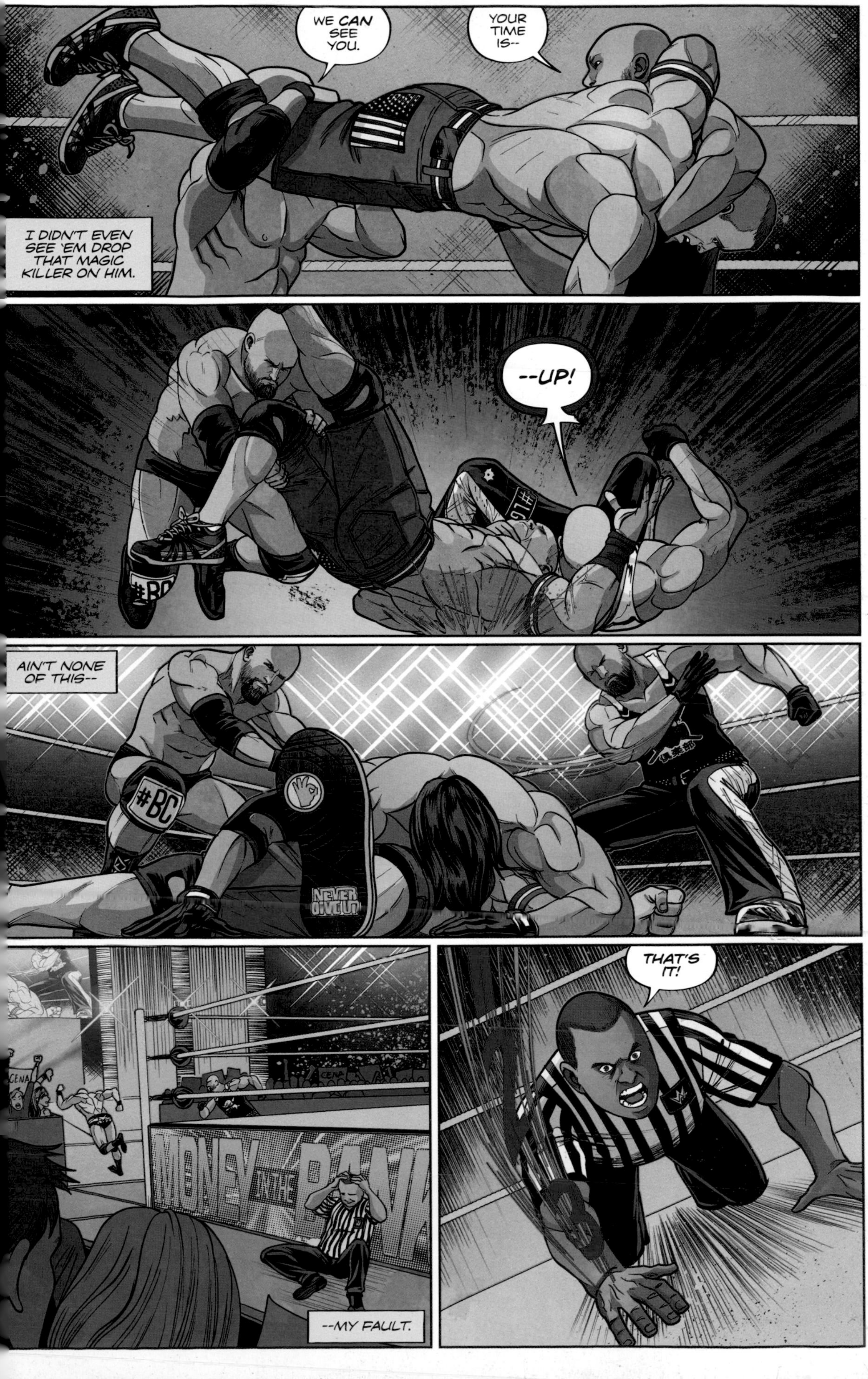

WE CAN SEE YOU.
YOUR TIME IS--
I DIDN'T EVEN SEE 'EM DROP THAT MAGIC KILLER ON HIM.
--UP!
AIN'T NONE OF THIS--
--MY FAULT.
THAT'S IT!

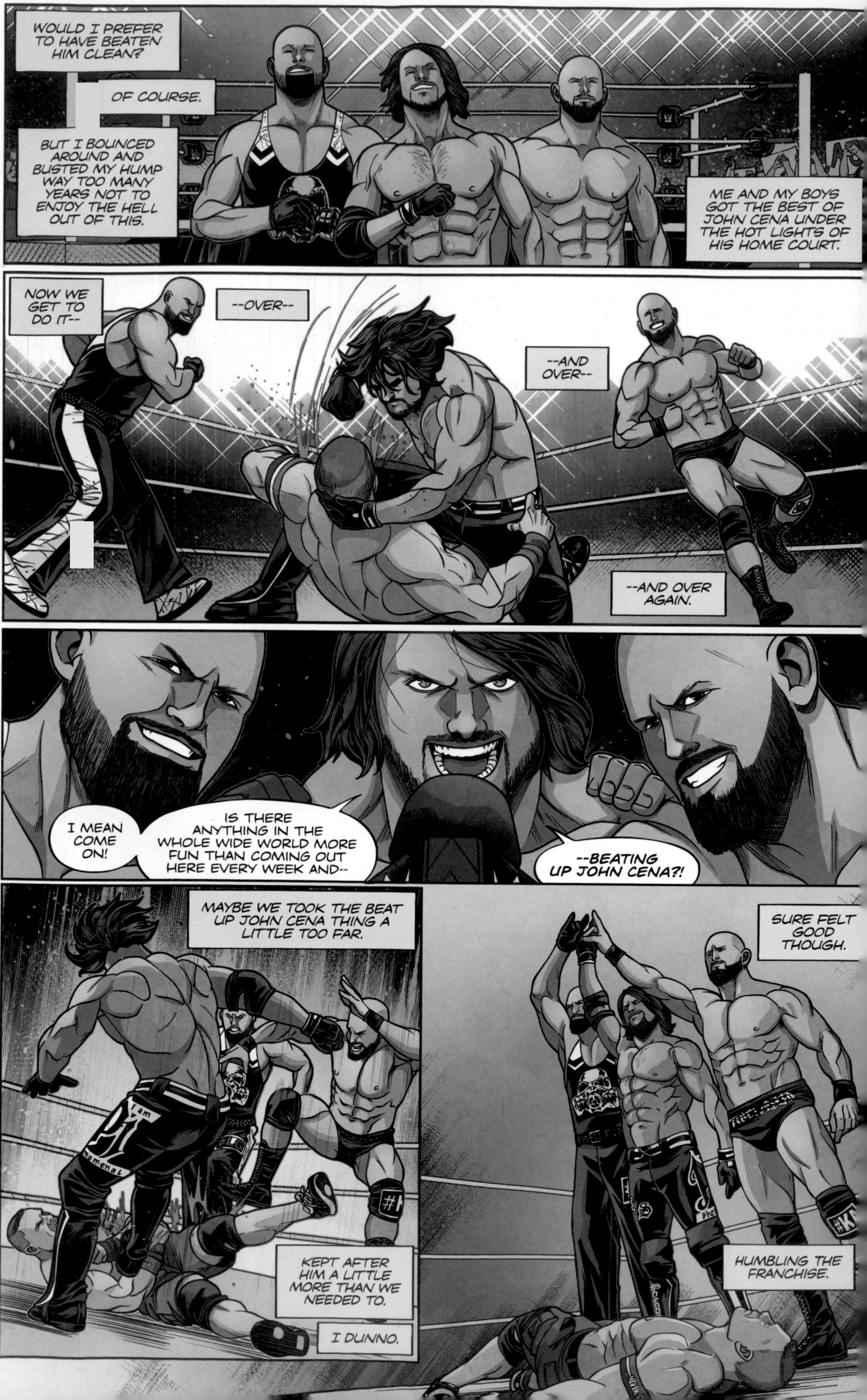
WOULD I PREFER TO HAVE BEATEN HIM CLEAN?
OF COURSE.
BUT I BOUNCED AROUND AND BUSTED MY HUMP WAY TOO MANY YEARS NOT TO ENJOY THE HELL OUT OF THIS.
ME AND MY BOYS GOT THE BEST OF JOHN CENA UNDER THE HOT LIGHTS OF HIS HOME COURT.
NOW WE GET TO DO IT--
--OVER--
--AND OVER--
--AND OVER AGAIN.
I MEAN COME ON!
IS THERE ANYTHING IN THE WHOLE WIDE WORLD MORE FUN THAN COMING OUT HERE EVERY WEEK AND--
--BEATING UP JOHN CENA?!
MAYBE WE TOOK THE BEAT UP JOHN CENA THING A LITTLE TOO FAR.
KEPT AFTER HIM A LITTLE MORE THAN WE NEEDED TO.
I DUNNO.
SURE FELT GOOD THOUGH.
HUMBLING THE FRANCHISE.

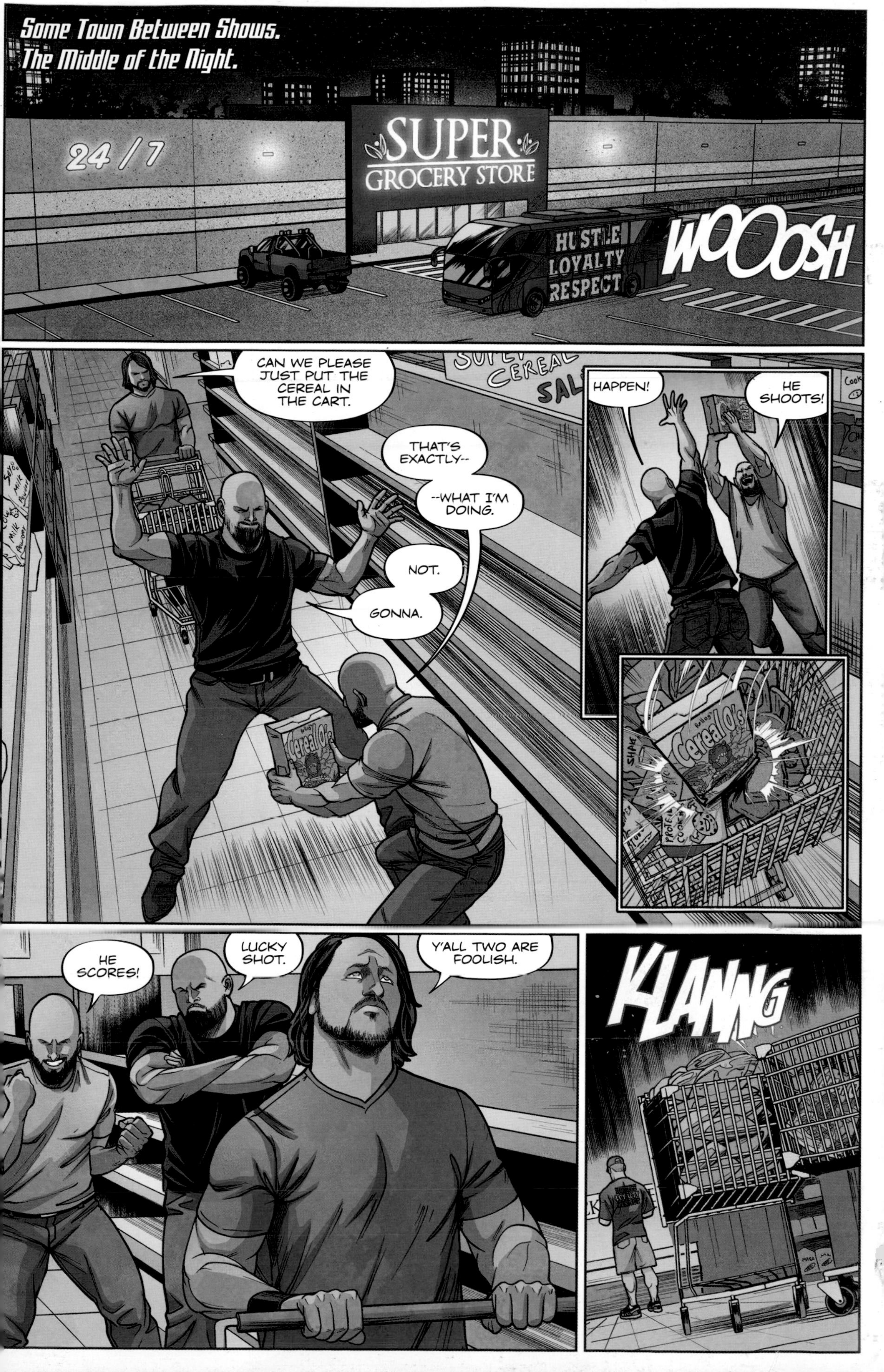
Some Town Between Shows.
The Middle of the Night.
24 / 7
SUPER
GROCERY STORE
HUSTLE
LOYALTY
RESPECT
WOOOSH
CAN WE PLEASE JUST PUT THE CEREAL IN THE CART.
THAT'S EXACTLY--
--WHAT I'M DOING.
NOT.
GONNA.
Cereal O's
HAPPEN!
HE SHOOTS!
Cereal O's
HE SCORES!
LUCKY SHOT.
Y'ALL TWO ARE FOOLISH.
KLANNG

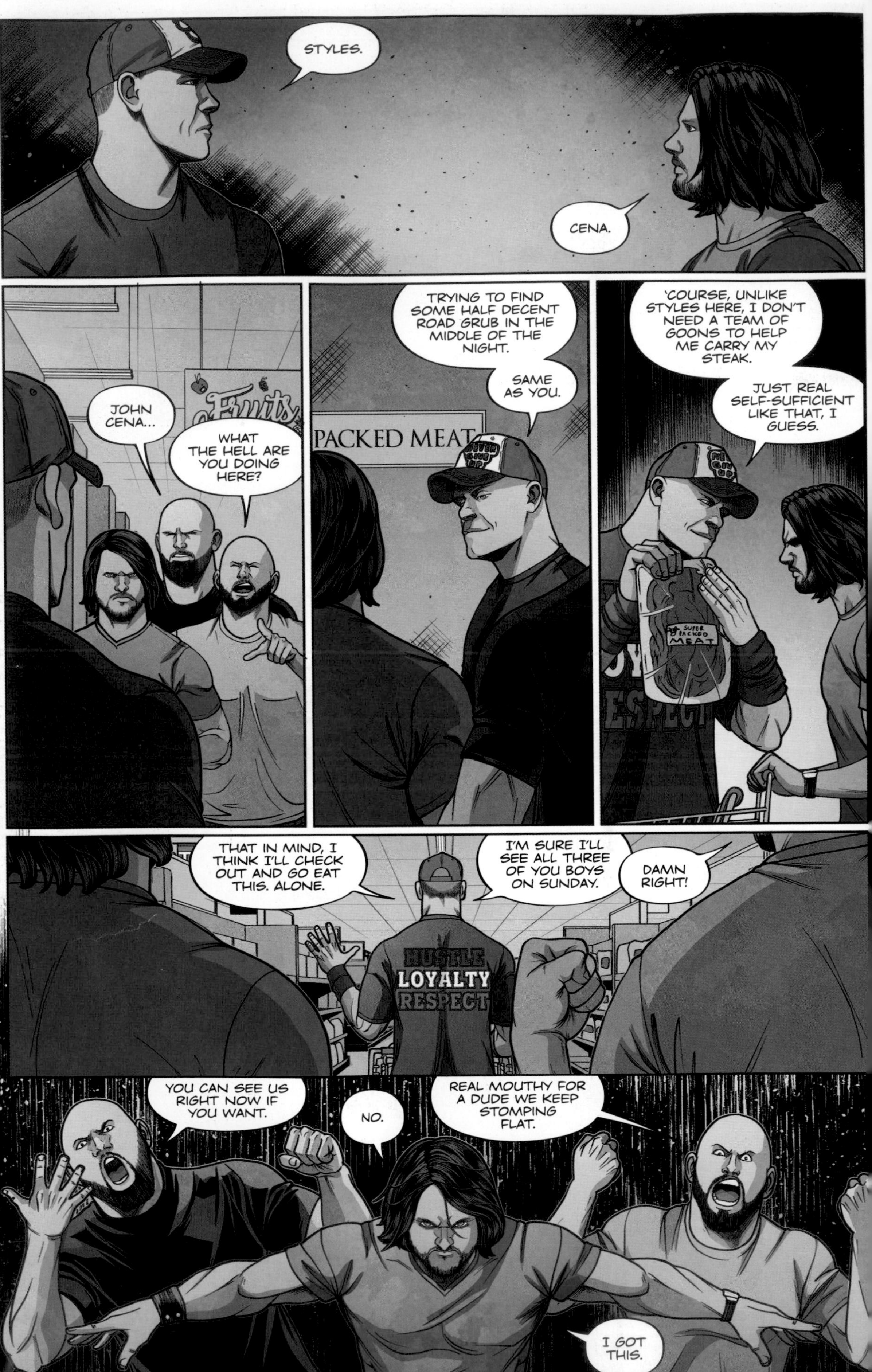
STYLES.
CENA.
JOHN CENA...
WHAT THE HELL ARE YOU DOING HERE?
FRUITS
PACKED MEAT
TRYING TO FIND SOME HALF DECENT ROAD GRUB IN THE MIDDLE OF THE NIGHT.
SAME AS YOU.
'COURSE, UNLIKE STYLES HERE, I DON'T NEED A TEAM OF GOONS TO HELP ME CARRY MY STEAK.
JUST REAL SELF-SUFFICIENT LIKE THAT, I GUESS.
SUPER PACKED MEAT
THAT IN MIND, I THINK I'LL CHECK OUT AND GO EAT THIS. ALONE.
I'M SURE I'LL SEE ALL THREE OF YOU BOYS ON SUNDAY.
DAMN RIGHT!
HUSTLE
LOYALTY
RESPECT
YOU CAN SEE US RIGHT NOW IF YOU WANT.
NO.
REAL MOUTHY FOR A DUDE WE KEEP STOMPING FLAT.
I GOT THIS.

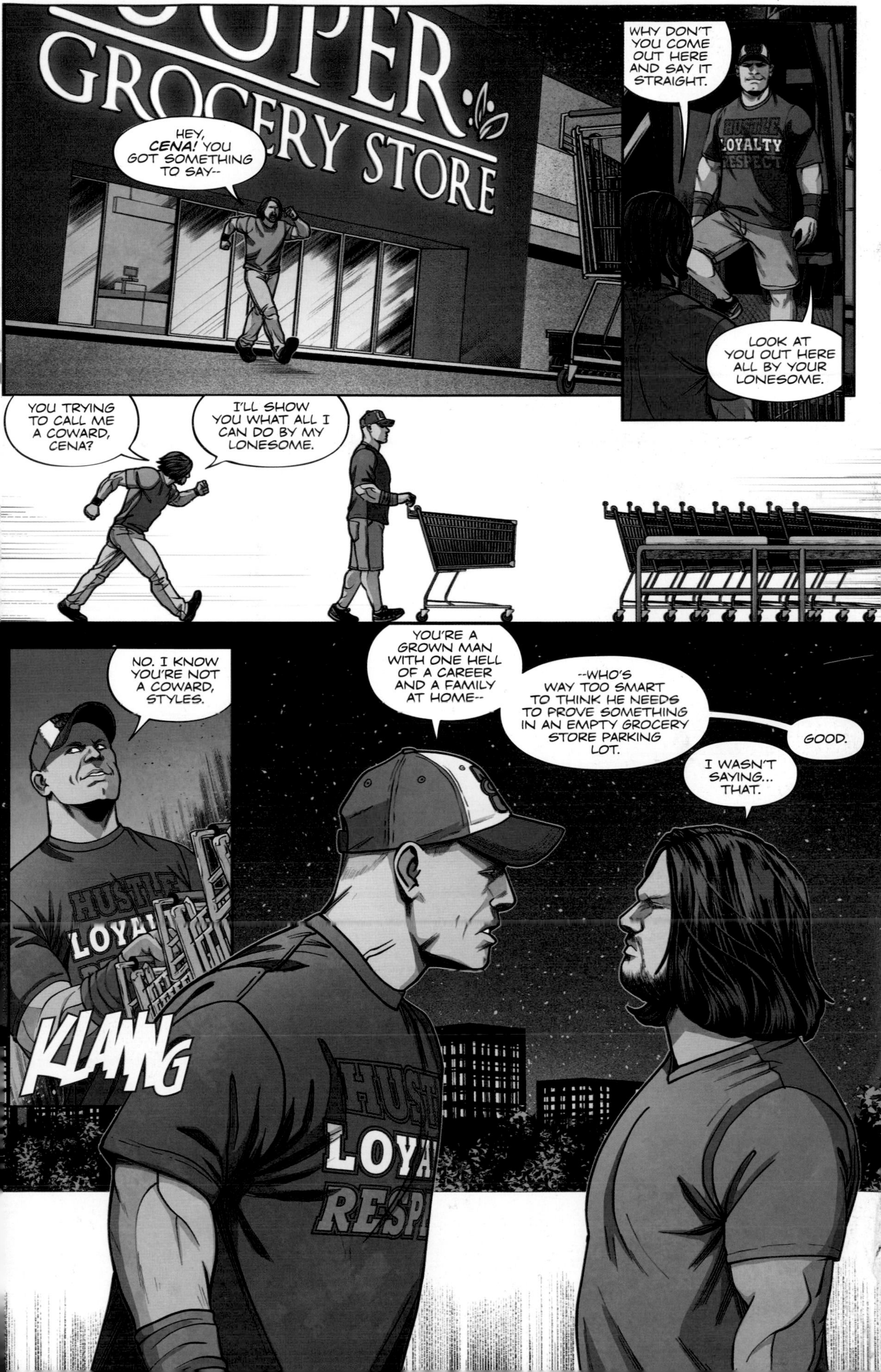
SUPER
GROCERY STORE
HEY, CENA! YOU GOT SOMETHING TO SAY--
WHY DON'T YOU COME OUT HERE AND SAY IT STRAIGHT.
HUSTLE LOYALTY RESPECT
LOOK AT YOU OUT HERE ALL BY YOUR LONESOME.
YOU TRYING TO CALL ME A COWARD, CENA?
I'LL SHOW YOU WHAT ALL I CAN DO BY MY LONESOME.
NO. I KNOW YOU'RE NOT A COWARD, STYLES.
KLANNG
YOU'RE A GROWN MAN WITH ONE HELL OF A CAREER AND A FAMILY AT HOME--
--WHO'S WAY TOO SMART TO THINK HE NEEDS TO PROVE SOMETHING IN AN EMPTY GROCERY STORE PARKING LOT.
GOOD.
I WASN'T SAYING... THAT.

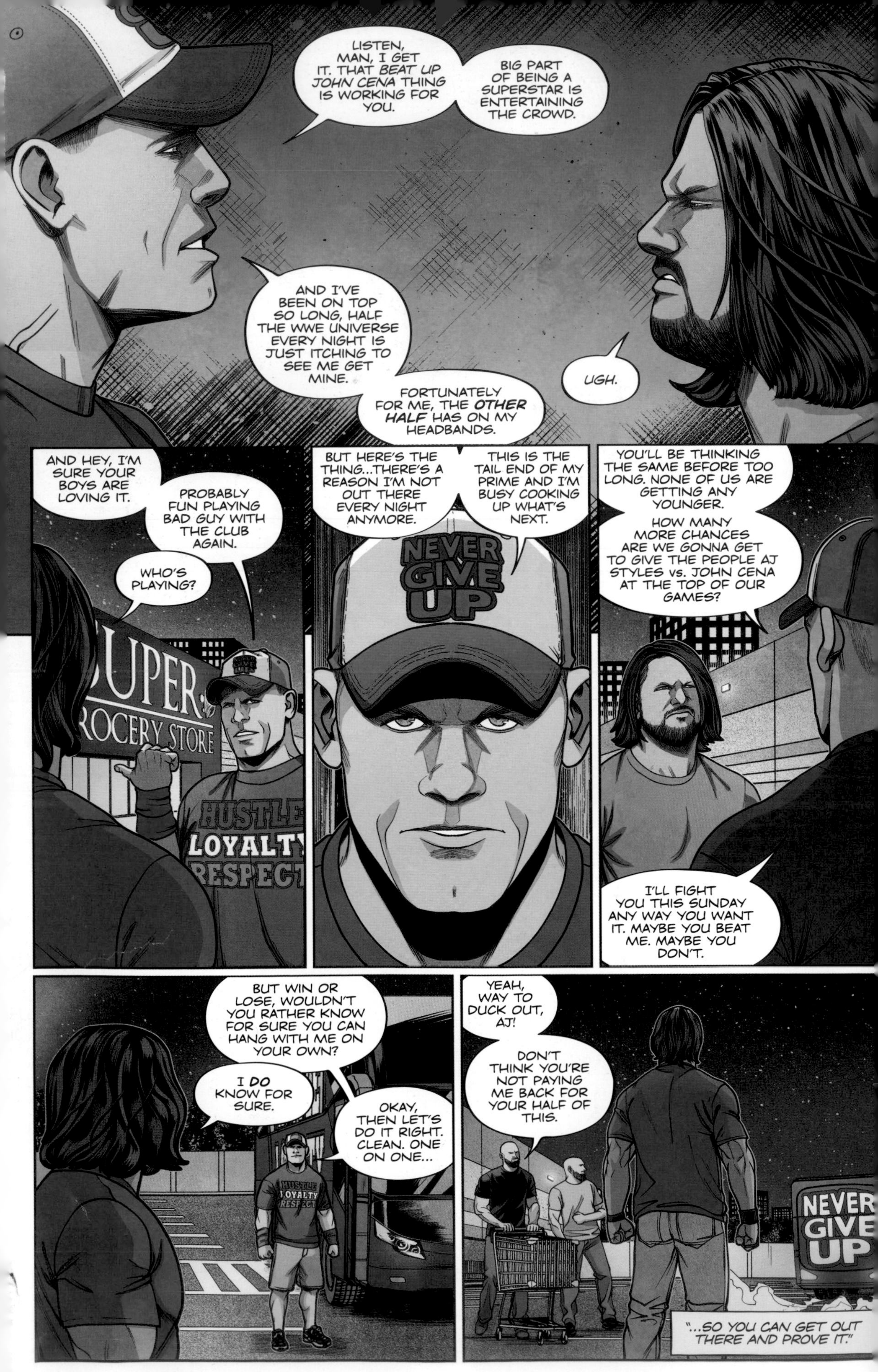
LISTEN, MAN, I GET IT. THAT BEAT UP JOHN CENA THING IS WORKING FOR YOU.
BIG PART OF BEING A SUPERSTAR IS ENTERTAINING THE CROWD.
AND I'VE BEEN ON TOP SO LONG, HALF THE WWE UNIVERSE EVERY NIGHT IS JUST ITCHING TO SEE ME GET MINE.
UGH.
FORTUNATELY FOR ME, THE OTHER HALF HAS ON MY HEADBANDS.
AND HEY, I'M SURE YOUR BOYS ARE LOVING IT.
PROBABLY FUN PLAYING BAD GUY WITH THE CLUB AGAIN.
WHO'S PLAYING?
SUPER GROCERY STORE
HUSTLE LOYALTY RESPECT
BUT HERE'S THE THING...THERE'S A REASON I'M NOT OUT THERE EVERY NIGHT ANYMORE.
THIS IS THE TAIL END OF MY PRIME AND I'M BUSY COOKING UP WHAT'S NEXT.
NEVER GIVE UP
YOU'LL BE THINKING THE SAME BEFORE TOO LONG. NONE OF US ARE GETTING ANY YOUNGER.
HOW MANY MORE CHANCES ARE WE GONNA GET TO GIVE THE PEOPLE AJ STYLES vs. JOHN CENA AT THE TOP OF OUR GAMES?
I'LL FIGHT YOU THIS SUNDAY ANY WAY YOU WANT IT. MAYBE YOU BEAT ME. MAYBE YOU DON'T.
BUT WIN OR LOSE, WOULDN'T YOU RATHER KNOW FOR SURE YOU CAN HANG WITH ME ON YOUR OWN?
I DO KNOW FOR SURE.
OKAY, THEN LET'S DO IT RIGHT. CLEAN. ONE ON ONE...
HUSTLE LOYALTY RESPECT
YEAH, WAY TO DUCK OUT, AJ!
DON'T THINK YOU'RE NOT PAYING ME BACK FOR YOUR HALF OF THIS.
NEVER GIVE UP
"...SO YOU CAN GET OUT THERE AND PROVE IT."

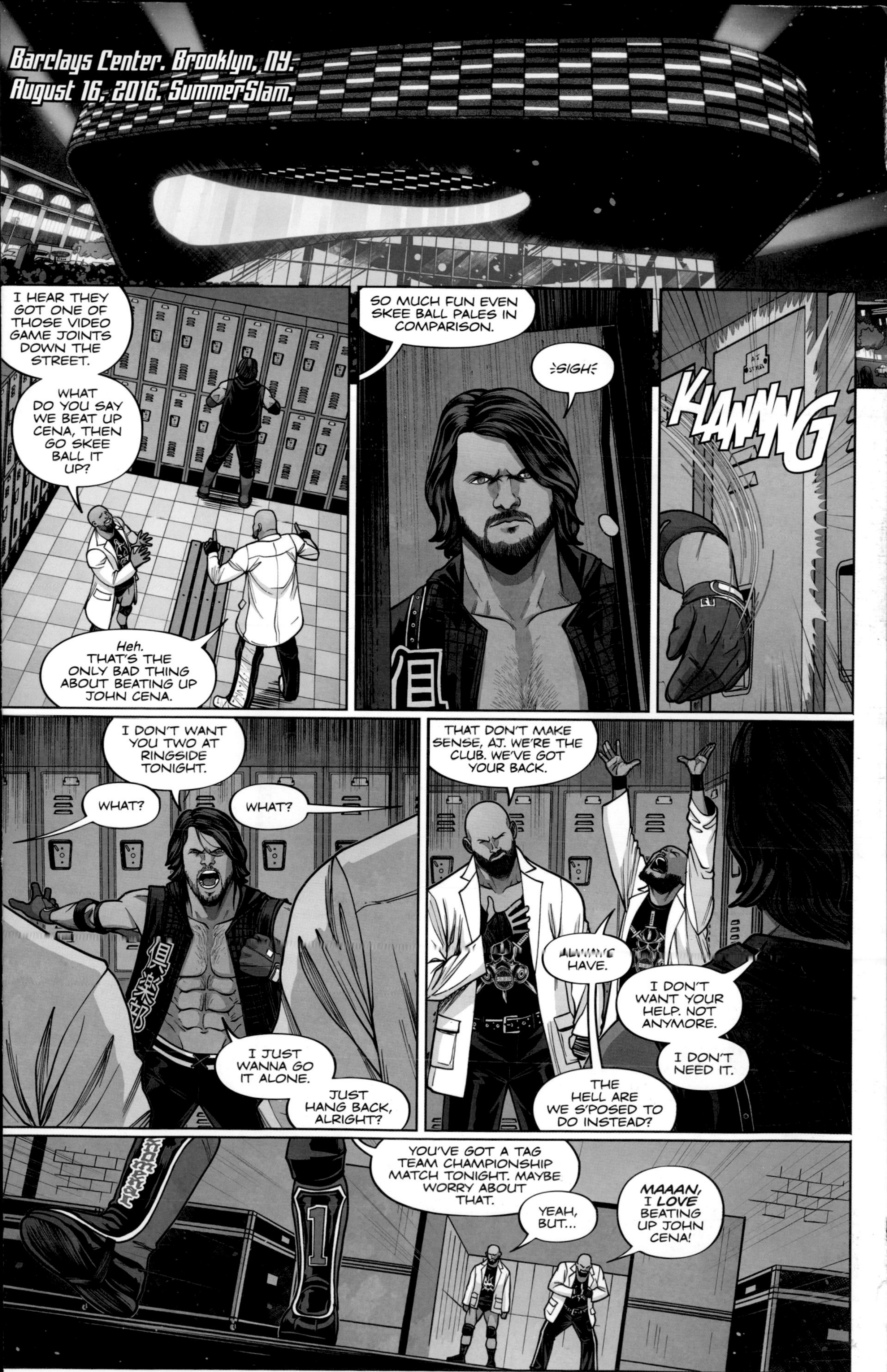
Barclays Center. Brooklyn, NY.
August 16, 2016. SummerSlam.
I HEAR THEY GOT ONE OF THOSE VIDEO GAME JOINTS DOWN THE STREET.
WHAT DO YOU SAY WE BEAT UP CENA, THEN GO SKEE BALL IT UP?
Heh. THAT'S THE ONLY BAD THING ABOUT BEATING UP JOHN CENA.
SO MUCH FUN EVEN SKEE BALL PALES IN COMPARISON.
SIGH
KLANNNG
I DON'T WANT YOU TWO AT RINGSIDE TONIGHT.
WHAT?
WHAT?
I JUST WANNA GO IT ALONE.
JUST HANG BACK, ALRIGHT?
THAT DON'T MAKE SENSE, AJ. WE'RE THE CLUB. WE'VE GOT YOUR BACK.
HAVE.
I DON'T WANT YOUR HELP. NOT ANYMORE.
I DON'T NEED IT.
THE HELL ARE WE S'POSED TO DO INSTEAD?
YOU'VE GOT A TAG TEAM CHAMPIONSHIP MATCH TONIGHT. MAYBE WORRY ABOUT THAT.
YEAH, BUT...
MAAAN, I LOVE BEATING UP JOHN CENA!

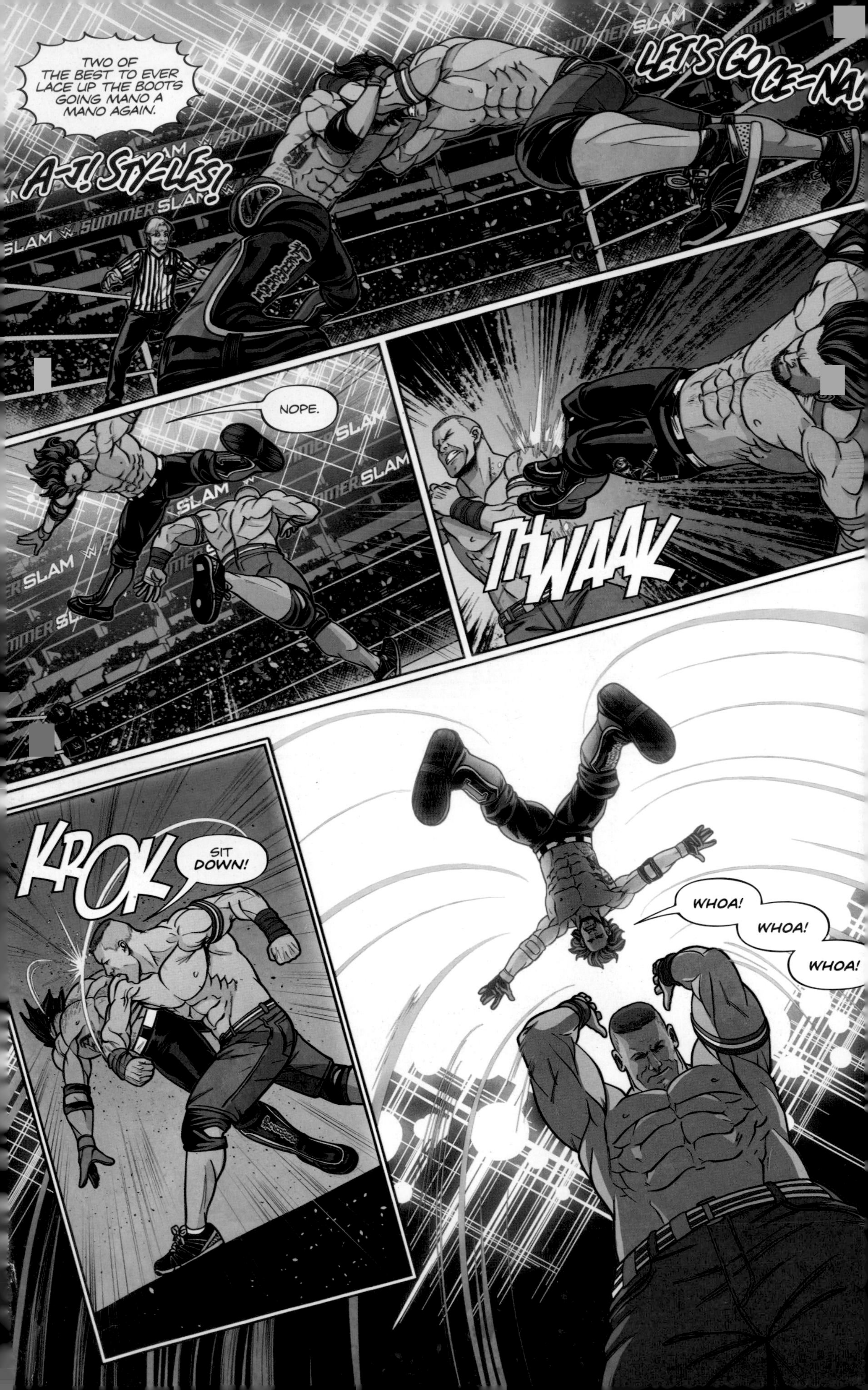
TWO OF THE BEST TO EVER LACE UP THE BOOTS GOING MANO A MANO AGAIN.
LET'S GO CE-NA!
A-J! STY-LES!
NOPE.
THWAAK
KROK
SIT DOWN!
WHOA!
WHOA!
WHOA!

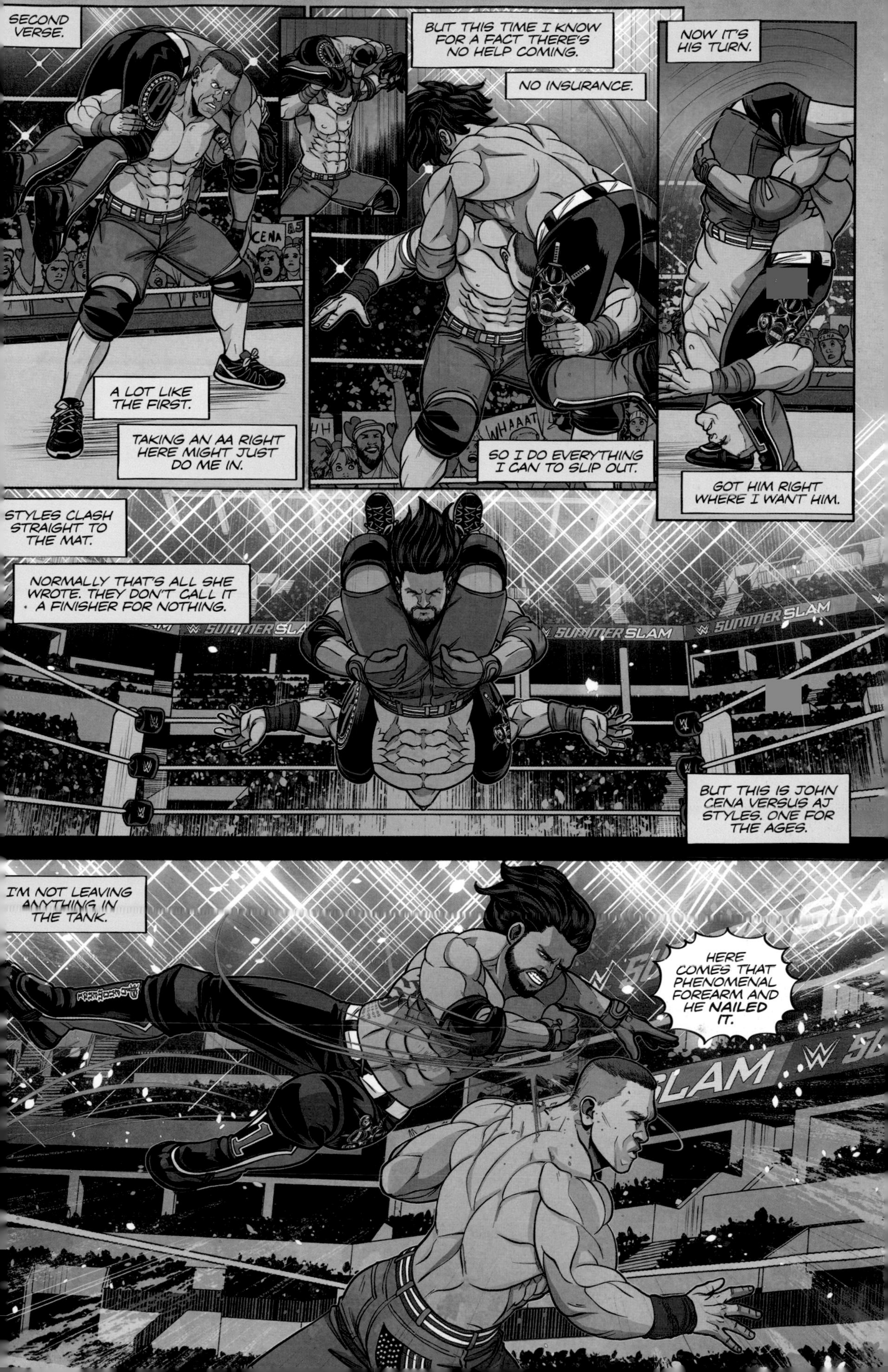
SECOND VERSE.
A LOT LIKE THE FIRST.
TAKING AN AA RIGHT HERE MIGHT JUST DO ME IN.
BUT THIS TIME I KNOW FOR A FACT THERE'S NO HELP COMING.
NO INSURANCE.
SO I DO EVERYTHING I CAN TO SLIP OUT.
NOW IT'S HIS TURN.
GOT HIM RIGHT WHERE I WANT HIM.
STYLES CLASH STRAIGHT TO THE MAT.
NORMALLY THAT'S ALL SHE WROTE. THEY DON'T CALL IT A FINISHER FOR NOTHING.
BUT THIS IS JOHN CENA VERSUS AJ STYLES. ONE FOR THE AGES.
I'M NOT LEAVING ANYTHING IN THE TANK.
HERE COMES THAT PHENOMENAL FOREARM AND HE NAILED IT.

AJ STYLES JUST BEAT JOHN CENA AT SUMMERSLAM!

YES!

LEGACY AFFIRMED. CAREER DEFINED. ONE HELL OF A VICTORY.

I KNOW JOHN CENA DID ME A SOLID TONIGHT.

CONVINCED ME TO STEP UP AND PROVE WHAT I'VE BEEN SAYING ALL THESE YEARS.

ALL BY MYSELF THIS TIME.

HE TALKED ME OUT OF MY OWN WAY.

NOW HE'S UP THERE SHOWING RESPECT.

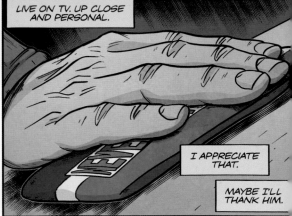

LIVE ON TV. UP CLOSE AND PERSONAL.

I APPRECIATE THAT.

MAYBE I'LL THANK HIM.

ONE DAY.

WHEN WE'RE BOTH LONG RETIRED.

AND NOBODY'S LISTENING.

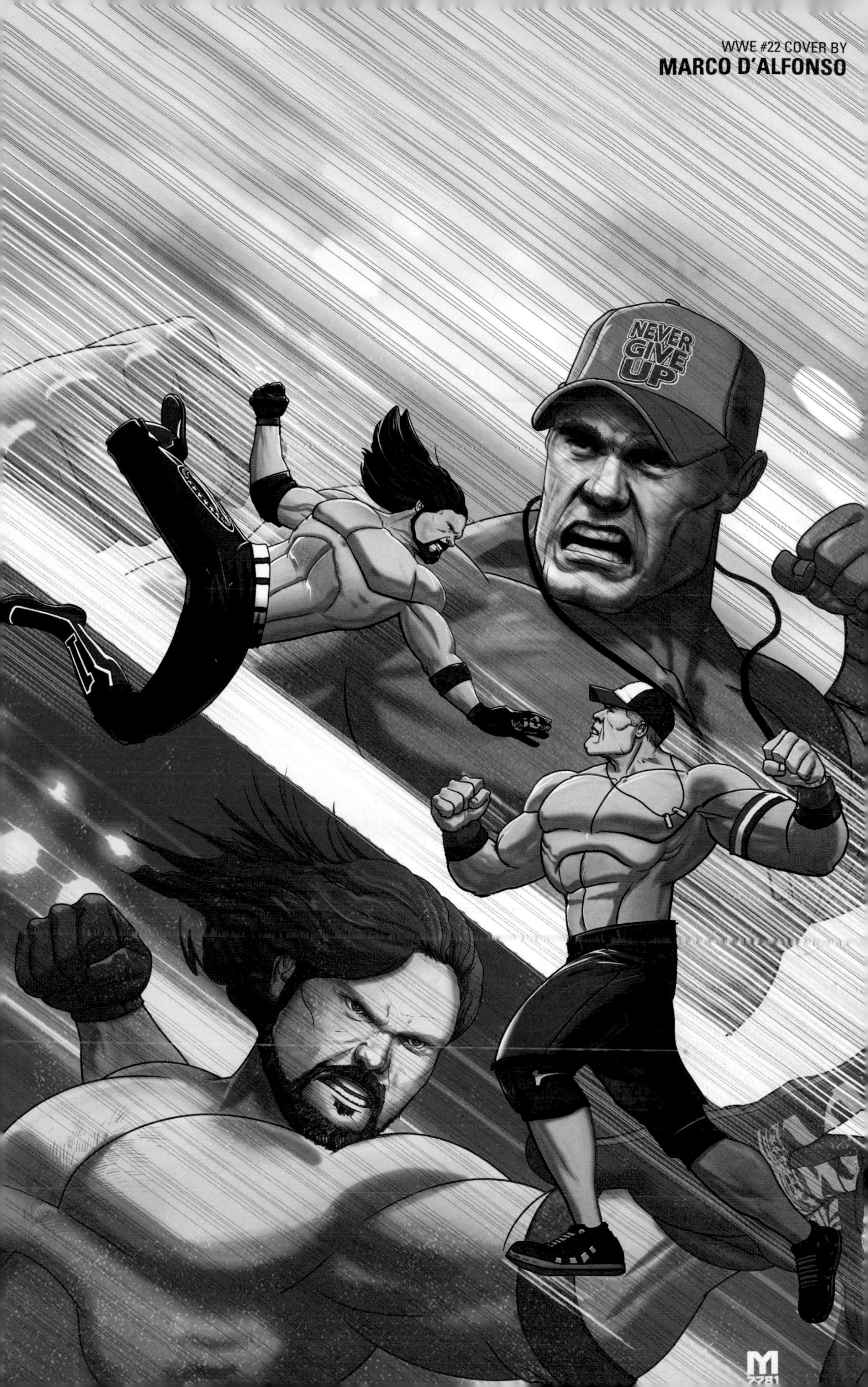
NEVER
GIVE
UP

WWE #22 COVER BY
MARCO D'ALFONSO

CHAPTER THREE

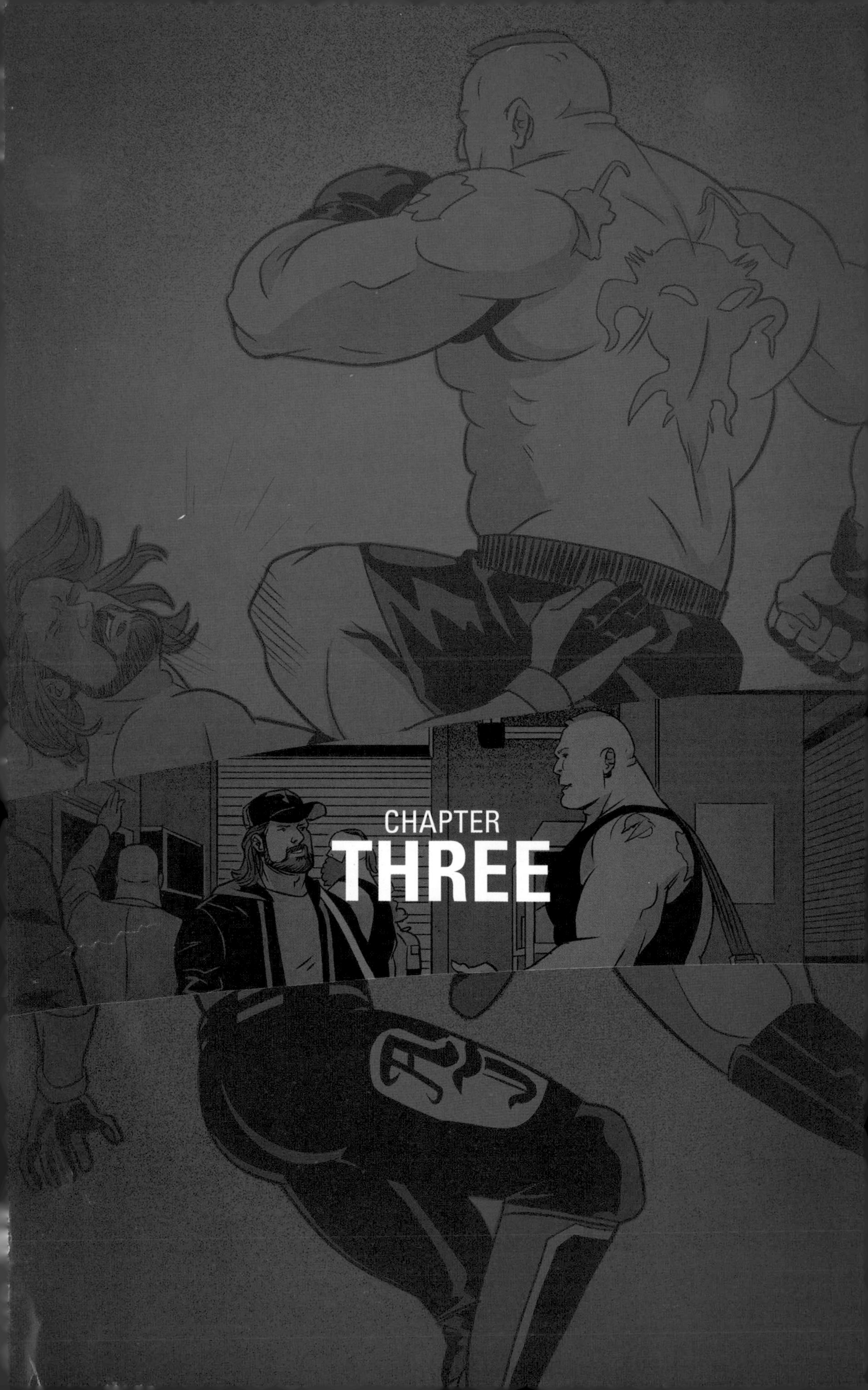

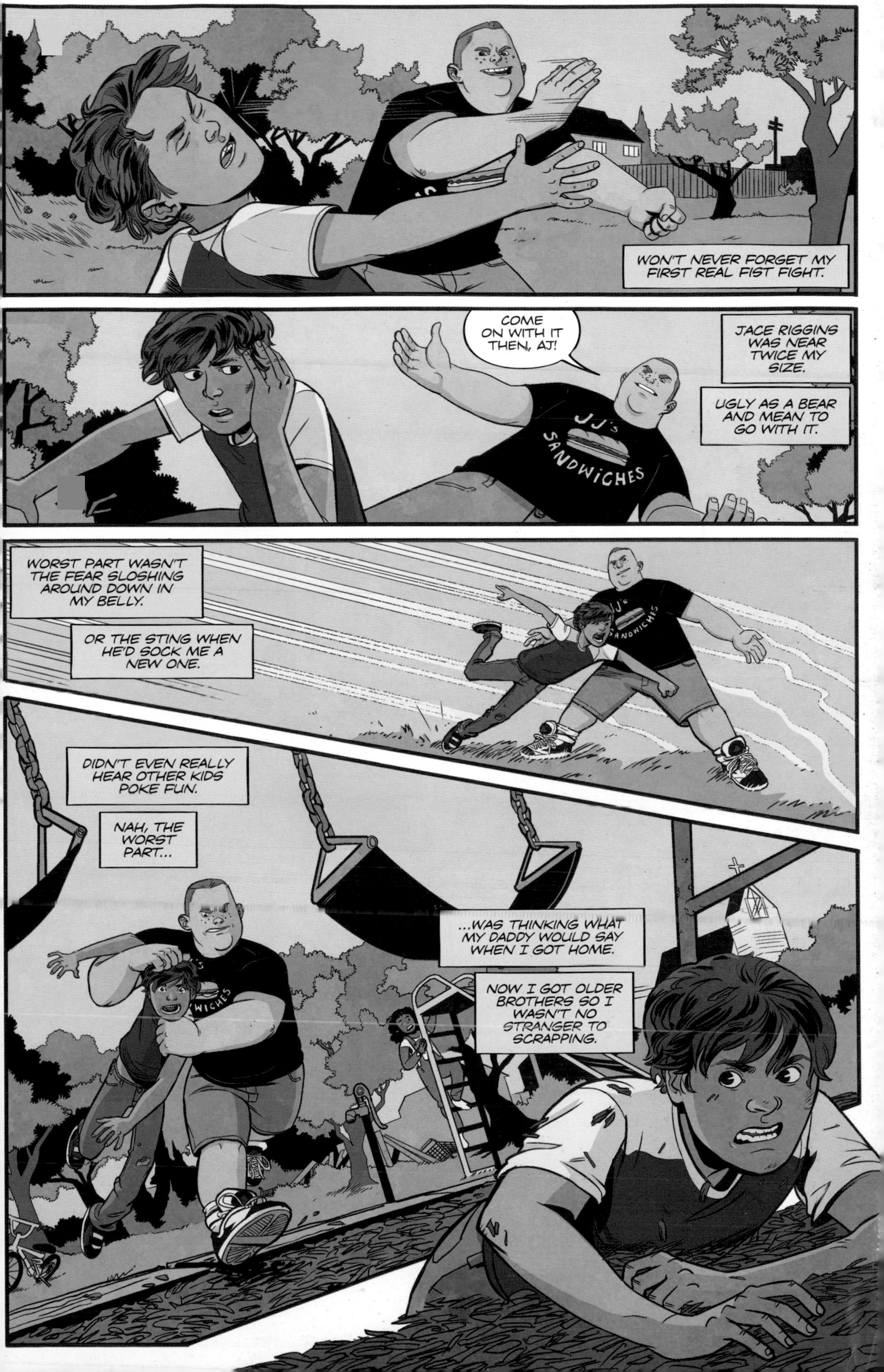
WON'T NEVER FORGET MY FIRST REAL FIST FIGHT.
COME ON WITH IT THEN, AJ!
JACE RIGGINS WAS NEAR TWICE MY SIZE.
UGLY AS A BEAR AND MEAN TO GO WITH IT.
JJ's SANDWICHES
WORST PART WASN'T THE FEAR SLOSHING AROUND DOWN IN MY BELLY.
OR THE STING WHEN HE'D SOCK ME A NEW ONE.
DIDN'T EVEN REALLY HEAR OTHER KIDS POKE FUN.
NAH, THE WORST PART...
...WAS THINKING WHAT MY DADDY WOULD SAY WHEN I GOT HOME.
NOW I GOT OLDER BROTHERS SO I WASN'T NO STRANGER TO SCRAPPING.

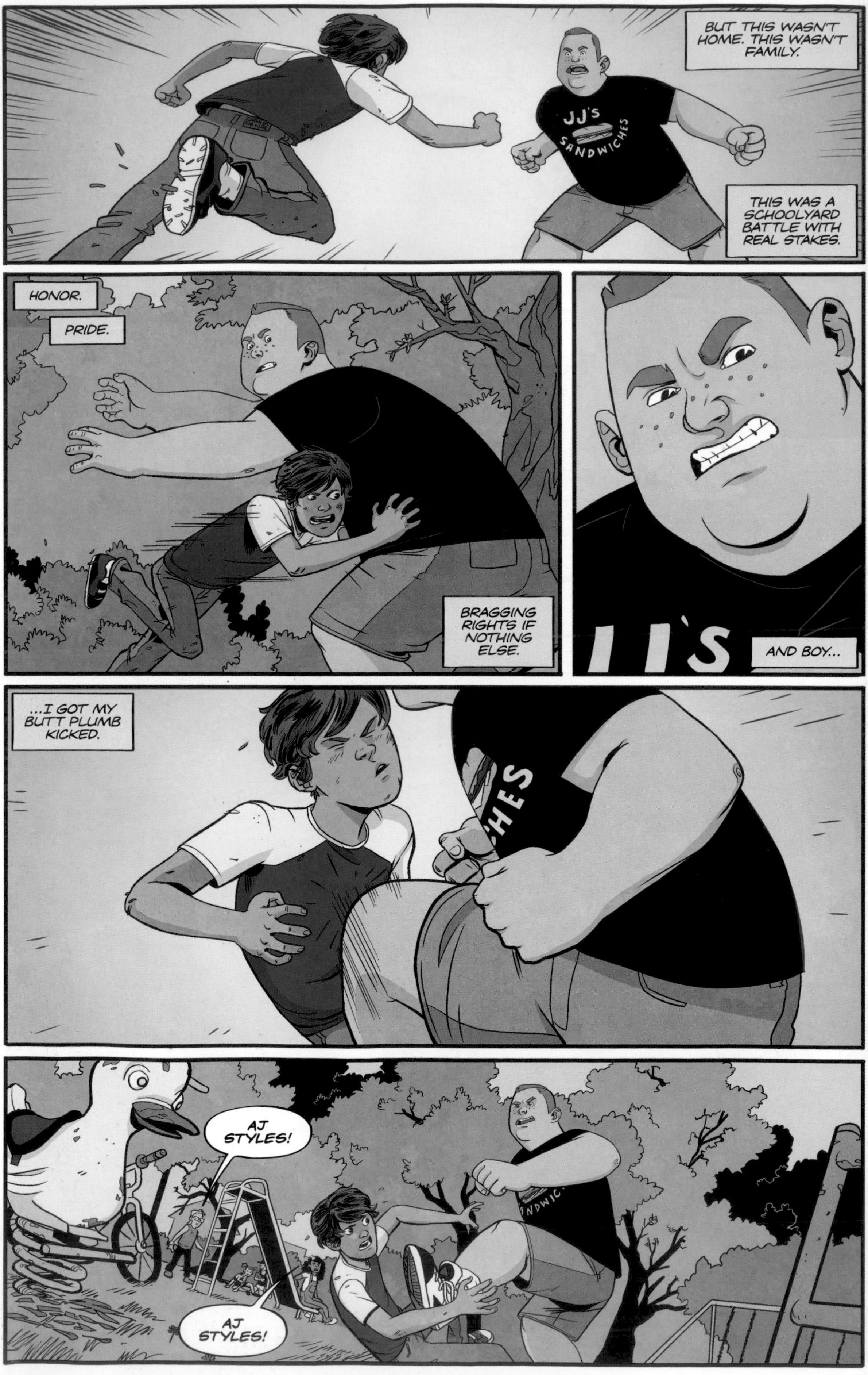
BUT THIS WASN'T HOME. THIS WASN'T FAMILY.
JJ'S SANDWICHES
THIS WAS A SCHOOLYARD BATTLE WITH REAL STAKES.
HONOR.
PRIDE.
BRAGGING RIGHTS IF NOTHING ELSE.
AND BOY...
...I GOT MY BUTT PLUMB KICKED.
AJ STYLES!
AJ STYLES!

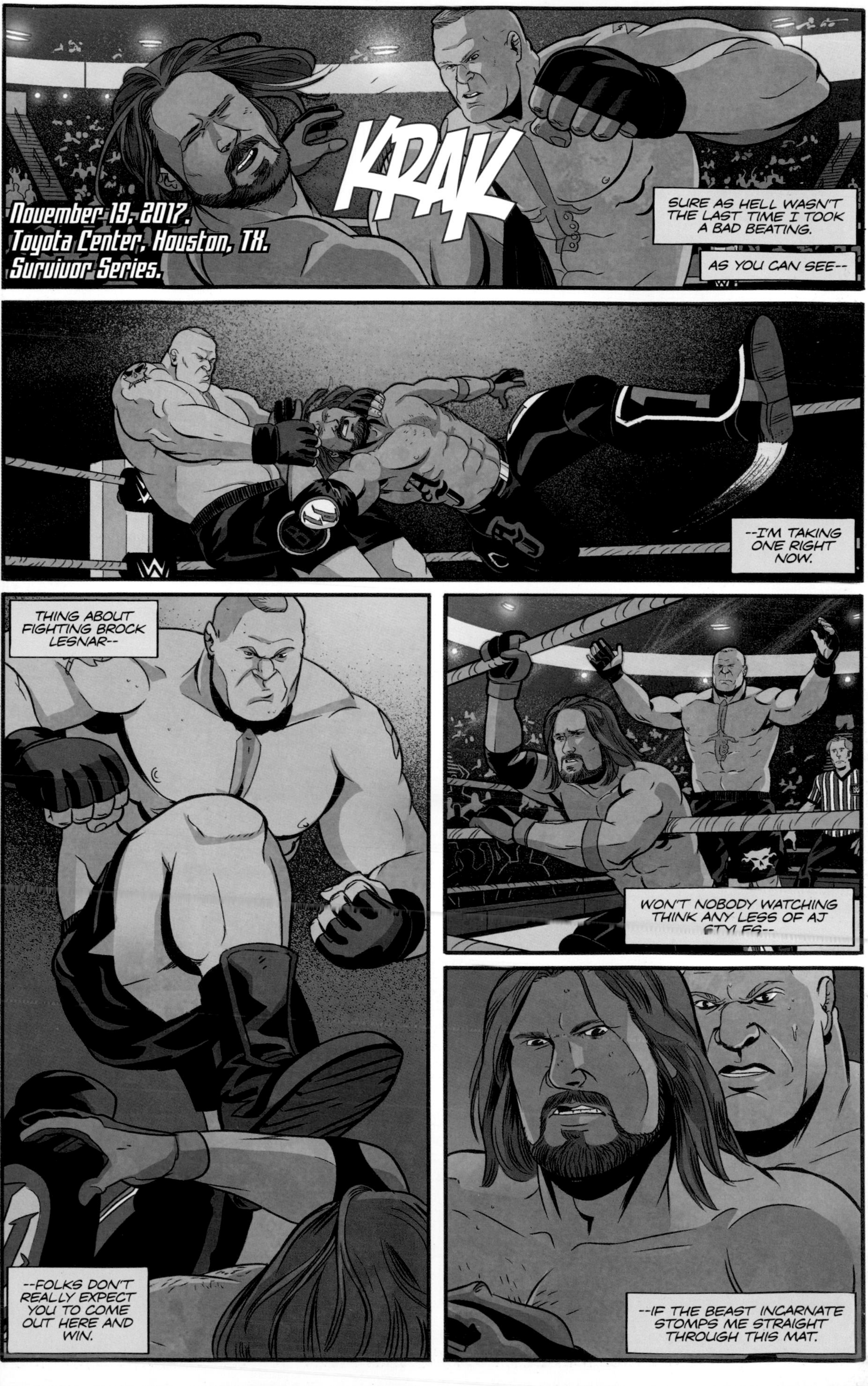
KRAK
November 19, 2017.
Toyota Center, Houston, TX.
Survivor Series.
SURE AS HELL WASN'T THE LAST TIME I TOOK A BAD BEATING.
AS YOU CAN SEE--
--I'M TAKING ONE RIGHT NOW.
THING ABOUT FIGHTING BROCK LESNAR--
--FOLKS DON'T REALLY EXPECT YOU TO COME OUT HERE AND WIN.
WON'T NOBODY WATCHING THINK ANY LESS OF AJ STYLES--
--IF THE BEAST INCARNATE STOMPS ME STRAIGHT THROUGH THIS MAT.

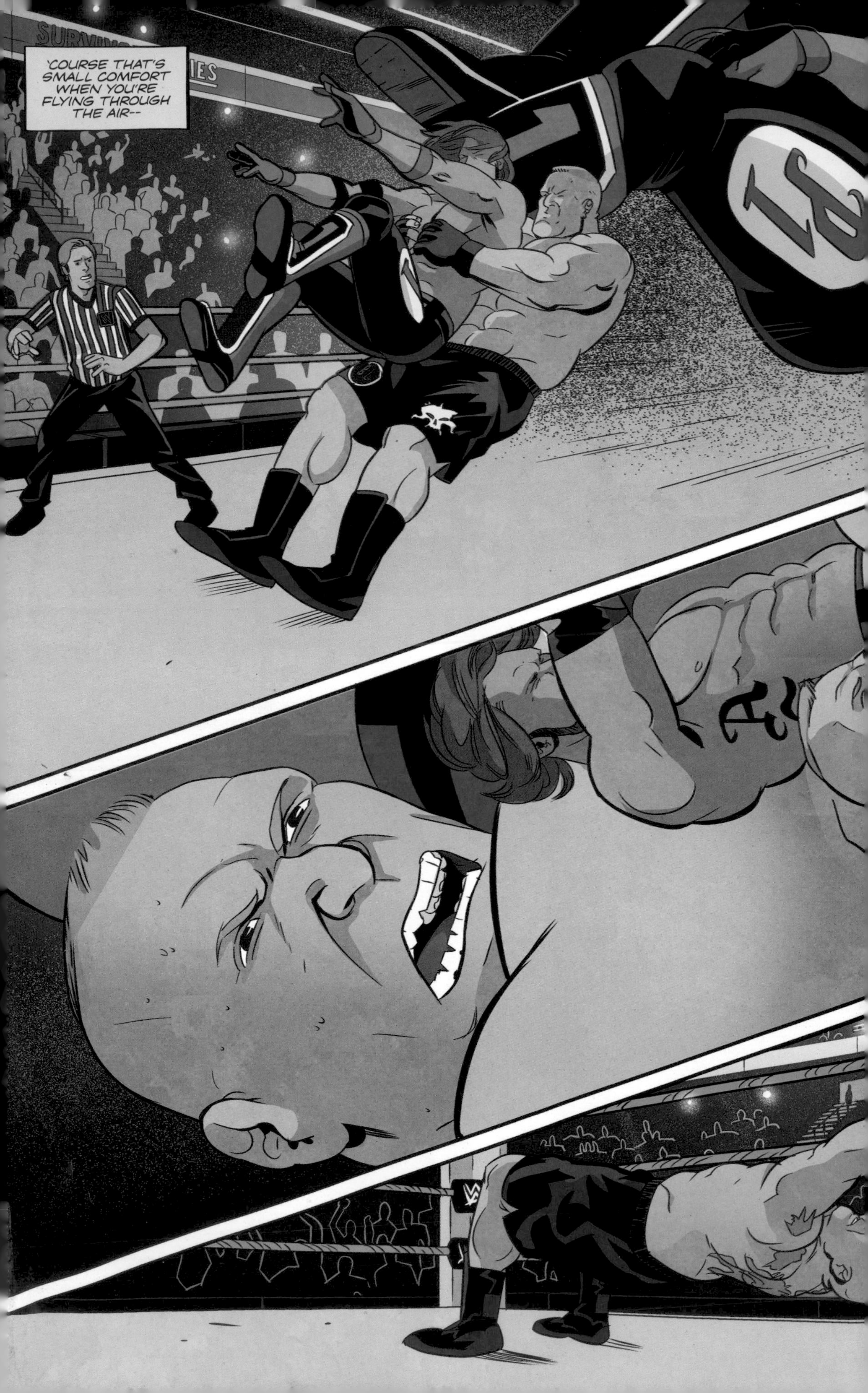
'COURSE THAT'S SMALL COMFORT WHEN YOU'RE FLYING THROUGH THE AIR--

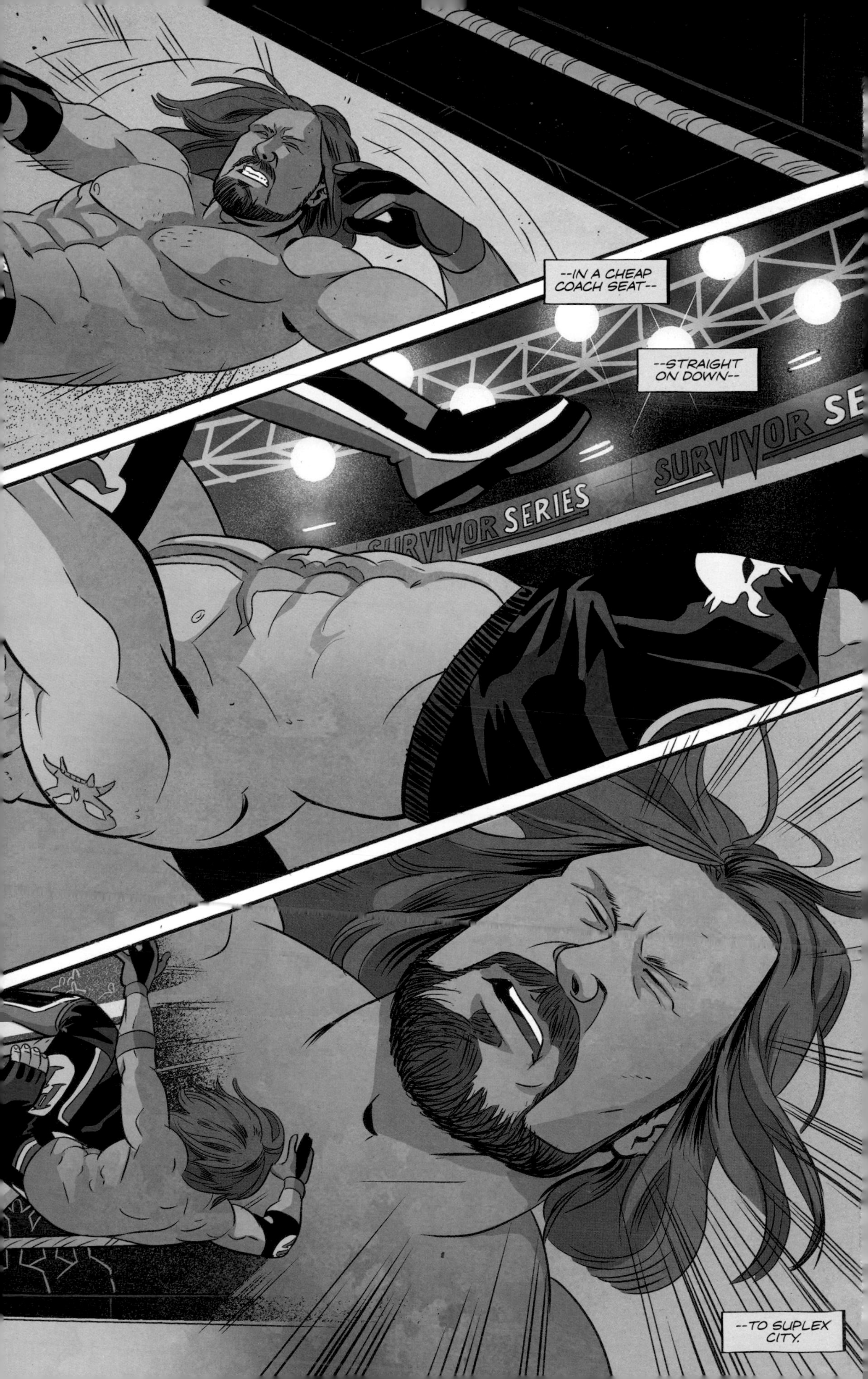
--IN A CHEAP COACH SEAT--
--STRAIGHT ON DOWN--
SURVIVOR SERIES
--TO SUPLEX CITY.

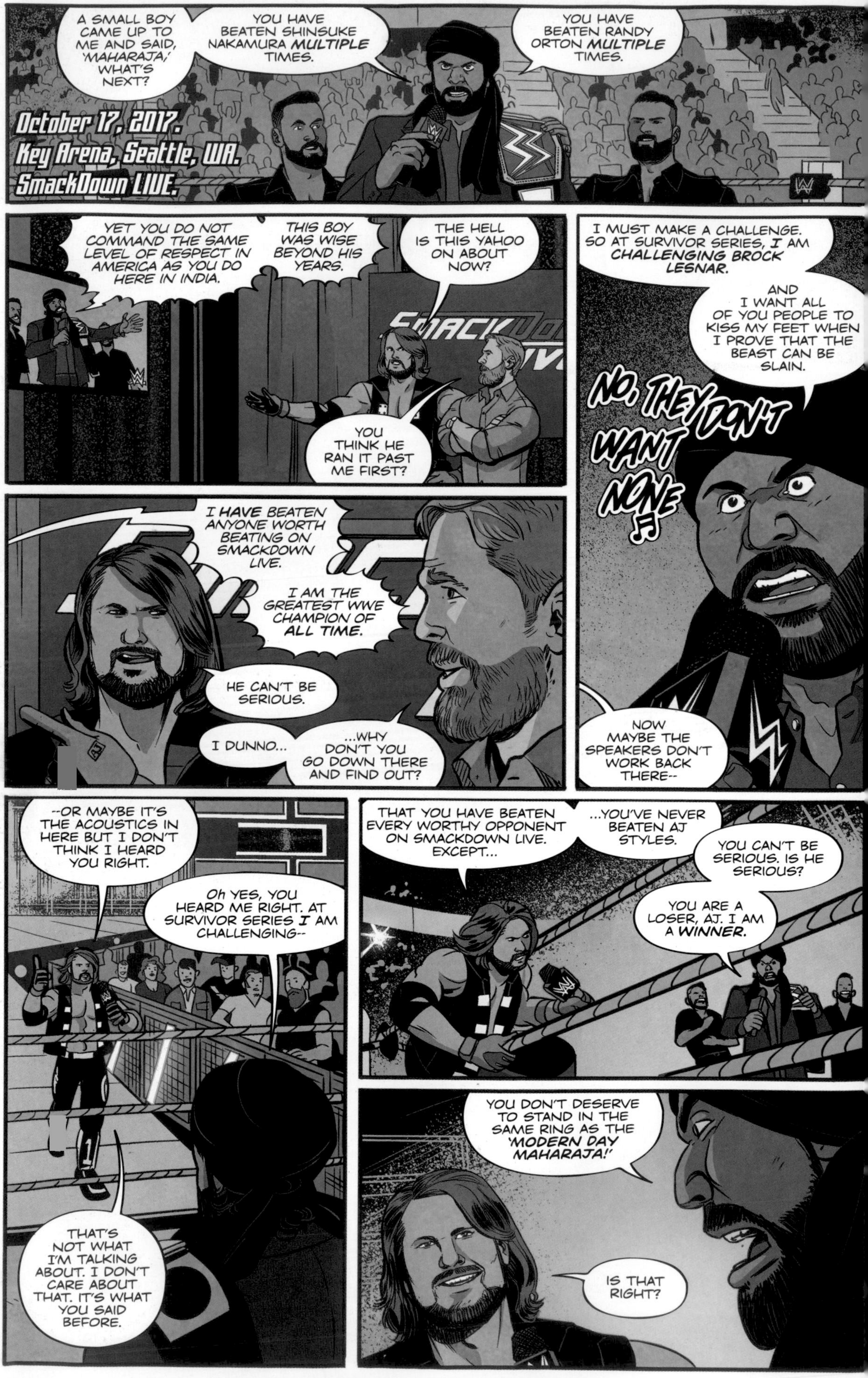
A SMALL BOY CAME UP TO ME AND SAID, 'MAHARAJA,' WHAT'S NEXT?
YOU HAVE BEATEN SHINSUKE NAKAMURA MULTIPLE TIMES.
YOU HAVE BEATEN RANDY ORTON MULTIPLE TIMES.
October 17, 2017.
Key Arena, Seattle, WA.
SmackDown LIVE.
YET YOU DO NOT COMMAND THE SAME LEVEL OF RESPECT IN AMERICA AS YOU DO HERE IN INDIA.
THIS BOY WAS WISE BEYOND HIS YEARS.
THE HELL IS THIS YAHOO ON ABOUT NOW?
YOU THINK HE RAN IT PAST ME FIRST?
I MUST MAKE A CHALLENGE. SO AT SURVIVOR SERIES, I AM CHALLENGING BROCK LESNAR.
AND I WANT ALL OF YOU PEOPLE TO KISS MY FEET WHEN I PROVE THAT THE BEAST CAN BE SLAIN.
NO, THEY DON'T WANT NONE ♫
I HAVE BEATEN ANYONE WORTH BEATING ON SMACKDOWN LIVE.
I AM THE GREATEST WWE CHAMPION OF ALL TIME.
HE CAN'T BE SERIOUS.
I DUNNO...
...WHY DON'T YOU GO DOWN THERE AND FIND OUT?
NOW MAYBE THE SPEAKERS DON'T WORK BACK THERE--
--OR MAYBE IT'S THE ACOUSTICS IN HERE BUT I DON'T THINK I HEARD YOU RIGHT.
Oh YES, YOU HEARD ME RIGHT. AT SURVIVOR SERIES I AM CHALLENGING--
THAT'S NOT WHAT I'M TALKING ABOUT. I DON'T CARE ABOUT THAT. IT'S WHAT YOU SAID BEFORE.
THAT YOU HAVE BEATEN EVERY WORTHY OPPONENT ON SMACKDOWN LIVE. EXCEPT...
...YOU'VE NEVER BEATEN AJ STYLES.
YOU CAN'T BE SERIOUS. IS HE SERIOUS?
YOU ARE A LOSER, AJ. I AM A WINNER.
YOU DON'T DESERVE TO STAND IN THE SAME RING AS THE 'MODERN DAY MAHARAJA!'
IS THAT RIGHT?

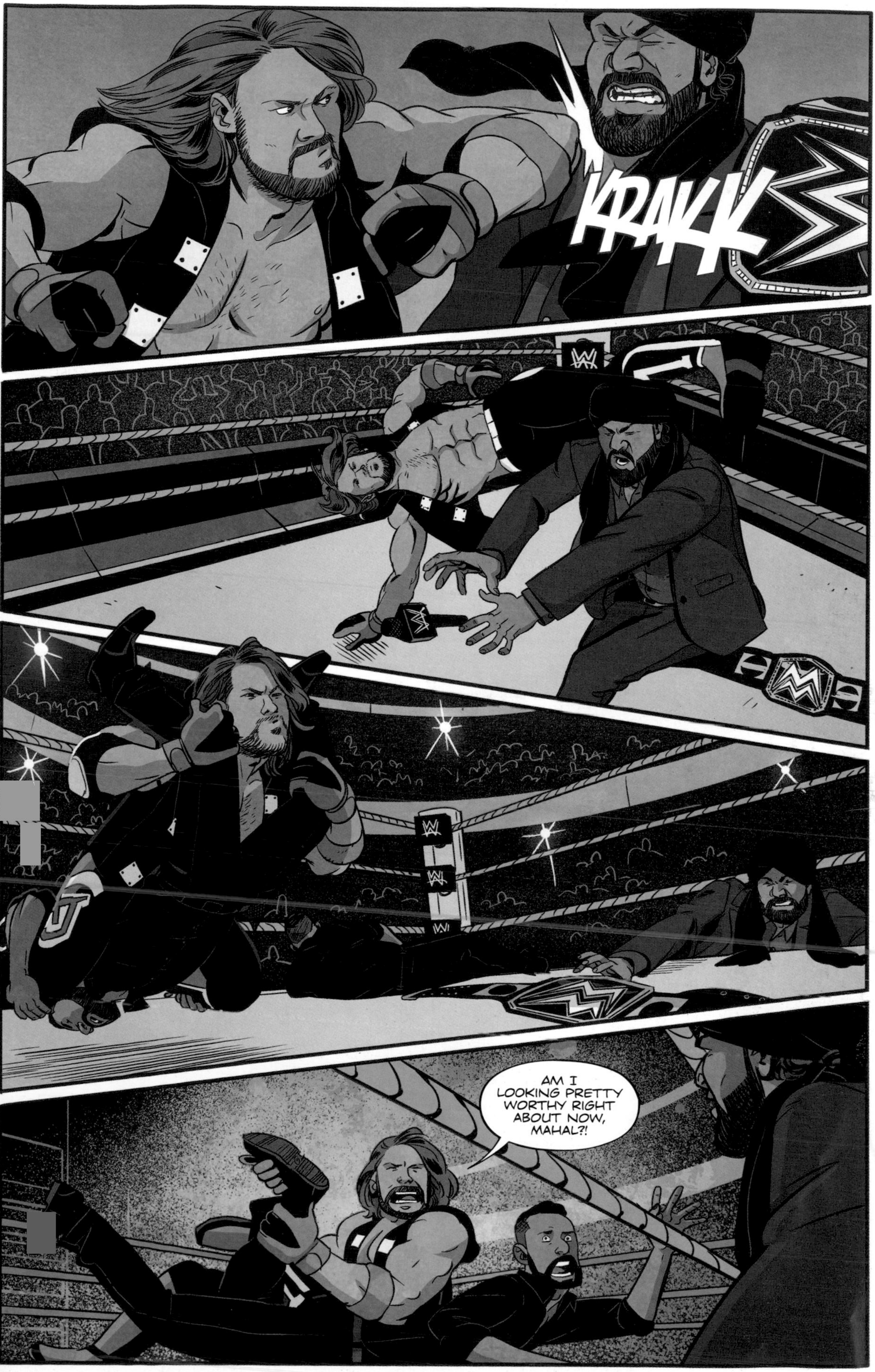
KRAKK
AM I LOOKING PRETTY WORTHY RIGHT ABOUT NOW, MAHAL?!

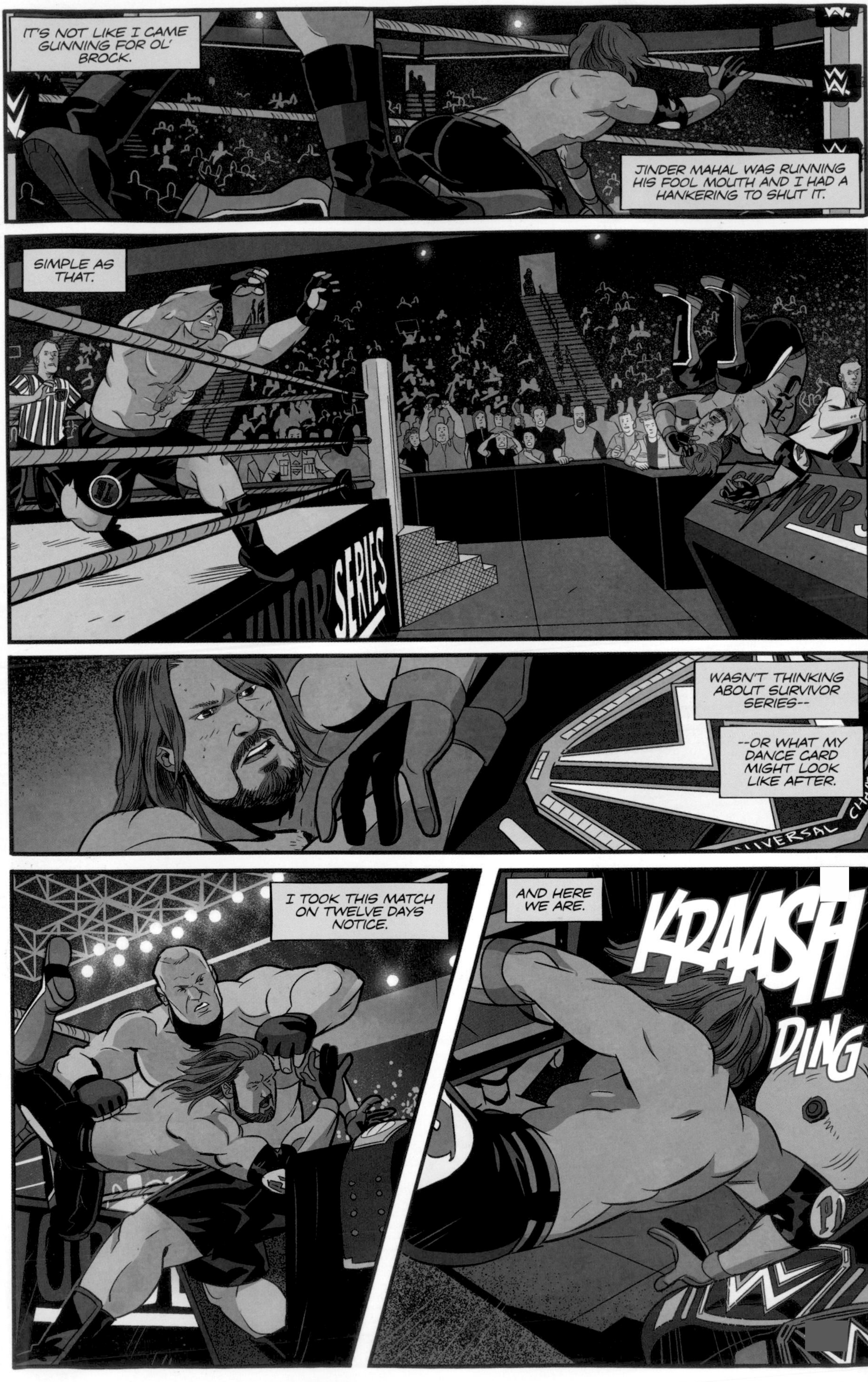
IT'S NOT LIKE I CAME GUNNING FOR OL' BROCK.
JINDER MAHAL WAS RUNNING HIS FOOL MOUTH AND I HAD A HANKERING TO SHUT IT.
SIMPLE AS THAT.
SURVIVOR SERIES
WASN'T THINKING ABOUT SURVIVOR SERIES--
--OR WHAT MY DANCE CARD MIGHT LOOK LIKE AFTER.
I TOOK THIS MATCH ON TWELVE DAYS NOTICE.
AND HERE WE ARE.
KRAASH
DING

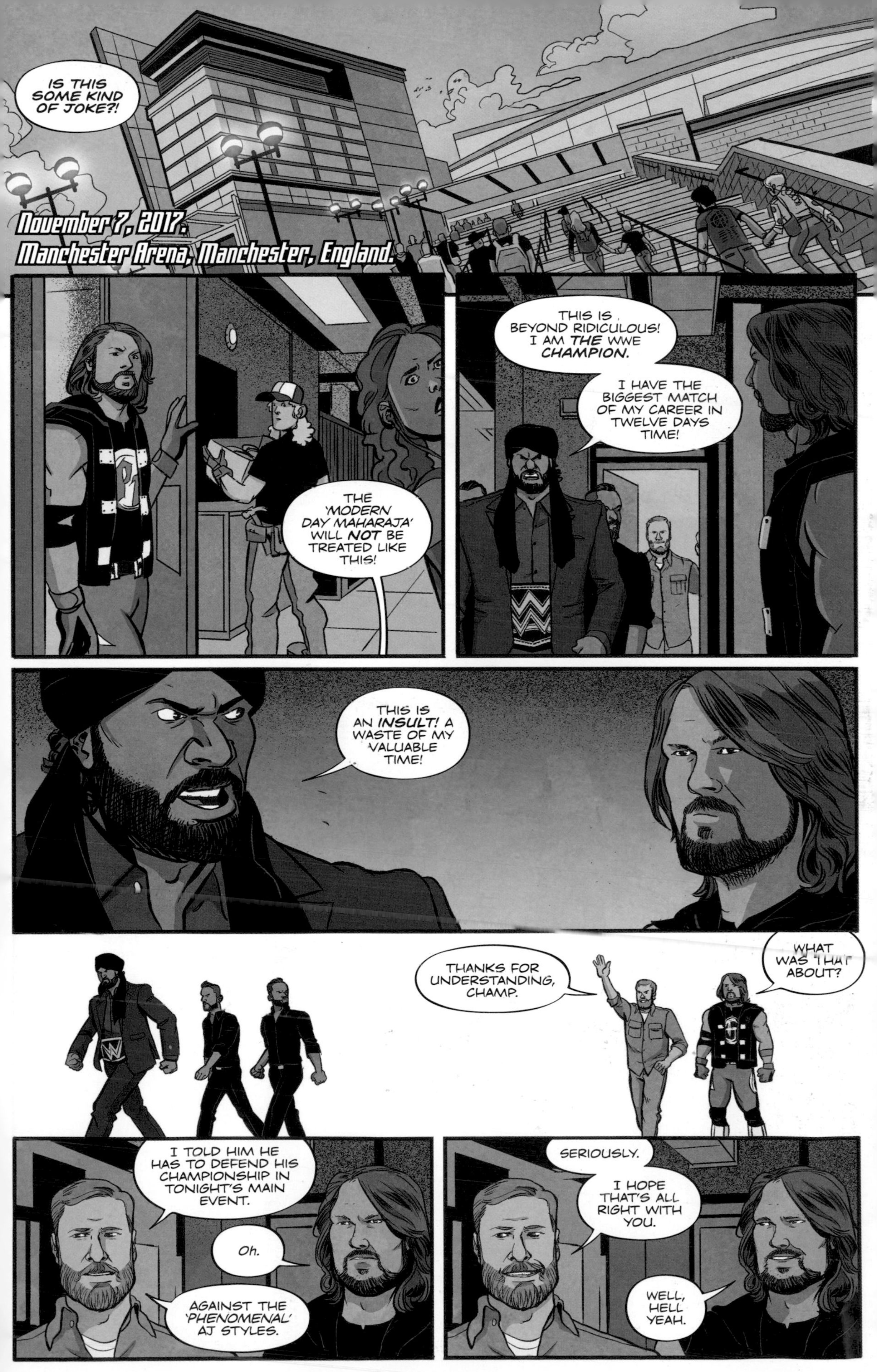

IS THIS SOME KIND OF JOKE?!
November 7, 2017. Manchester Arena, Manchester, England.
THE 'MODERN DAY MAHARAJA' WILL NOT BE TREATED LIKE THIS!
THIS IS BEYOND RIDICULOUS! I AM THE WWE CHAMPION.
I HAVE THE BIGGEST MATCH OF MY CAREER IN TWELVE DAYS TIME!
THIS IS AN INSULT! A WASTE OF MY VALUABLE TIME!
THANKS FOR UNDERSTANDING, CHAMP.
WHAT WAS THAT ABOUT?
I TOLD HIM HE HAS TO DEFEND HIS CHAMPIONSHIP IN TONIGHT'S MAIN EVENT.
Oh.
AGAINST THE 'PHENOMENAL' AJ STYLES.
SERIOUSLY.
I HOPE THAT'S ALL RIGHT WITH YOU.
WELL, HELL YEAH.

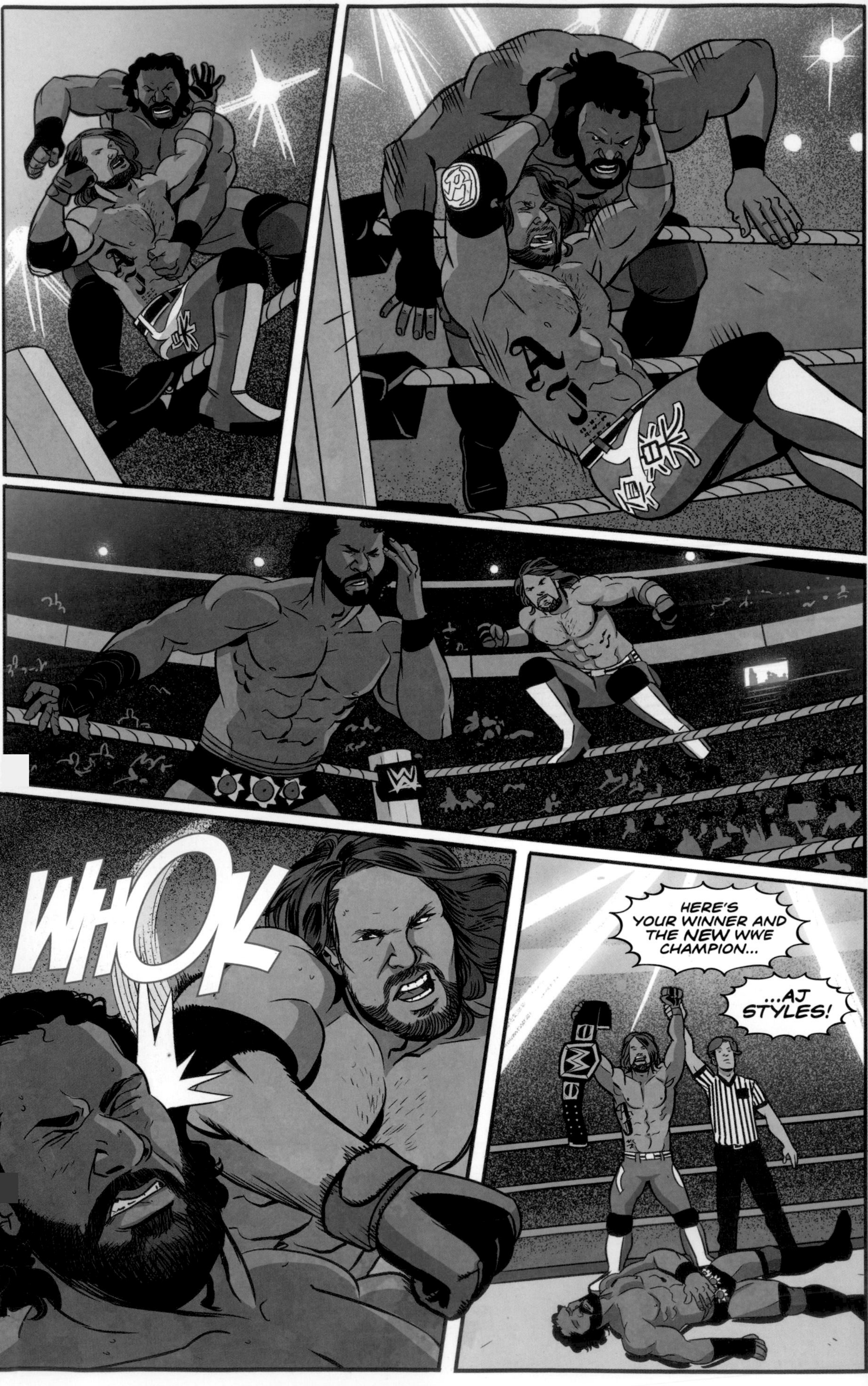
WHOK
HERE'S YOUR WINNER AND THE NEW WWE CHAMPION...
...AJ STYLES!

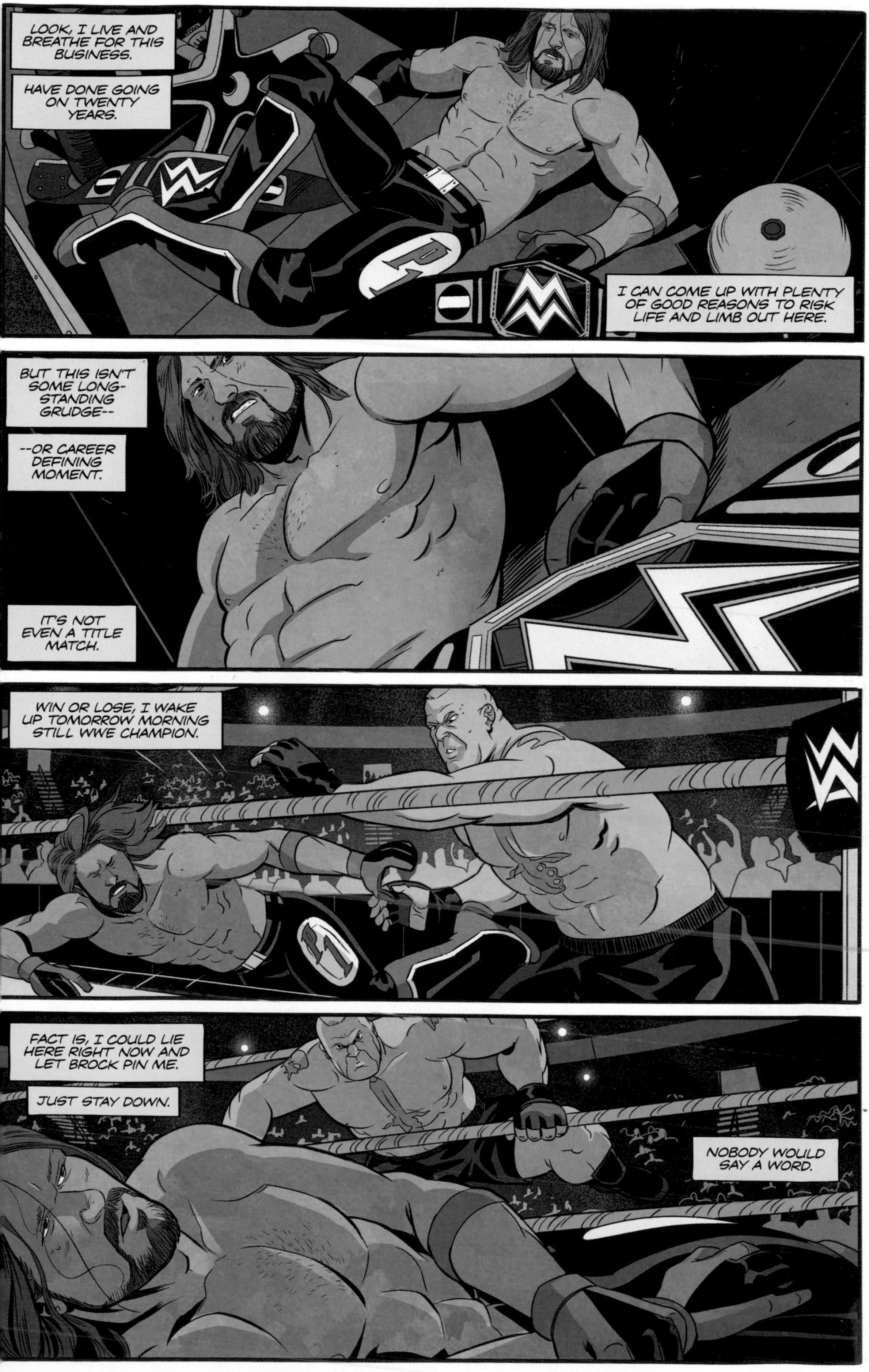
LOOK, I LIVE AND BREATHE FOR THIS BUSINESS.
HAVE DONE GOING ON TWENTY YEARS.
I CAN COME UP WITH PLENTY OF GOOD REASONS TO RISK LIFE AND LIMB OUT HERE.
BUT THIS ISN'T SOME LONG-STANDING GRUDGE--
--OR CAREER DEFINING MOMENT.
IT'S NOT EVEN A TITLE MATCH.
WIN OR LOSE, I WAKE UP TOMORROW MORNING STILL WWE CHAMPION.
FACT IS, I COULD LIE HERE RIGHT NOW AND LET BROCK PIN ME.
JUST STAY DOWN.
NOBODY WOULD SAY A WORD.

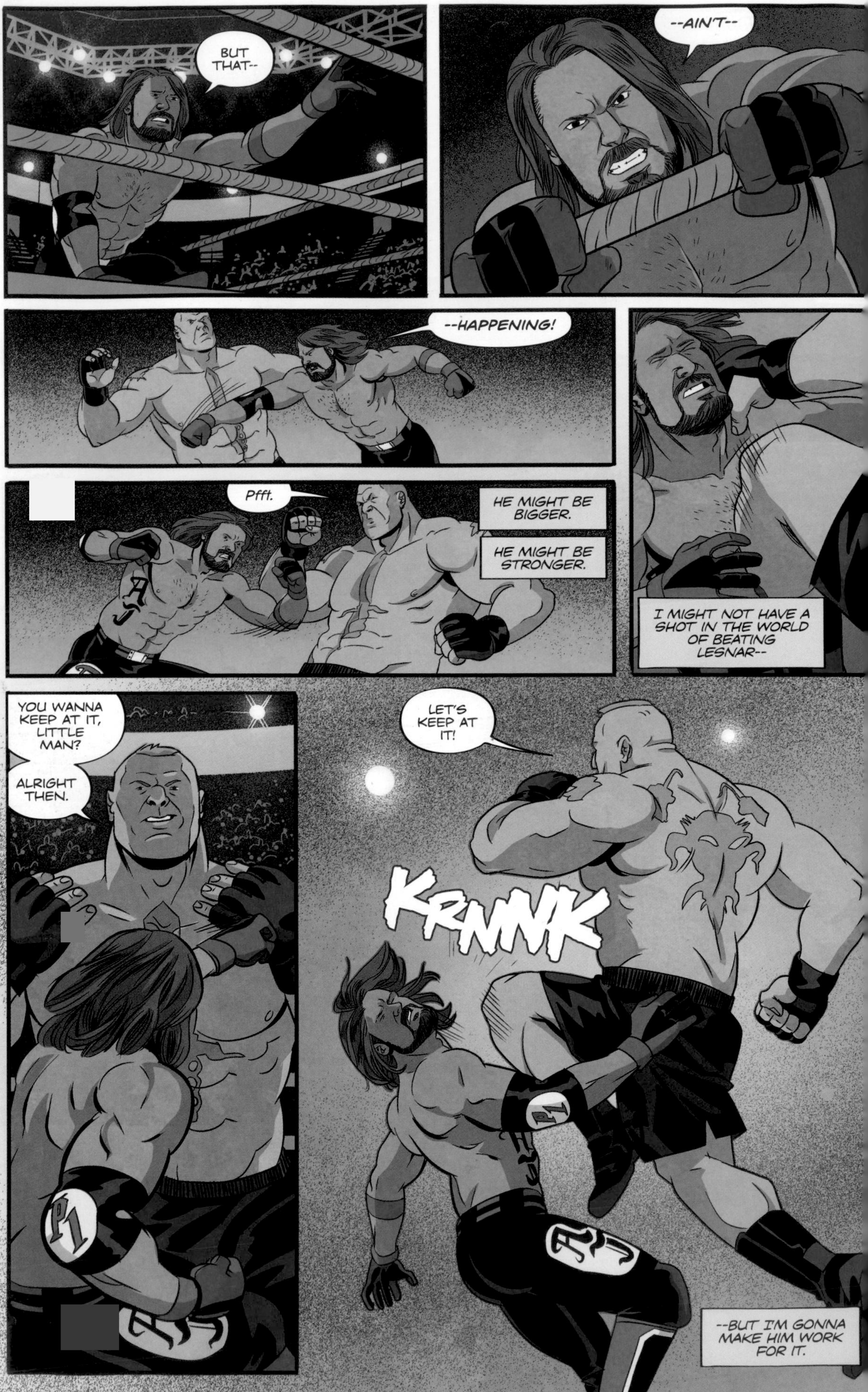
BUT THAT--
--AIN'T--
--HAPPENING!
I MIGHT NOT HAVE A SHOT IN THE WORLD OF BEATING LESNAR--
Pfft.
HE MIGHT BE BIGGER.
HE MIGHT BE STRONGER.
YOU WANNA KEEP AT IT, LITTLE MAN?
ALRIGHT THEN.
LET'S KEEP AT IT!
KRNNK
--BUT I'M GONNA MAKE HIM WORK FOR IT.

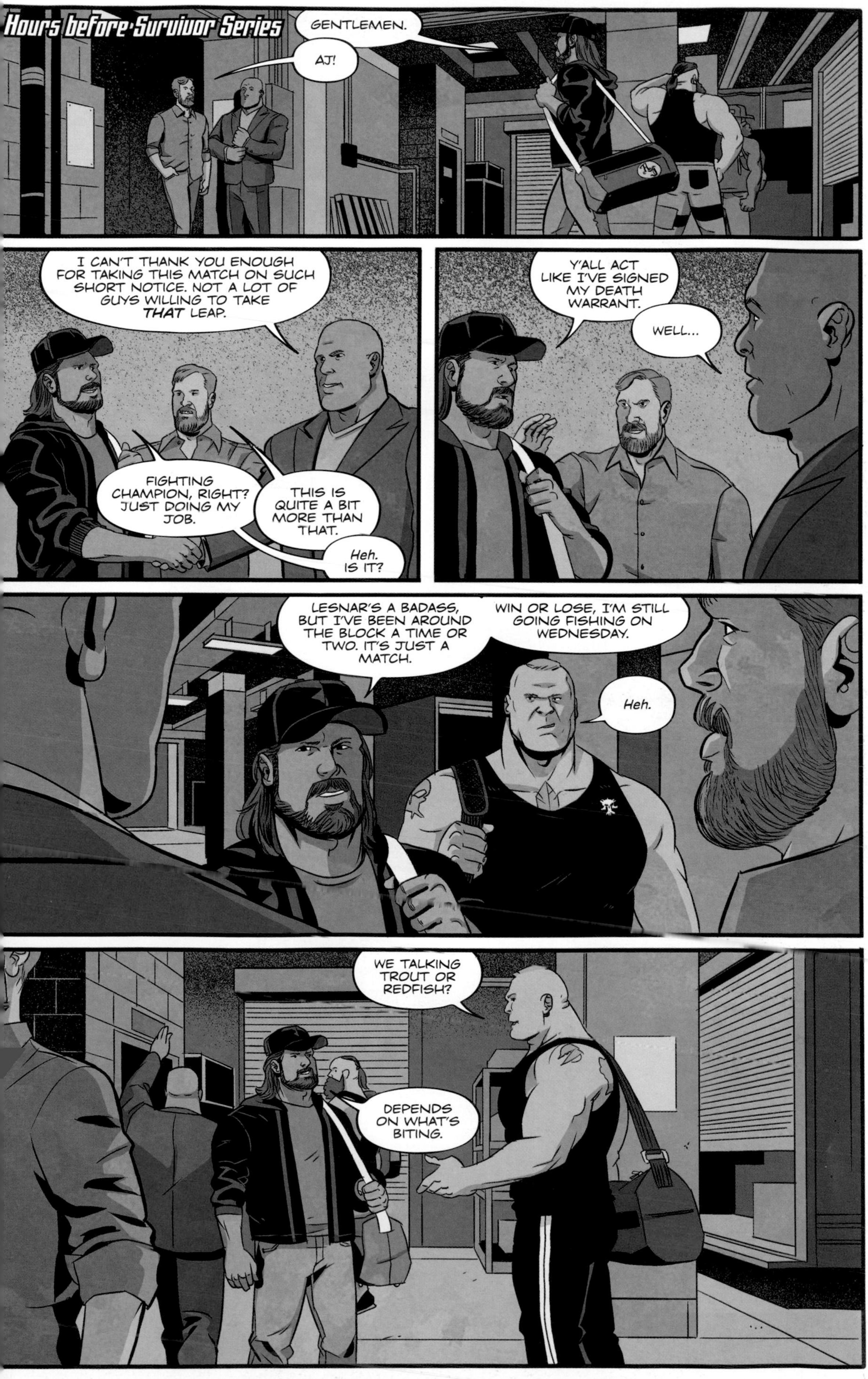
Hours before Survivor Series
GENTLEMEN.
AJ!
I CAN'T THANK YOU ENOUGH FOR TAKING THIS MATCH ON SUCH SHORT NOTICE. NOT A LOT OF GUYS WILLING TO TAKE THAT LEAP.
FIGHTING CHAMPION, RIGHT? JUST DOING MY JOB.
THIS IS QUITE A BIT MORE THAN THAT.
Heh. IS IT?
Y'ALL ACT LIKE I'VE SIGNED MY DEATH WARRANT.
WELL...
LESNAR'S A BADASS, BUT I'VE BEEN AROUND THE BLOCK A TIME OR TWO. IT'S JUST A MATCH.
WIN OR LOSE, I'M STILL GOING FISHING ON WEDNESDAY.
Heh.
WE TALKING TROUT OR REDFISH?
DEPENDS ON WHAT'S BITING.

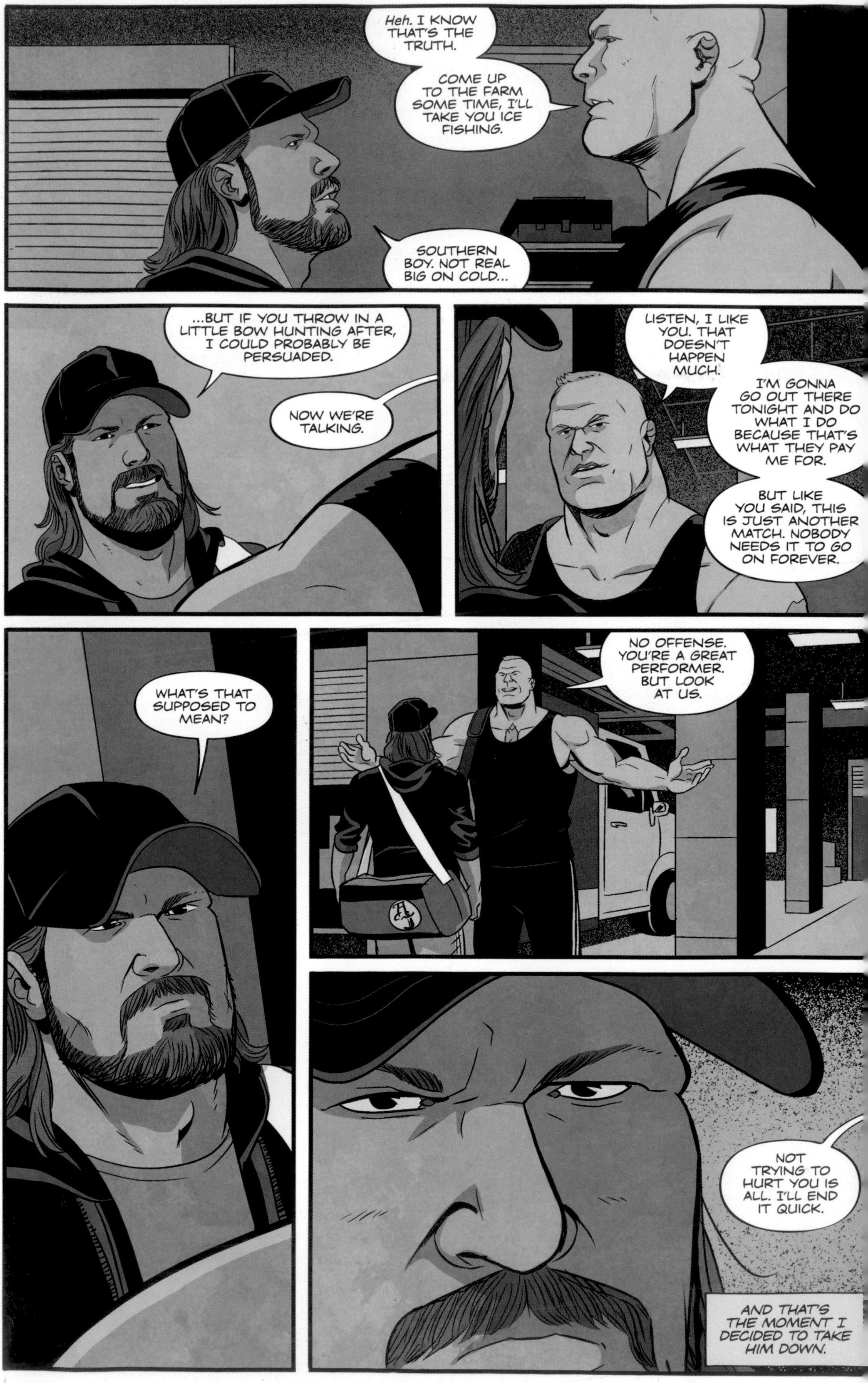
Heh. I KNOW THAT'S THE TRUTH.
COME UP TO THE FARM SOME TIME, I'LL TAKE YOU ICE FISHING.
SOUTHERN BOY. NOT REAL BIG ON COLD...
...BUT IF YOU THROW IN A LITTLE BOW HUNTING AFTER, I COULD PROBABLY BE PERSUADED.
NOW WE'RE TALKING.
LISTEN, I LIKE YOU. THAT DOESN'T HAPPEN MUCH.
I'M GONNA GO OUT THERE TONIGHT AND DO WHAT I DO BECAUSE THAT'S WHAT THEY PAY ME FOR.
BUT LIKE YOU SAID, THIS IS JUST ANOTHER MATCH. NOBODY NEEDS IT TO GO ON FOREVER.
WHAT'S THAT SUPPOSED TO MEAN?
NO OFFENSE. YOU'RE A GREAT PERFORMER. BUT LOOK AT US.
NOT TRYING TO HURT YOU IS ALL. I'LL END IT QUICK.
AND THAT'S THE MOMENT I DECIDED TO TAKE HIM DOWN.

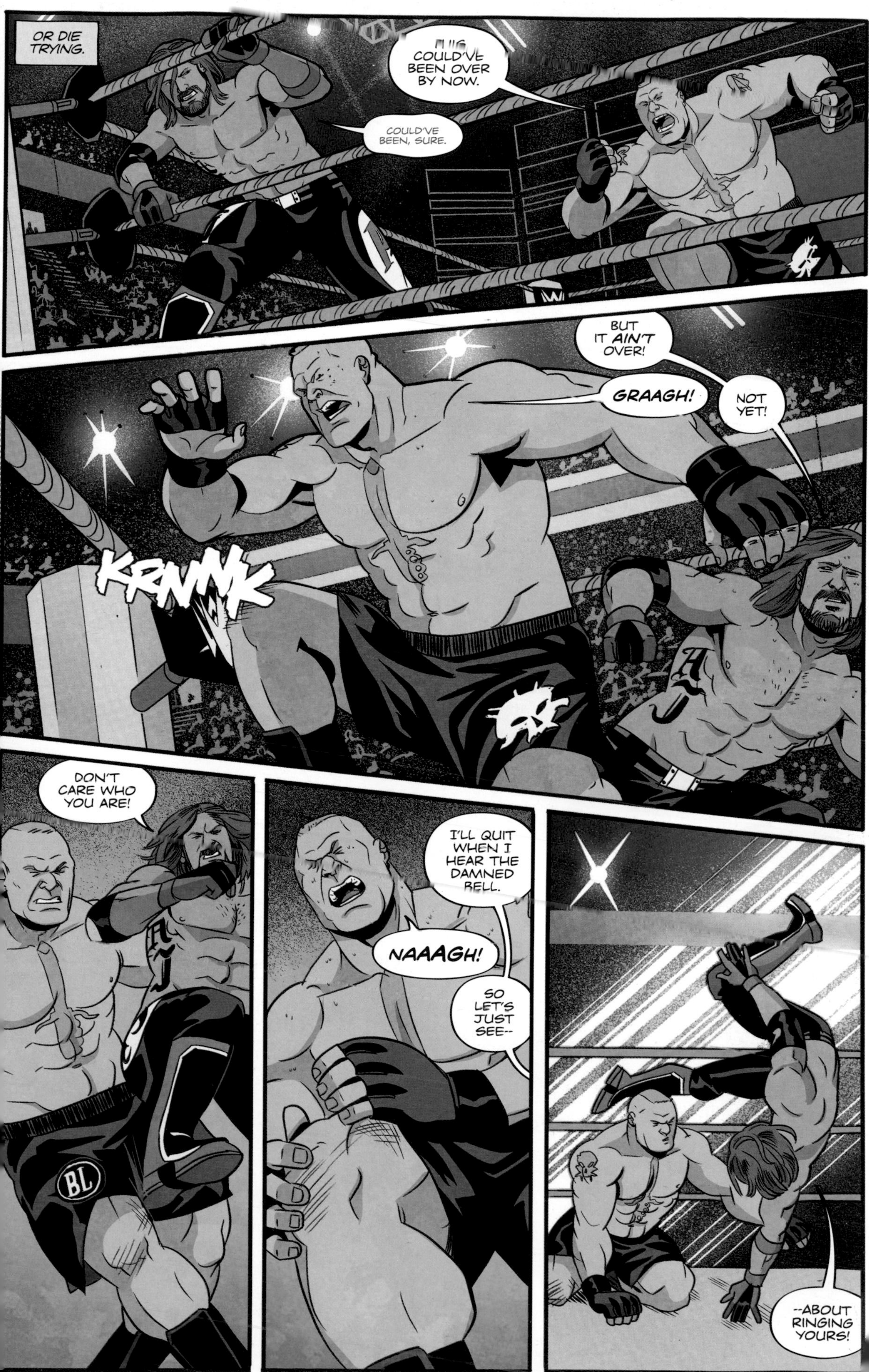
OR DIE TRYING.
COULD'VE BEEN OVER BY NOW.
COULD'VE BEEN, SURE.
BUT IT AIN'T OVER!
GRAAGH!
NOT YET!
KRNNK
DON'T CARE WHO YOU ARE!
I'LL QUIT WHEN I HEAR THE DAMNED BELL.
NAAAGH!
SO LET'S JUST SEE--
--ABOUT RINGING YOURS!

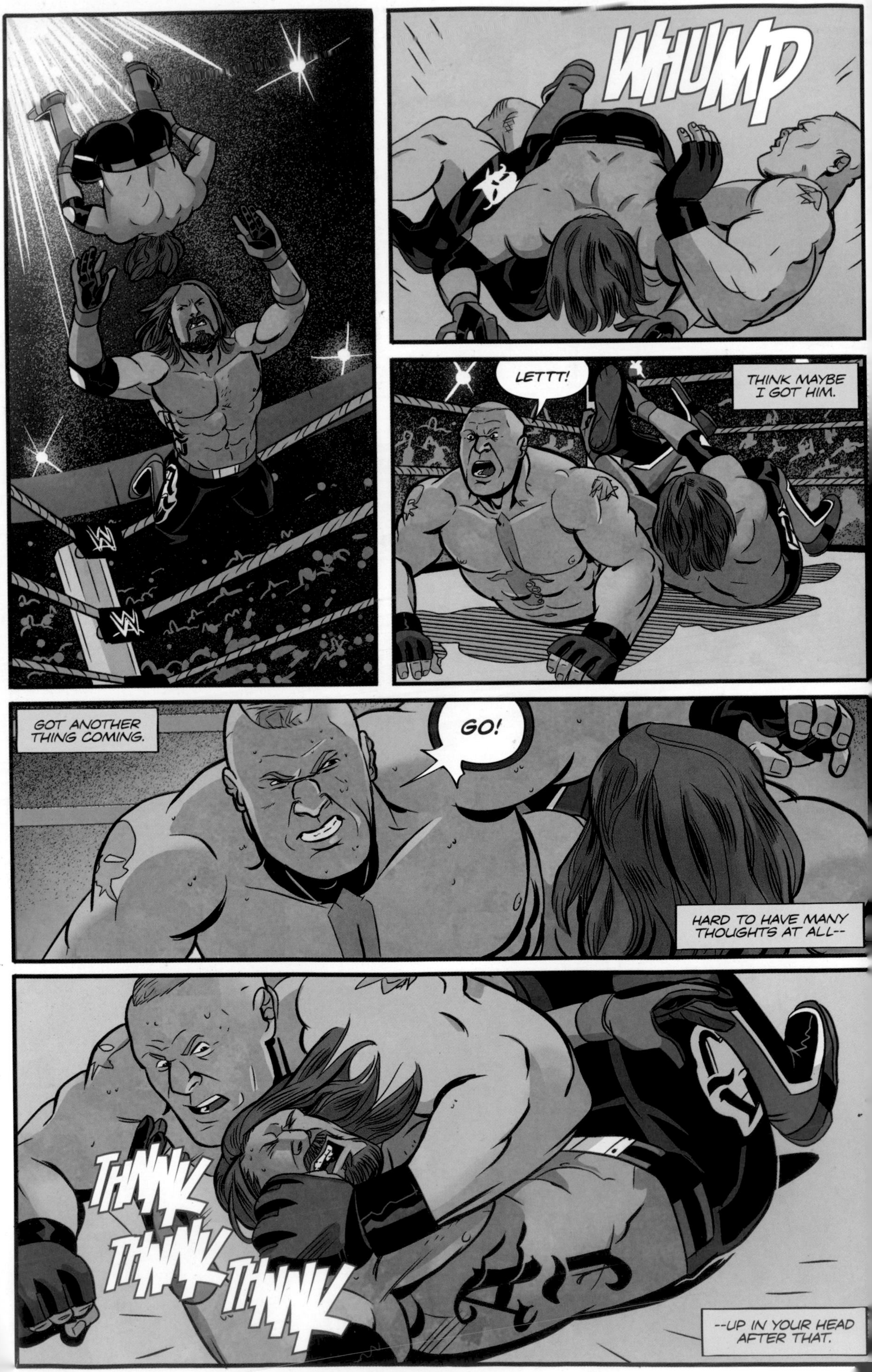
WHUMP
LETTT!
THINK MAYBE I GOT HIM.
GOT ANOTHER THING COMING.
GO!
HARD TO HAVE MANY THOUGHTS AT ALL--
THNNK THNNK THNNK
--UP IN YOUR HEAD AFTER THAT.

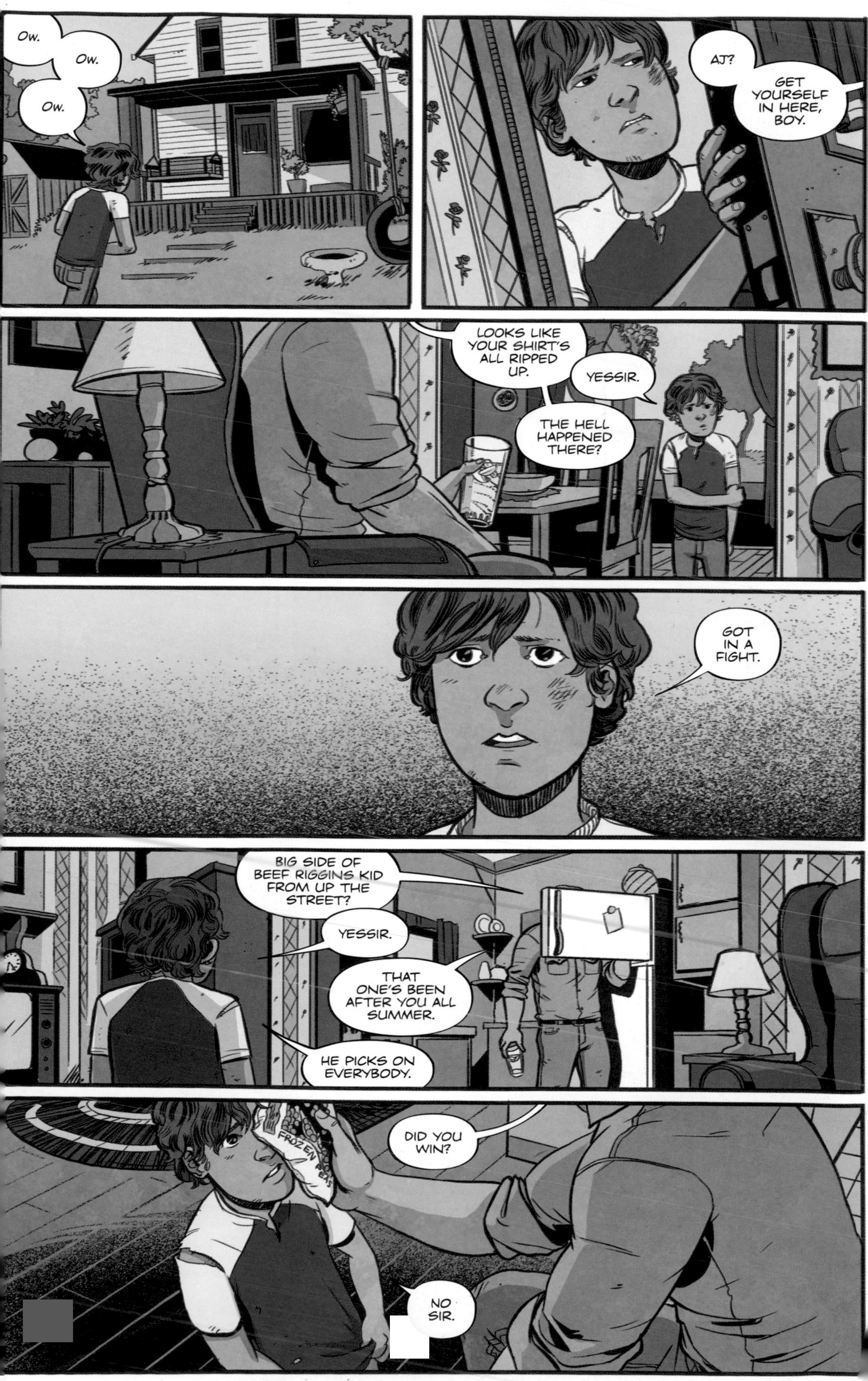
Ow.
Ow.
Ow.
AJ?
GET YOURSELF IN HERE, BOY.
LOOKS LIKE YOUR SHIRT'S ALL RIPPED UP.
YESSIR.
THE HELL HAPPENED THERE?
GOT IN A FIGHT.
BIG SIDE OF BEEF RIGGINS KID FROM UP THE STREET?
YESSIR.
THAT ONE'S BEEN AFTER YOU ALL SUMMER.
HE PICKS ON EVERYBODY.
DID YOU WIN?
FROZEN PEAS
NO SIR.

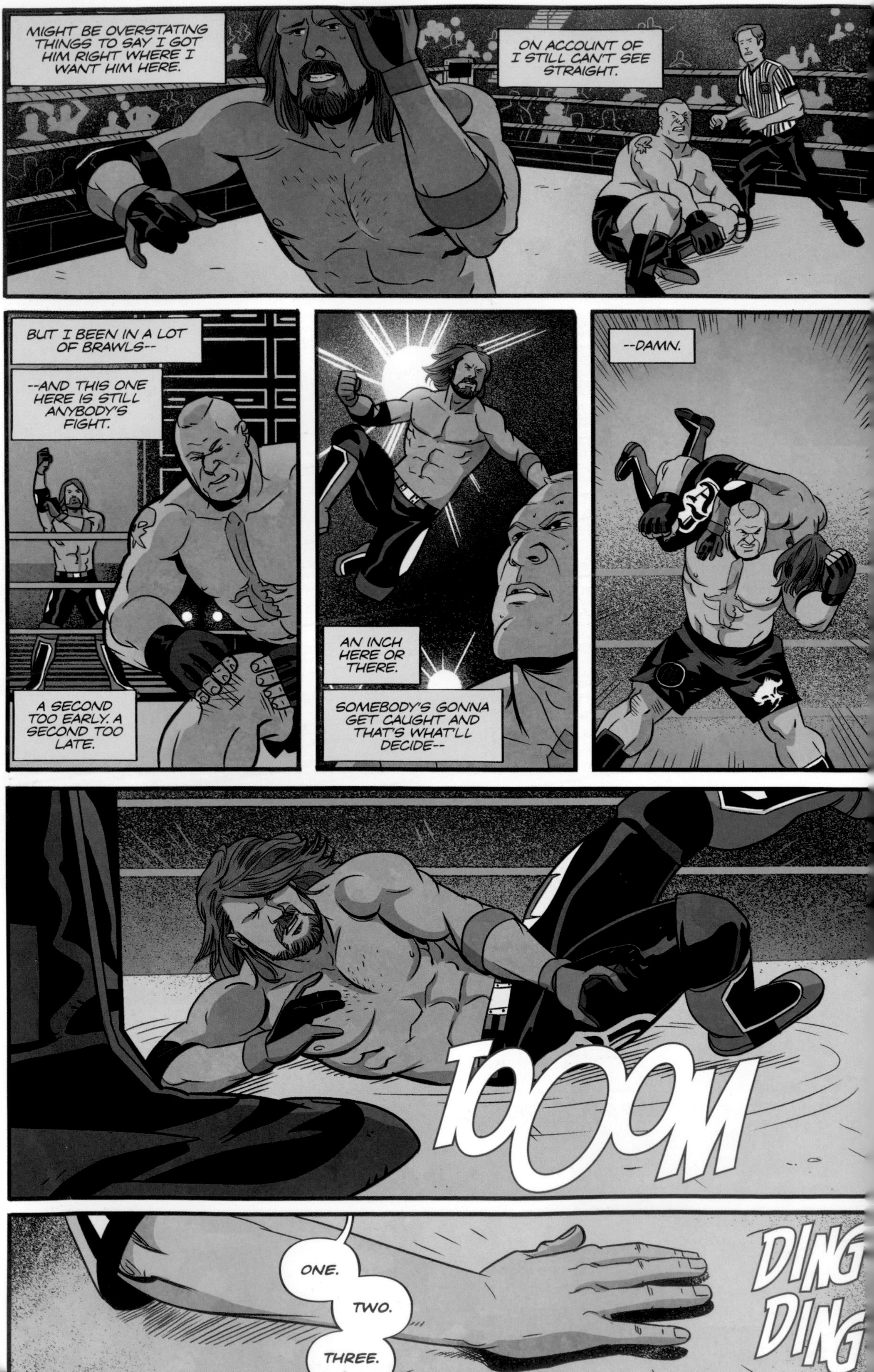
MIGHT BE OVERSTATING THINGS TO SAY I GOT HIM RIGHT WHERE I WANT HIM HERE.
ON ACCOUNT OF I STILL CAN'T SEE STRAIGHT.
BUT I BEEN IN A LOT OF BRAWLS--
--AND THIS ONE HERE IS STILL ANYBODY'S FIGHT.
A SECOND TOO EARLY. A SECOND TOO LATE.
AN INCH HERE OR THERE.
SOMEBODY'S GONNA GET CAUGHT AND THAT'S WHAT'LL DECIDE--
--DAMN.
TOOOM
ONE.
TWO.
THREE.
DING DING

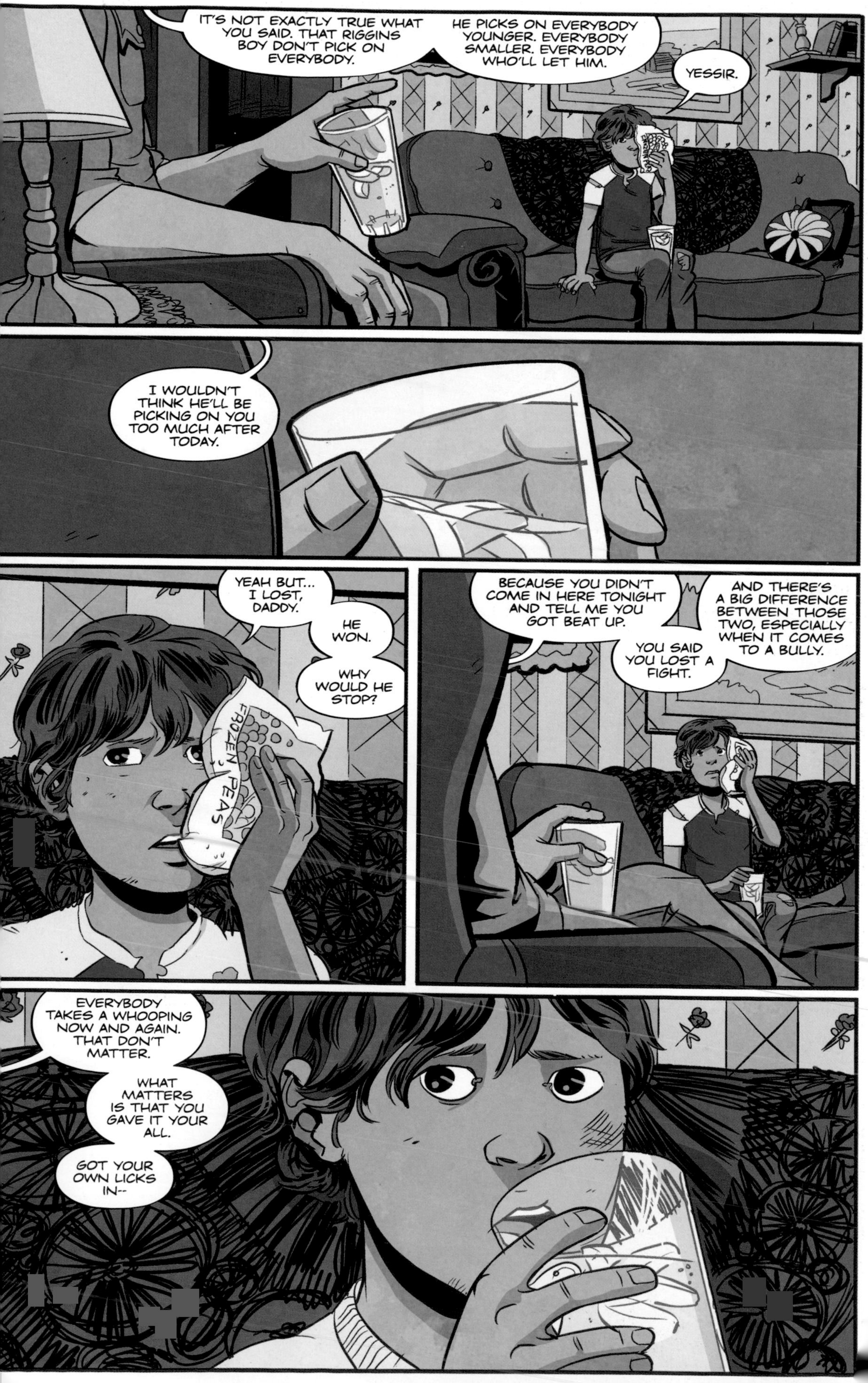
IT'S NOT EXACTLY TRUE WHAT YOU SAID. THAT RIGGINS BOY DON'T PICK ON EVERYBODY.
HE PICKS ON EVERYBODY YOUNGER. EVERYBODY SMALLER. EVERYBODY WHO'LL LET HIM.
YESSIR.
I WOULDN'T THINK HE'LL BE PICKING ON YOU TOO MUCH AFTER TODAY.
YEAH BUT... I LOST, DADDY.
HE WON.
WHY WOULD HE STOP?
FROZEN PEAS
BECAUSE YOU DIDN'T COME IN HERE TONIGHT AND TELL ME YOU GOT BEAT UP.
YOU SAID YOU LOST A FIGHT.
AND THERE'S A BIG DIFFERENCE BETWEEN THOSE TWO, ESPECIALLY WHEN IT COMES TO A BULLY.
EVERYBODY TAKES A WHOOPING NOW AND AGAIN. THAT DON'T MATTER.
WHAT MATTERS IS THAT YOU GAVE IT YOUR ALL.
GOT YOUR OWN LICKS IN--

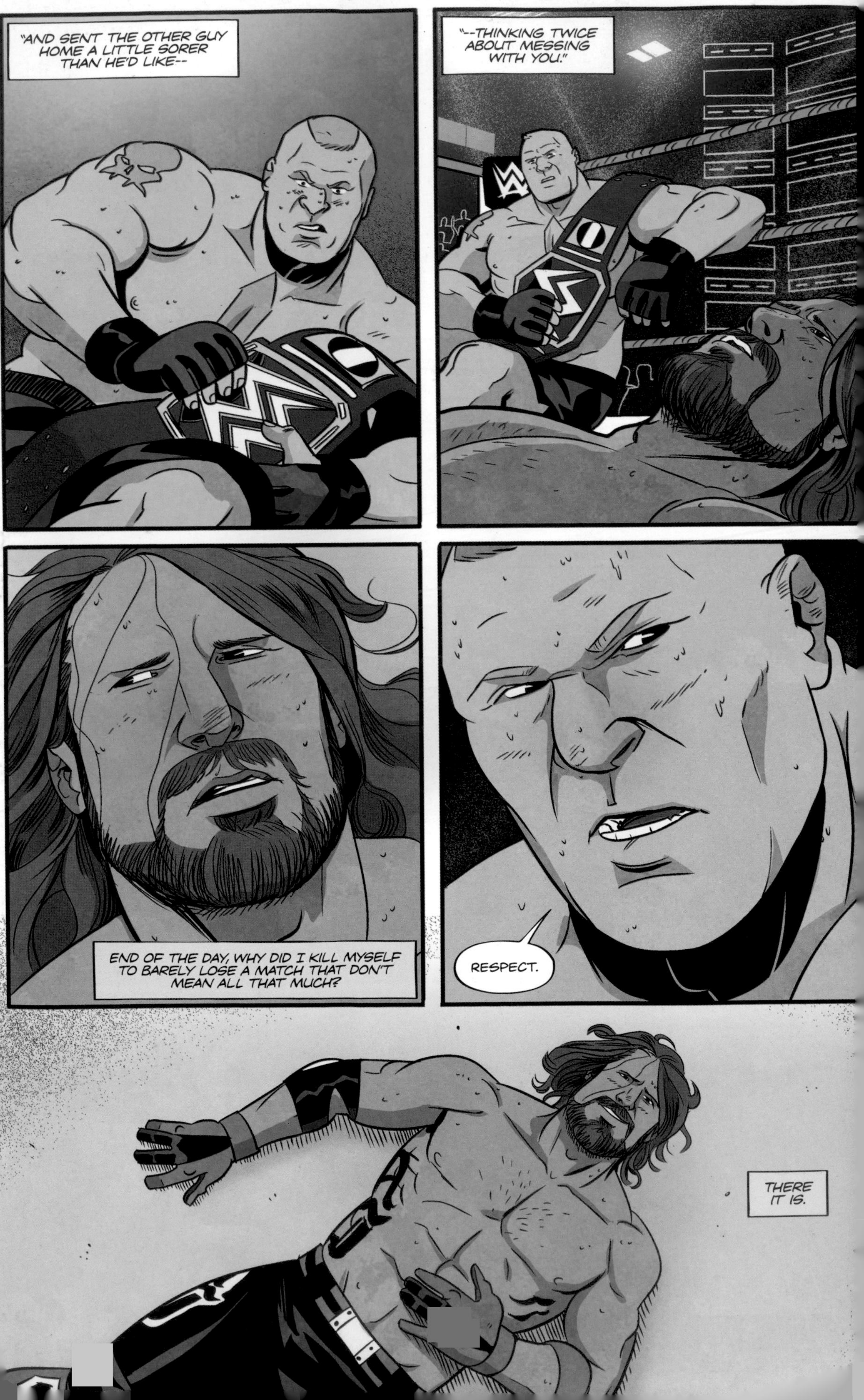
"AND SENT THE OTHER GUY HOME A LITTLE SORER THAN HE'D LIKE--
"--THINKING TWICE ABOUT MESSING WITH YOU."
END OF THE DAY, WHY DID I KILL MYSELF TO BARELY LOSE A MATCH THAT DON'T MEAN ALL THAT MUCH?
RESPECT.
THERE IT IS.

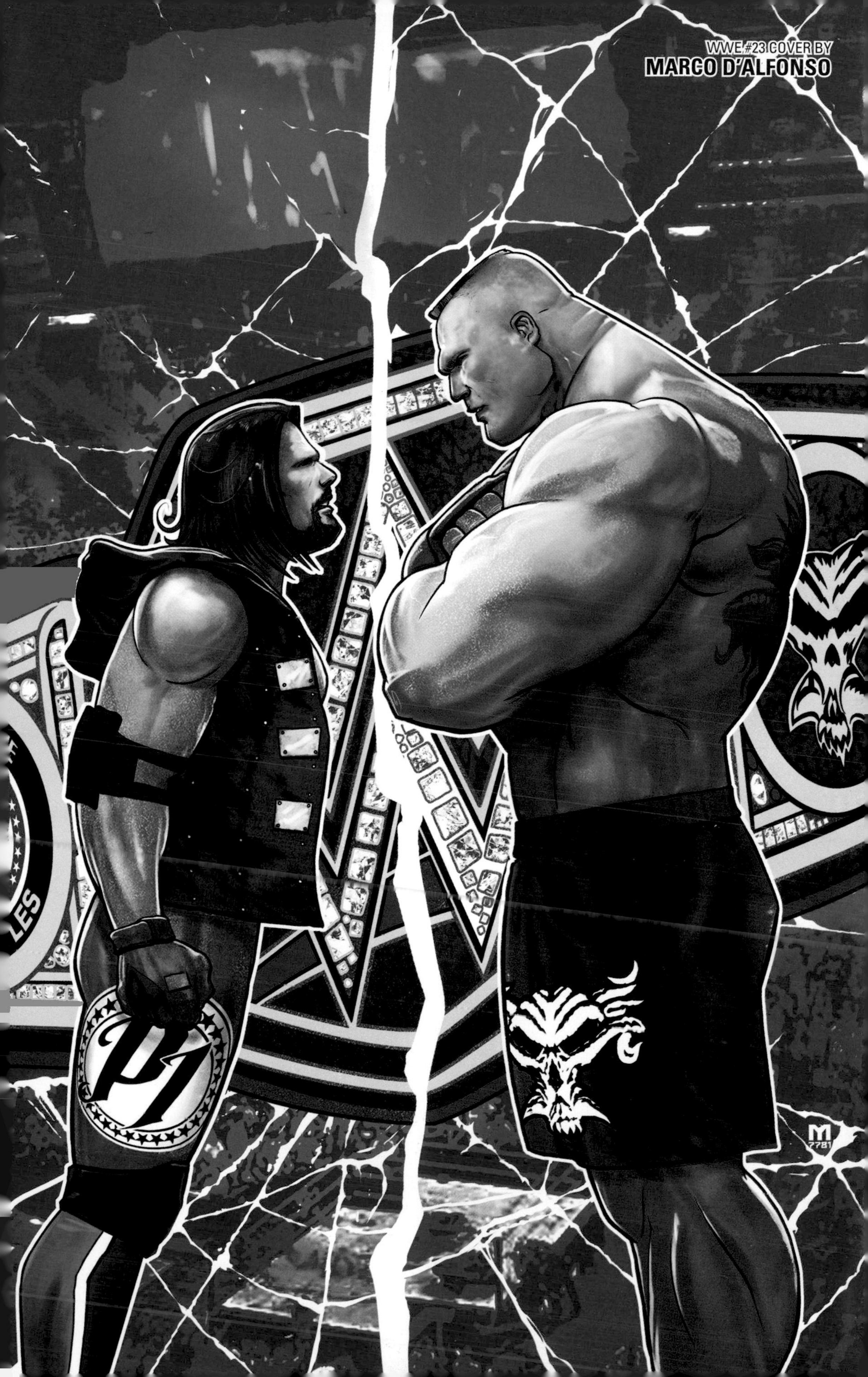

WWE #23 COVER BY
MARCO D'ALFONSO

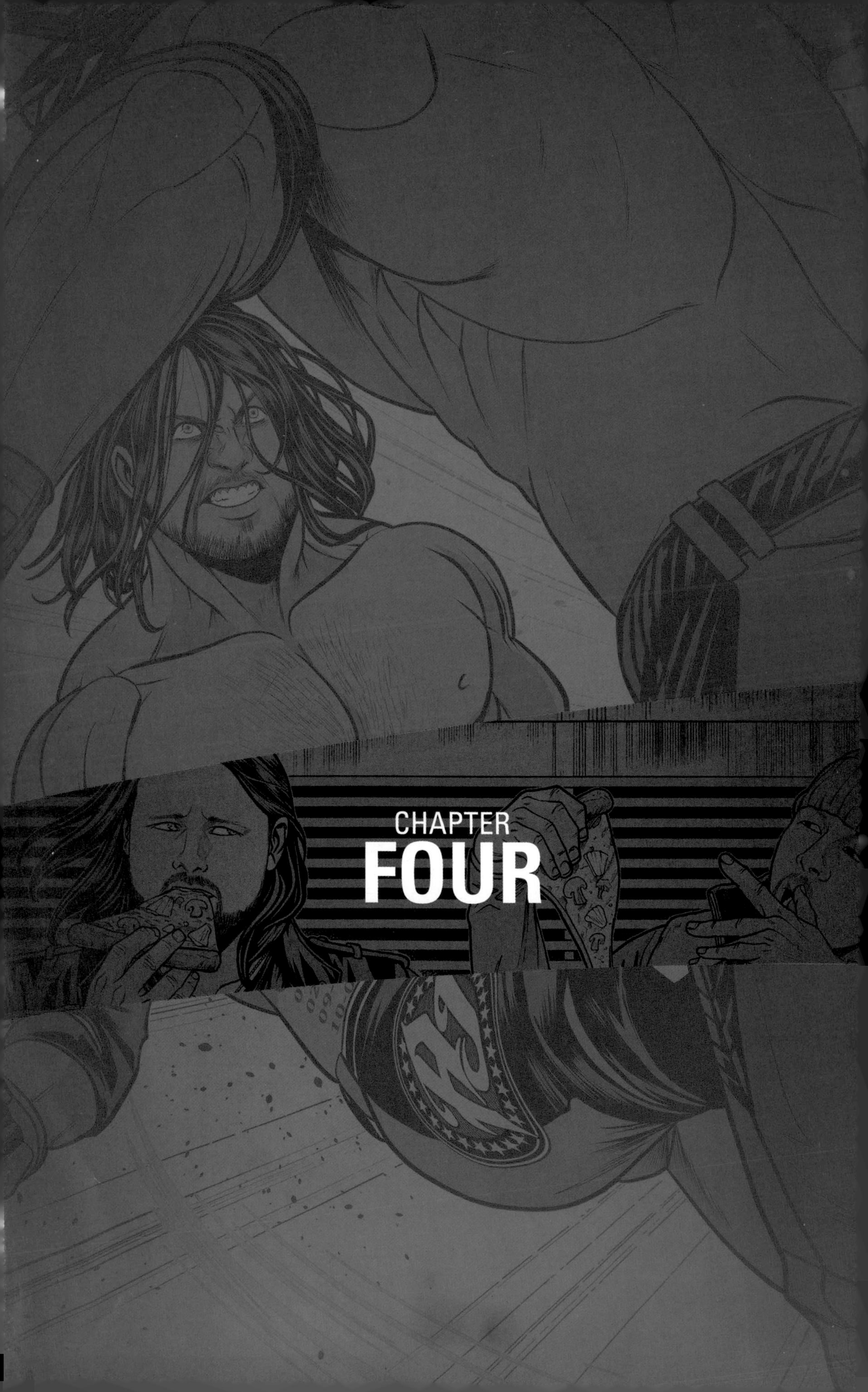
CHAPTER
FOUR

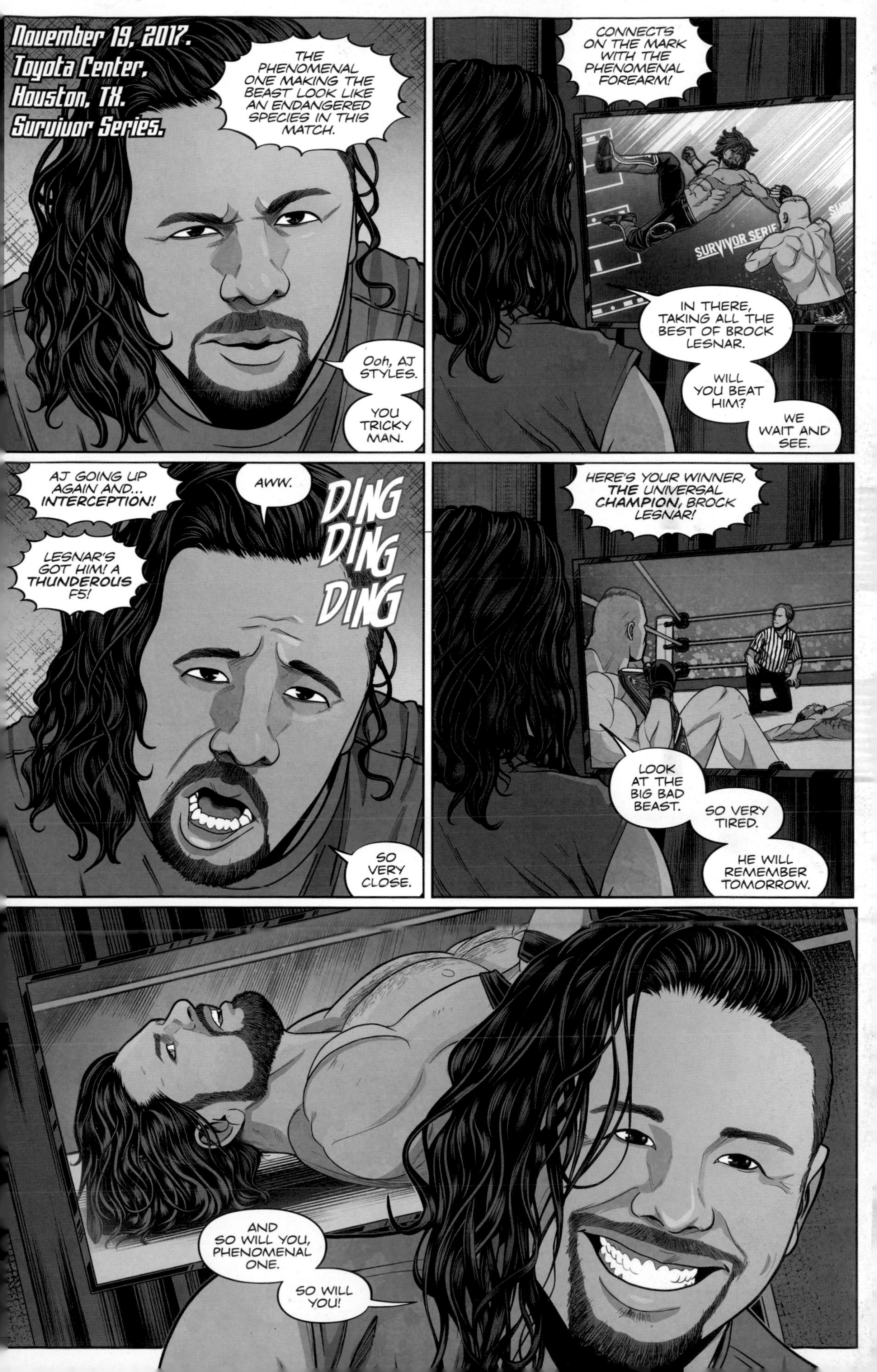
November 19, 2017. Toyota Center, Houston, TX. Survivor Series.
THE PHENOMENAL ONE MAKING THE BEAST LOOK LIKE AN ENDANGERED SPECIES IN THIS MATCH.
Ooh, AJ STYLES.
YOU TRICKY MAN.
CONNECTS ON THE MARK WITH THE PHENOMENAL FOREARM!
SURVIVOR SERIE
IN THERE, TAKING ALL THE BEST OF BROCK LESNAR.
WILL YOU BEAT HIM?
WE WAIT AND SEE.
AJ GOING UP AGAIN AND... INTERCEPTION!
AWW.
DING DING DING
LESNAR'S GOT HIM! A THUNDEROUS F5!
SO VERY CLOSE.
HERE'S YOUR WINNER, THE UNIVERSAL CHAMPION, BROCK LESNAR!
LOOK AT THE BIG BAD BEAST.
SO VERY TIRED.
HE WILL REMEMBER TOMORROW.
AND SO WILL YOU, PHENOMENAL ONE.
SO WILL YOU!

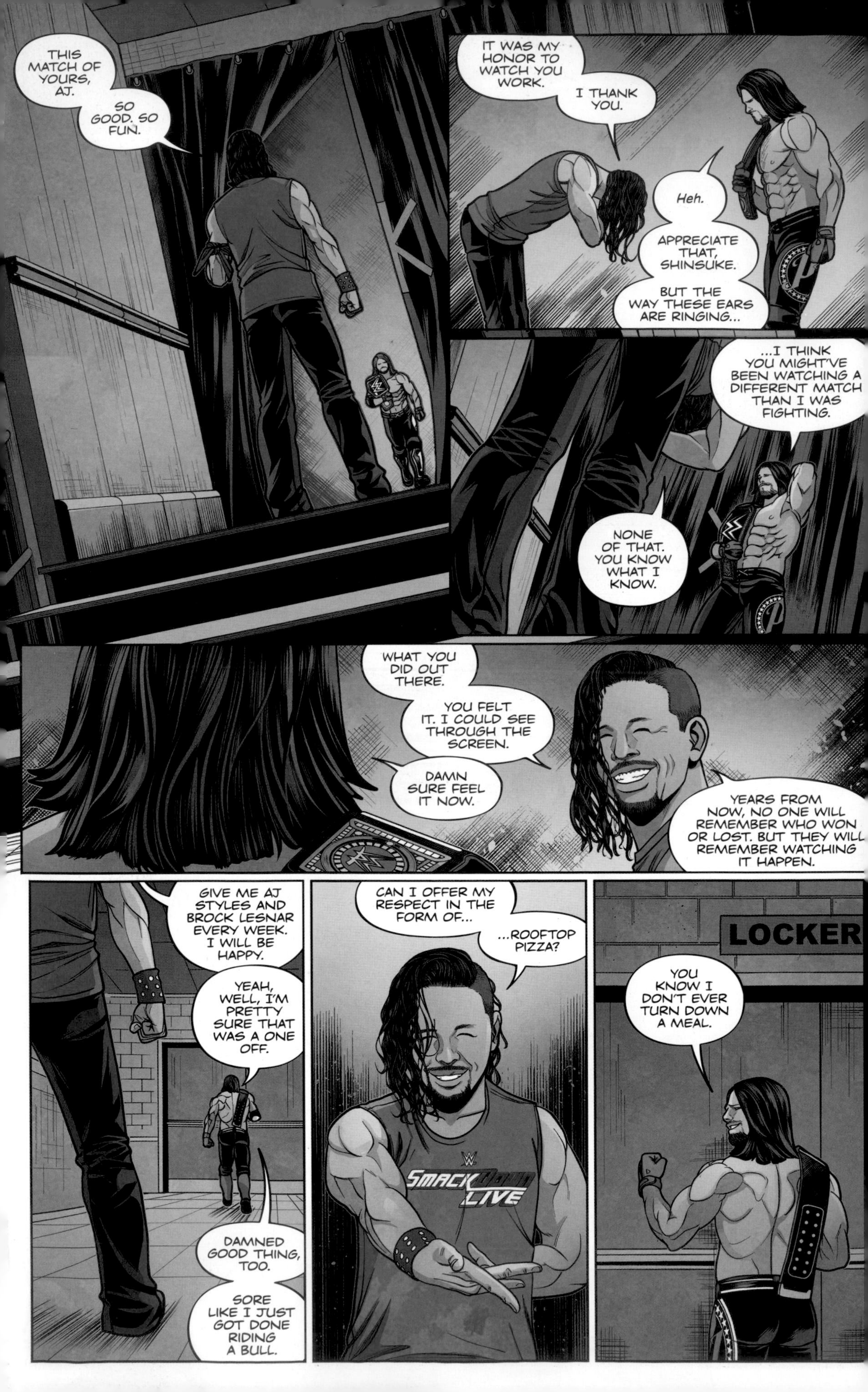

THIS MATCH OF YOURS, AJ.
SO GOOD. SO FUN.
IT WAS MY HONOR TO WATCH YOU WORK.
I THANK YOU.
Heh.
APPRECIATE THAT, SHINSUKE.
BUT THE WAY THESE EARS ARE RINGING...
...I THINK YOU MIGHT'VE BEEN WATCHING A DIFFERENT MATCH THAN I WAS FIGHTING.
NONE OF THAT. YOU KNOW WHAT I KNOW.
WHAT YOU DID OUT THERE.
YOU FELT IT. I COULD SEE THROUGH THE SCREEN.
DAMN SURE FEEL IT NOW.
YEARS FROM NOW, NO ONE WILL REMEMBER WHO WON OR LOST. BUT THEY WILL REMEMBER WATCHING IT HAPPEN.
GIVE ME AJ STYLES AND BROCK LESNAR EVERY WEEK. I WILL BE HAPPY.
YEAH, WELL, I'M PRETTY SURE THAT WAS A ONE OFF.
DAMNED GOOD THING, TOO.
SORE LIKE I JUST GOT DONE RIDING A BULL.
CAN I OFFER MY RESPECT IN THE FORM OF...
...ROOFTOP PIZZA?
SMACKDOWN LIVE
LOCKER
YOU KNOW I DON'T EVER TURN DOWN A MEAL.

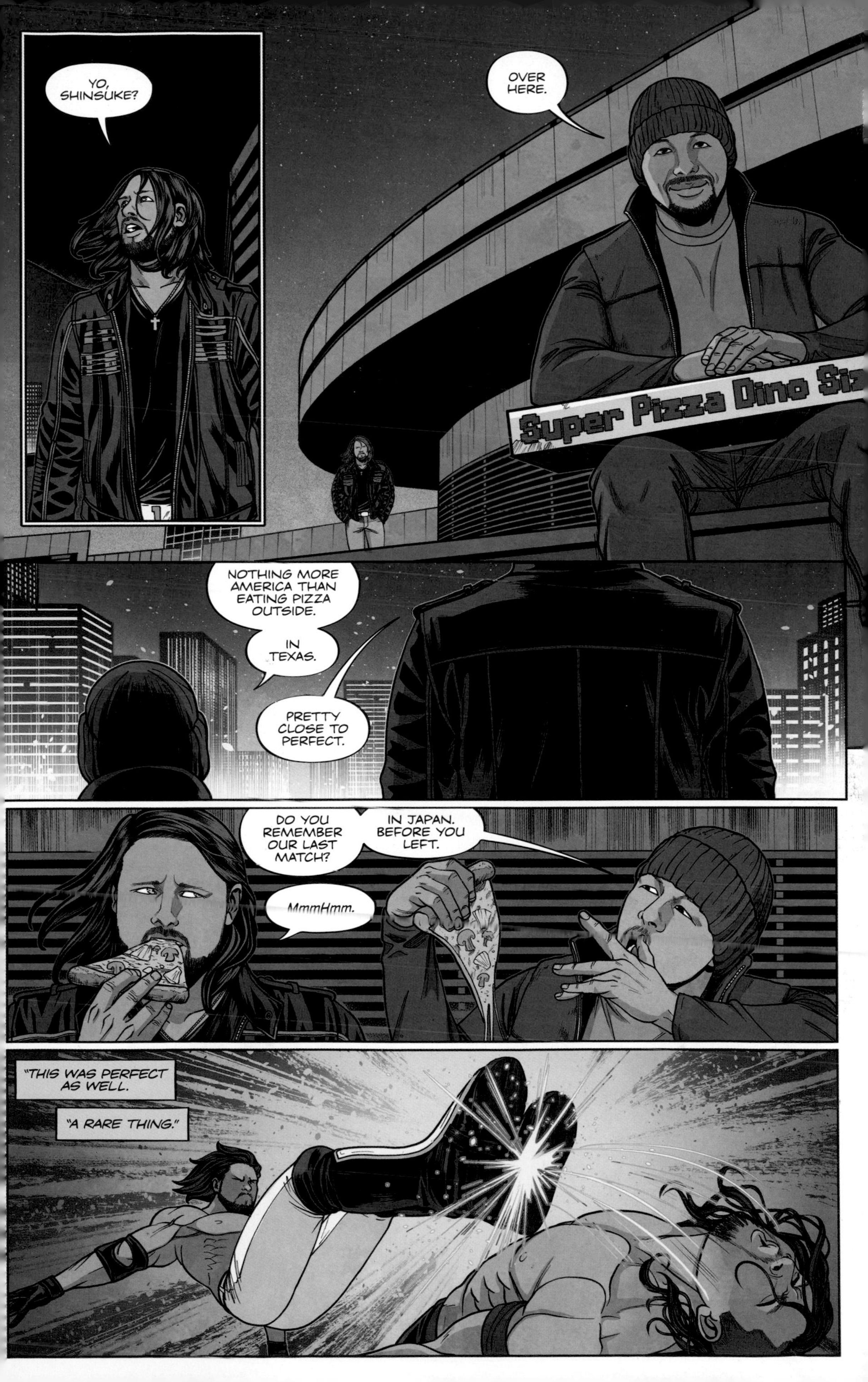
YO, SHINSUKE?
OVER HERE.
Super Pizza Dino Siz
NOTHING MORE AMERICA THAN EATING PIZZA OUTSIDE.
IN TEXAS.
PRETTY CLOSE TO PERFECT.
DO YOU REMEMBER OUR LAST MATCH?
IN JAPAN. BEFORE YOU LEFT.
MmmHmm.
"THIS WAS PERFECT AS WELL.
"A RARE THING."

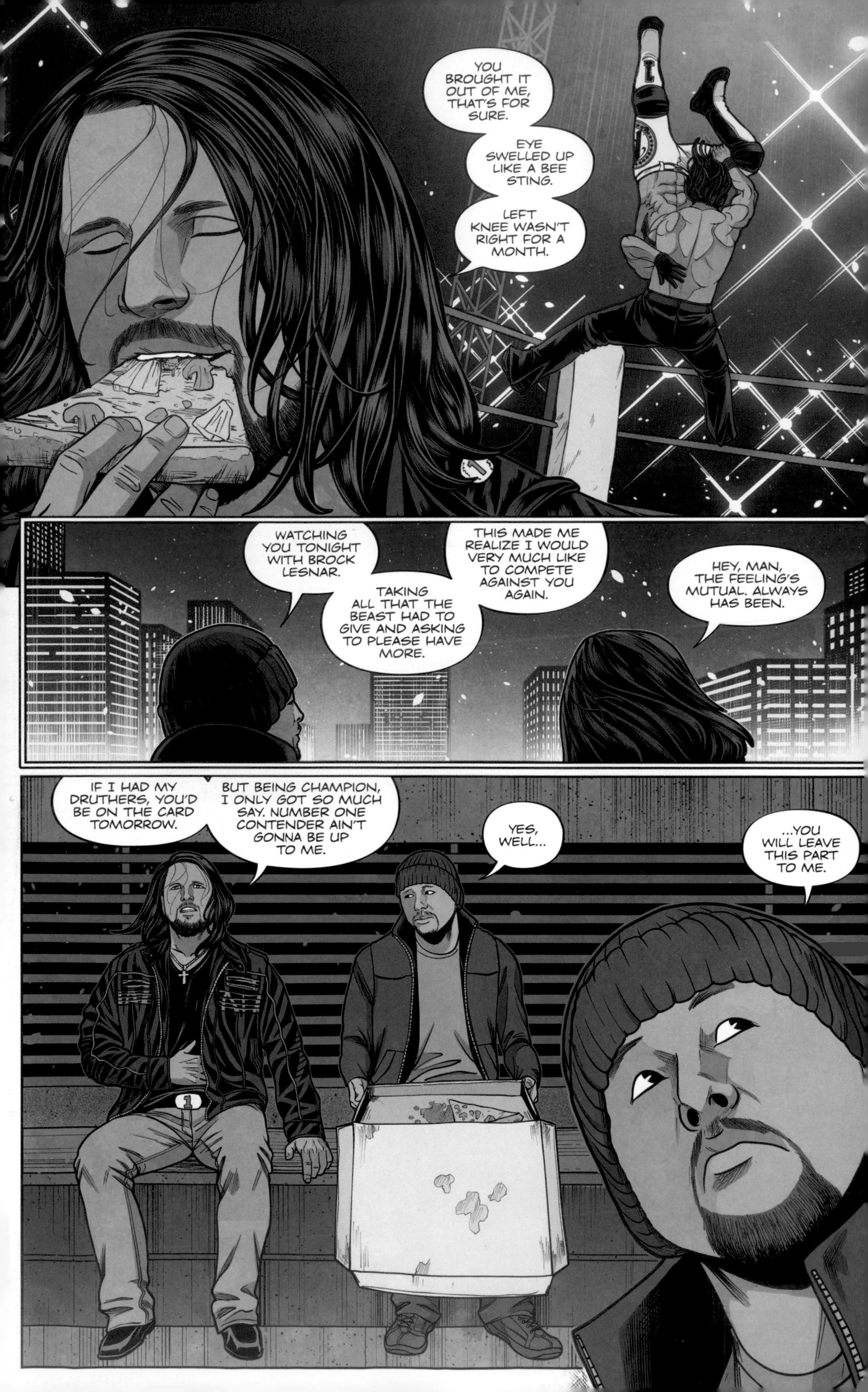
YOU BROUGHT IT OUT OF ME, THAT'S FOR SURE.
EYE SWELLED UP LIKE A BEE STING.
LEFT KNEE WASN'T RIGHT FOR A MONTH.
WATCHING YOU TONIGHT WITH BROCK LESNAR.
TAKING ALL THAT THE BEAST HAD TO GIVE AND ASKING TO PLEASE HAVE MORE.
THIS MADE ME REALIZE I WOULD VERY MUCH LIKE TO COMPETE AGAINST YOU AGAIN.
HEY, MAN, THE FEELING'S MUTUAL. ALWAYS HAS BEEN.
IF I HAD MY DRUTHERS, YOU'D BE ON THE CARD TOMORROW.
BUT BEING CHAMPION, I ONLY GOT SO MUCH SAY. NUMBER ONE CONTENDER AIN'T GONNA BE UP TO ME.
YES, WELL...
...YOU WILL LEAVE THIS PART TO ME.

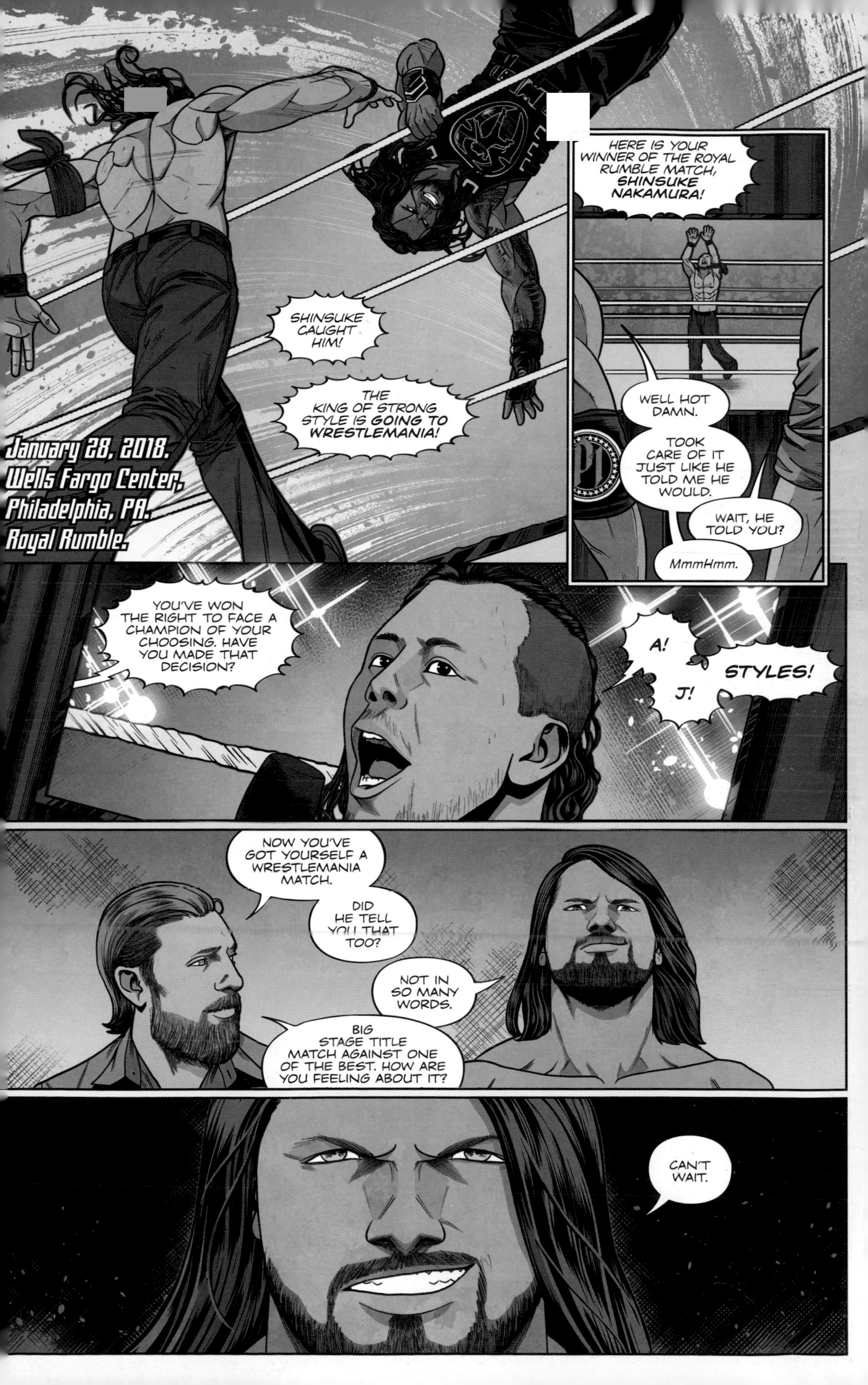
January 28, 2018.
Wells Fargo Center,
Philadelphia, PA.
Royal Rumble.
SHINSUKE CAUGHT HIM!
THE KING OF STRONG STYLE IS GOING TO WRESTLEMANIA!
HERE IS YOUR WINNER OF THE ROYAL RUMBLE MATCH, SHINSUKE NAKAMURA!
WELL HOT DAMN.
TOOK CARE OF IT JUST LIKE HE TOLD ME HE WOULD.
WAIT, HE TOLD YOU?
MmmHmm.
YOU'VE WON THE RIGHT TO FACE A CHAMPION OF YOUR CHOOSING. HAVE YOU MADE THAT DECISION?
A!
J!
STYLES!
NOW YOU'VE GOT YOURSELF A WRESTLEMANIA MATCH.
DID HE TELL YOU THAT TOO?
NOT IN SO MANY WORDS.
BIG STAGE TITLE MATCH AGAINST ONE OF THE BEST. HOW ARE YOU FEELING ABOUT IT?
CAN'T WAIT.

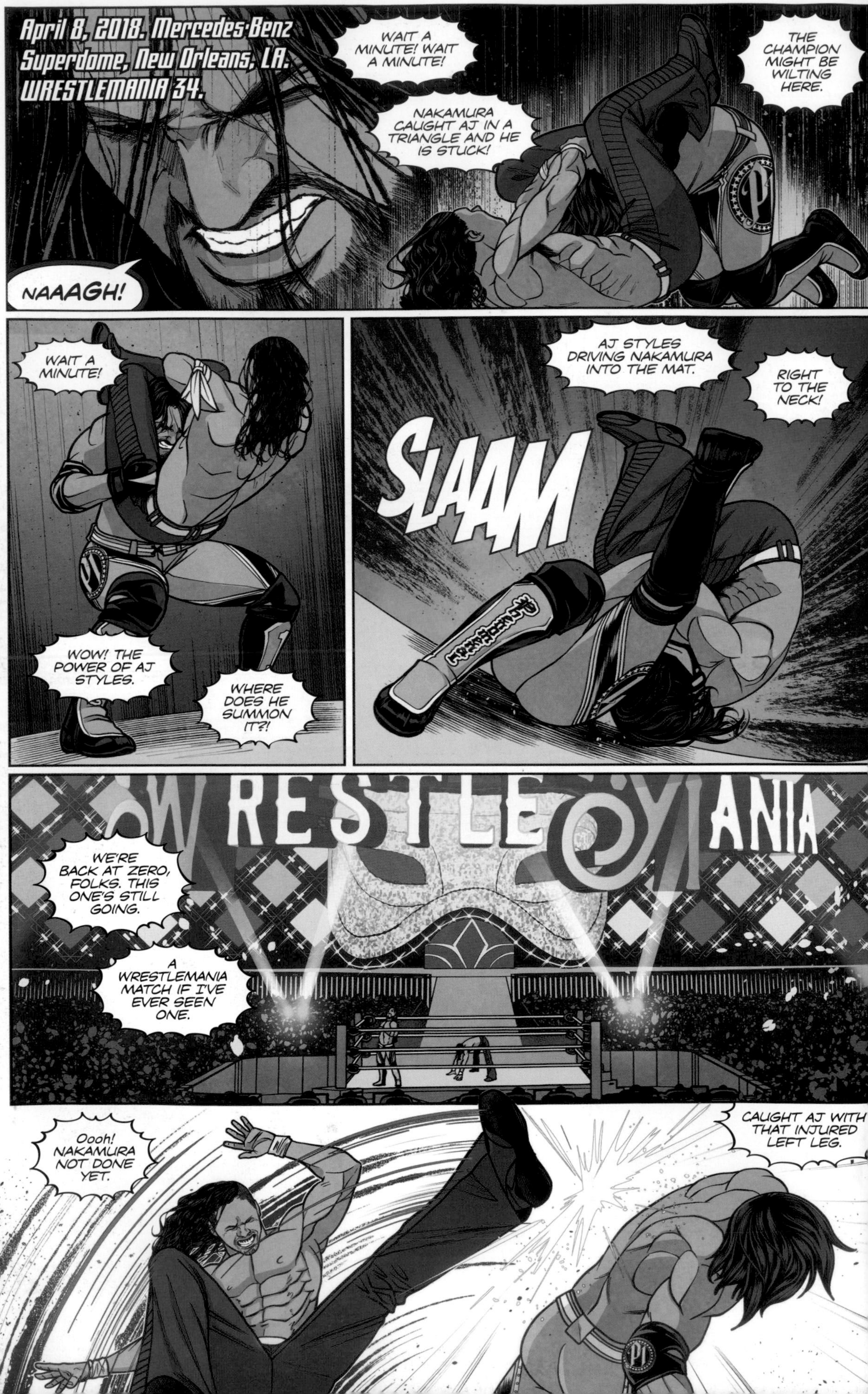

April 8, 2018. Mercedes-Benz Superdome, New Orleans, LA. WRESTLEMANIA 34.
WAIT A MINUTE! WAIT A MINUTE!
NAKAMURA CAUGHT AJ IN A TRIANGLE AND HE IS STUCK!
THE CHAMPION MIGHT BE WILTING HERE.
NAAAGH!
WAIT A MINUTE!
WOW! THE POWER OF AJ STYLES.
WHERE DOES HE SUMMON IT?!
AJ STYLES DRIVING NAKAMURA INTO THE MAT.
RIGHT TO THE NECK!
SLAAM
WRESTLEMANIA
WE'RE BACK AT ZERO, FOLKS. THIS ONE'S STILL GOING.
A WRESTLEMANIA MATCH IF I'VE EVER SEEN ONE.
Oooh! NAKAMURA NOT DONE YET.
CAUGHT AJ WITH THAT INJURED LEFT LEG.

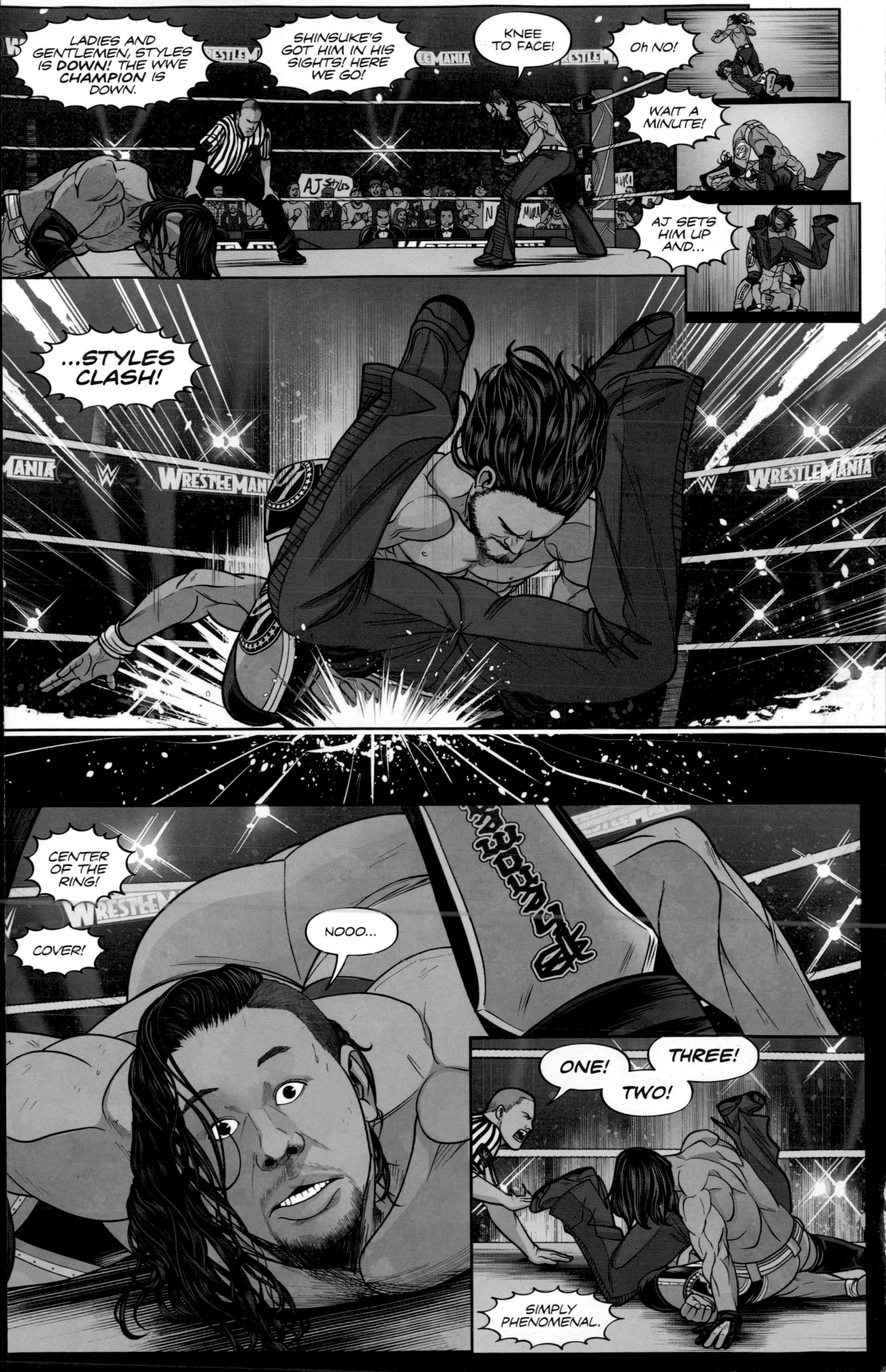
LADIES AND GENTLEMEN, STYLES IS DOWN! THE WWE CHAMPION IS DOWN.
SHINSUKE'S GOT HIM IN HIS SIGHTS! HERE WE GO!
KNEE TO FACE!
Oh NO!
WAIT A MINUTE!
AJ SETS HIM UP AND...
...STYLES CLASH!
CENTER OF THE RING!
COVER!
NOOO...
ONE!
TWO!
THREE!
SIMPLY PHENOMENAL.

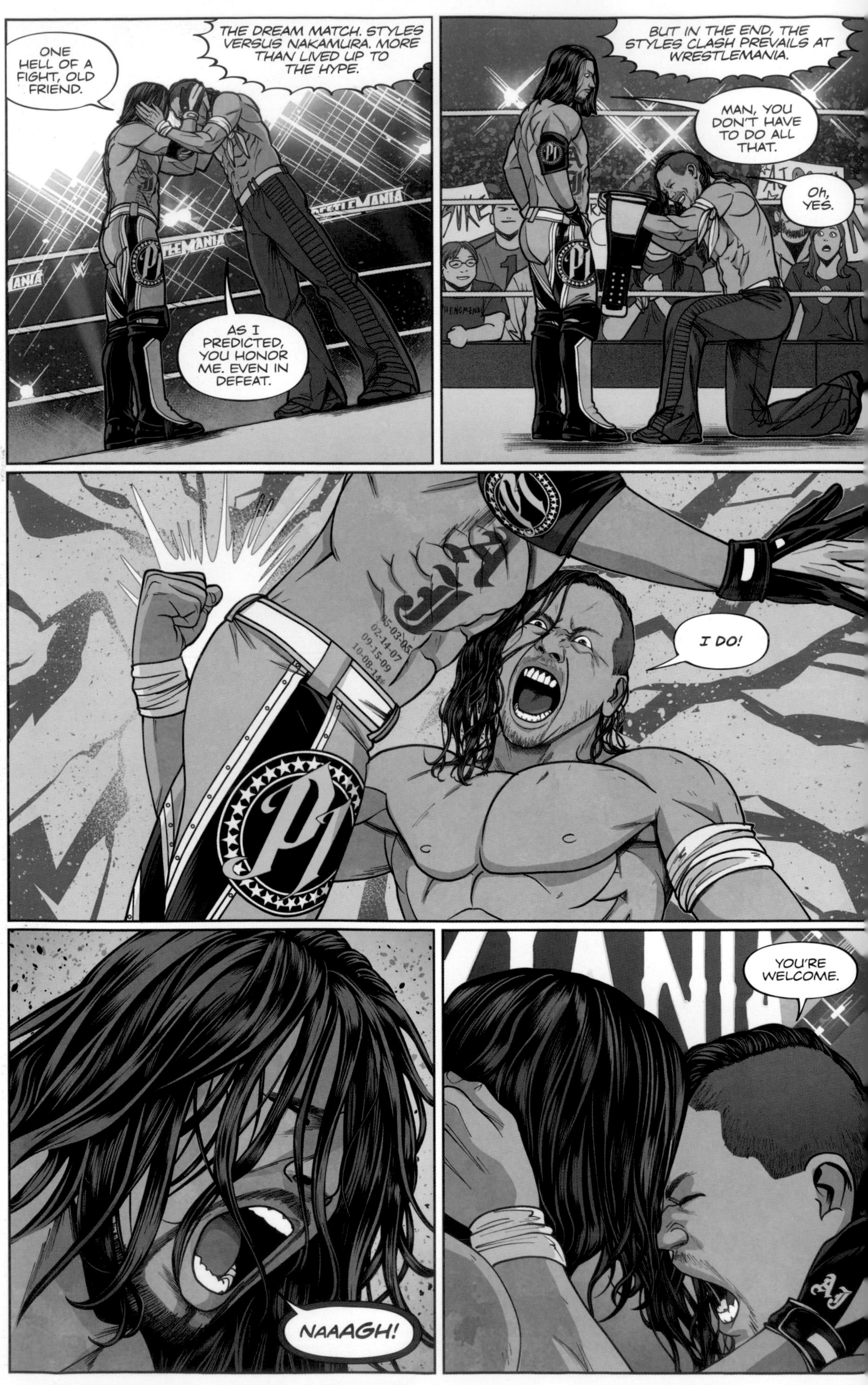
ONE HELL OF A FIGHT, OLD FRIEND.
THE DREAM MATCH. STYLES VERSUS NAKAMURA. MORE THAN LIVED UP TO THE HYPE.
AS I PREDICTED, YOU HONOR ME. EVEN IN DEFEAT.
BUT IN THE END, THE STYLES CLASH PREVAILS AT WRESTLEMANIA.
MAN, YOU DON'T HAVE TO DO ALL THAT.
Oh, YES.
I DO!
02-14-07
09-15-09
10-08-14
NAAAGH!
YOU'RE WELCOME.

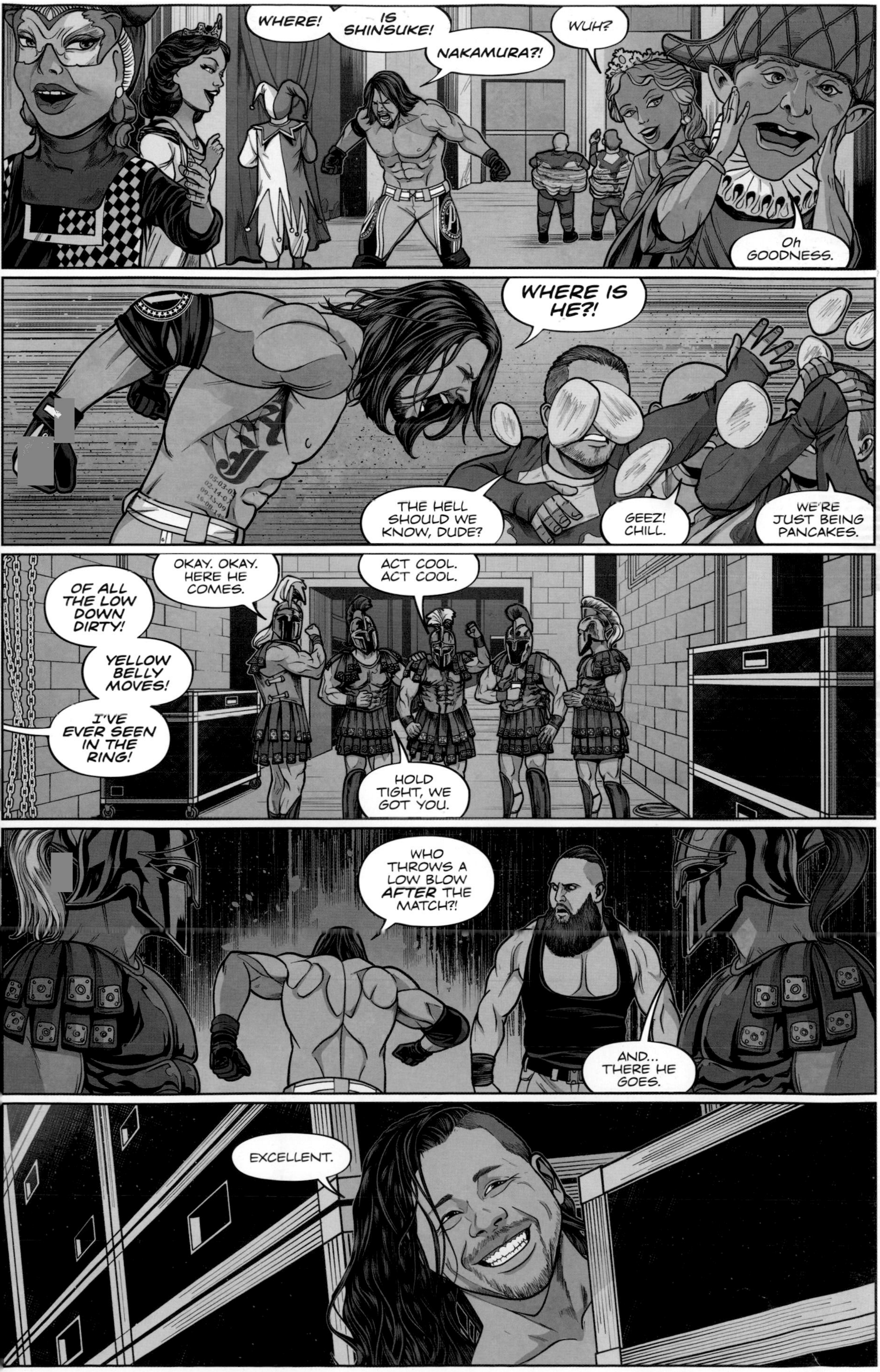
WHERE!
IS SHINSUKE!
NAKAMURA?!
WUH?
Oh GOODNESS.
WHERE IS HE?!
THE HELL SHOULD WE KNOW, DUDE?
GEEZ! CHILL.
WE'RE JUST BEING PANCAKES.
OF ALL THE LOW DOWN DIRTY!
YELLOW BELLY MOVES!
I'VE EVER SEEN IN THE RING!
OKAY. OKAY. HERE HE COMES.
ACT COOL. ACT COOL.
HOLD TIGHT, WE GOT YOU.
WHO THROWS A LOW BLOW AFTER THE MATCH?!
AND... THERE HE GOES.
EXCELLENT.

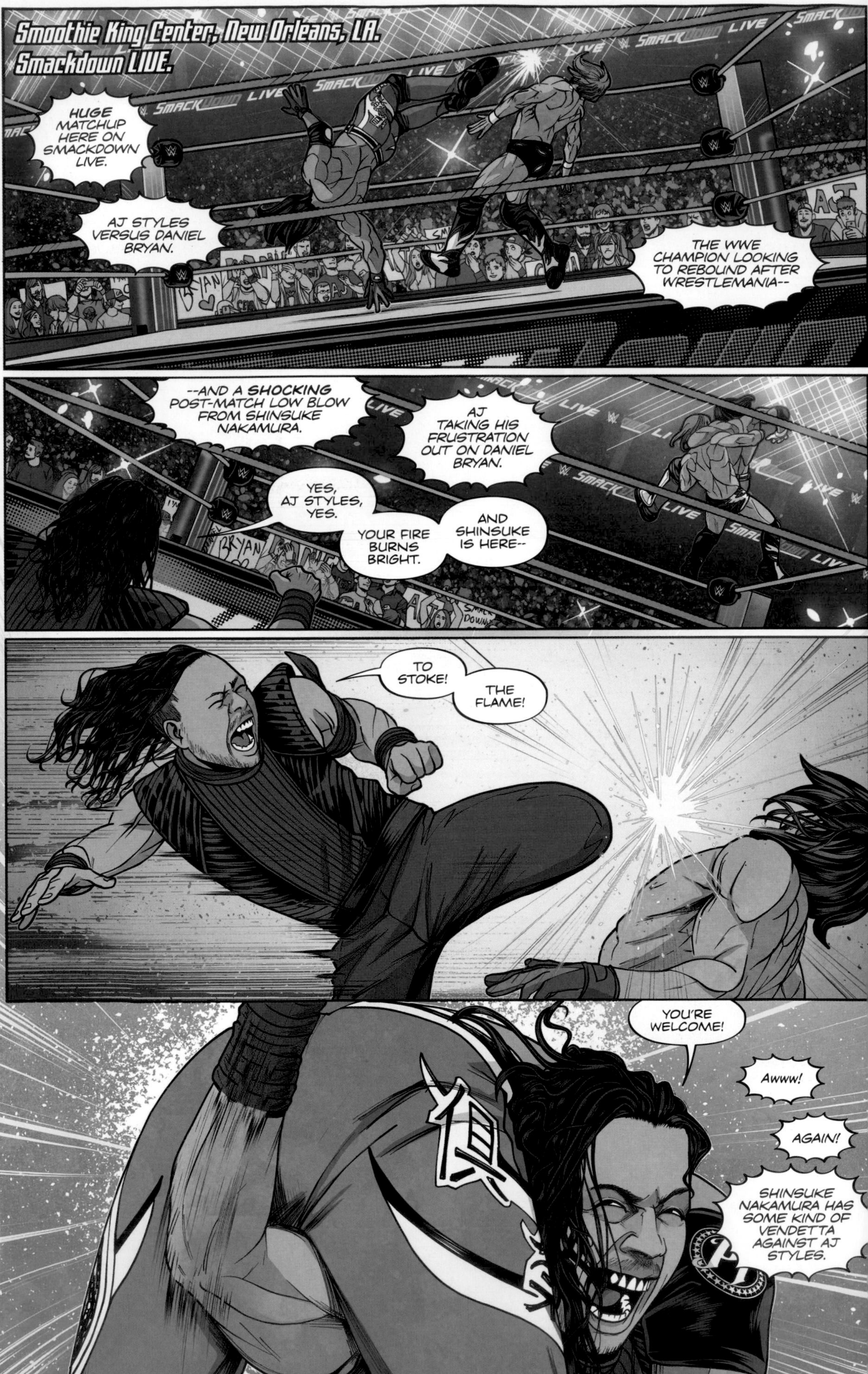

Smoothie King Center, New Orleans, LA.
Smackdown LIVE.
HUGE MATCHUP HERE ON SMACKDOWN LIVE.
AJ STYLES VERSUS DANIEL BRYAN.
THE WWE CHAMPION LOOKING TO REBOUND AFTER WRESTLEMANIA--
--AND A SHOCKING POST-MATCH LOW BLOW FROM SHINSUKE NAKAMURA.
AJ TAKING HIS FRUSTRATION OUT ON DANIEL BRYAN.
YES, AJ STYLES, YES.
YOUR FIRE BURNS BRIGHT.
AND SHINSUKE IS HERE--
TO STOKE!
THE FLAME!
YOU'RE WELCOME!
Awww!
AGAIN!
SHINSUKE NAKAMURA HAS SOME KIND OF VENDETTA AGAINST AJ STYLES.

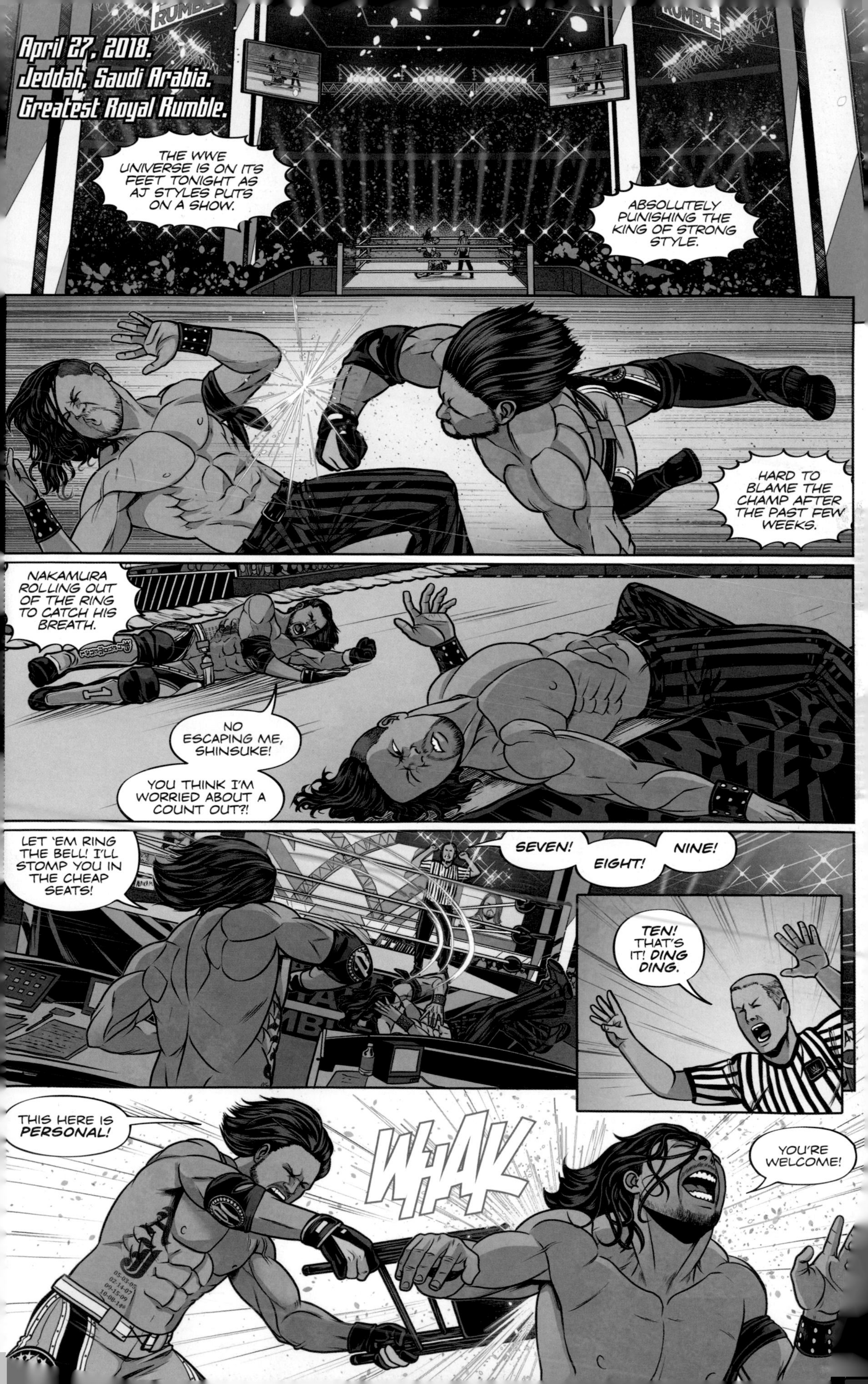
April 27, 2018.
Jeddah, Saudi Arabia.
Greatest Royal Rumble.
THE WWE UNIVERSE IS ON ITS FEET TONIGHT AS AJ STYLES PUTS ON A SHOW.
ABSOLUTELY PUNISHING THE KING OF STRONG STYLE.
HARD TO BLAME THE CHAMP AFTER THE PAST FEW WEEKS.
NAKAMURA ROLLING OUT OF THE RING TO CATCH HIS BREATH.
NO ESCAPING ME, SHINSUKE!
YOU THINK I'M WORRIED ABOUT A COUNT OUT?!
LET 'EM RING THE BELL! I'LL STOMP YOU IN THE CHEAP SEATS!
SEVEN!
EIGHT!
NINE!
TEN! THAT'S IT! DING DING.
THIS HERE IS PERSONAL!
WHAK
YOU'RE WELCOME!

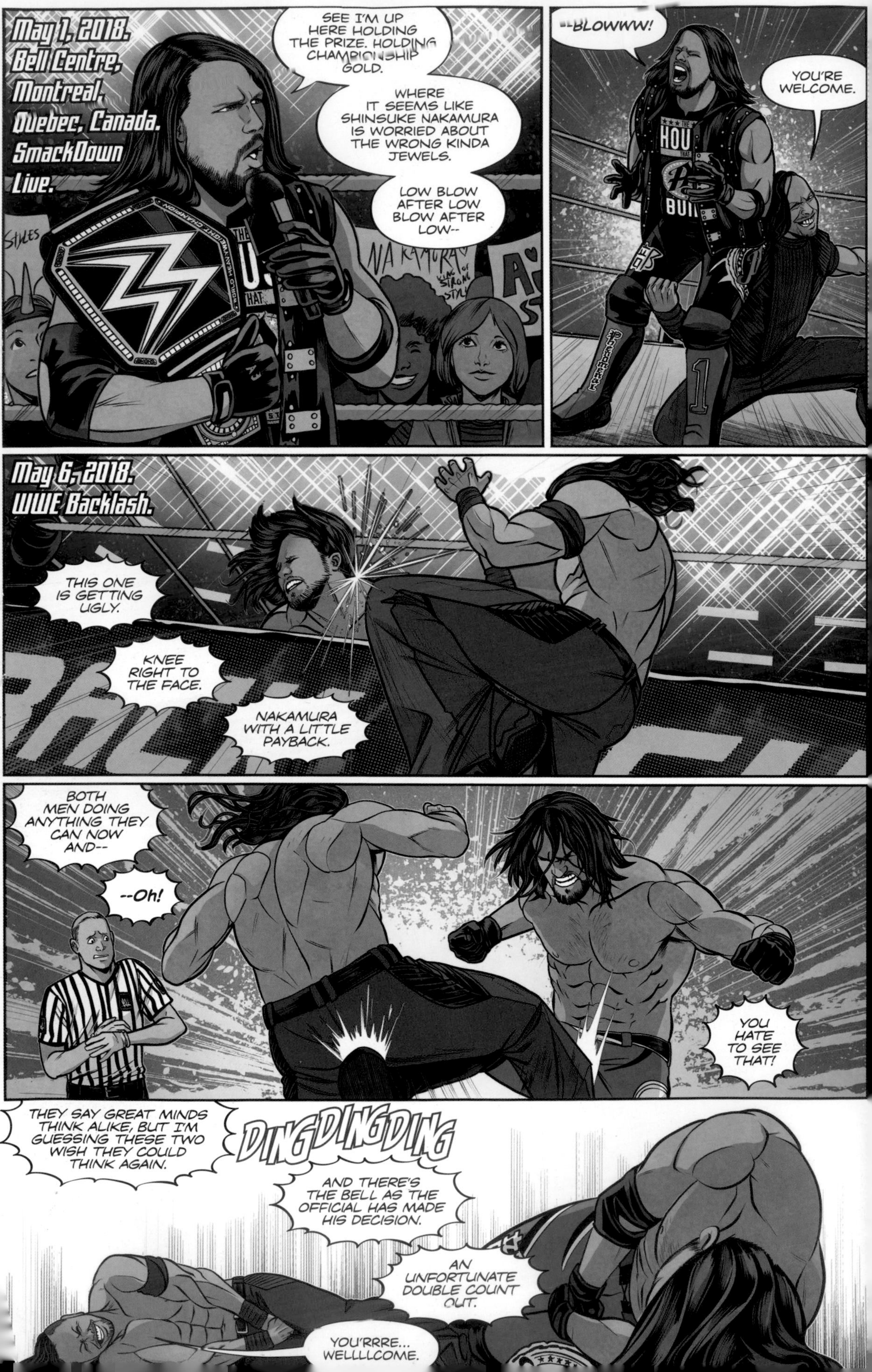
May 1, 2018. Bell Centre, Montreal, Quebec, Canada. SmackDown Live.
SEE I'M UP HERE HOLDING THE PRIZE. HOLDING CHAMPIONSHIP GOLD.
WHERE IT SEEMS LIKE SHINSUKE NAKAMURA IS WORRIED ABOUT THE WRONG KINDA JEWELS.
LOW BLOW AFTER LOW BLOW AFTER LOW--
--BLOWWW!
YOU'RE WELCOME.
May 6, 2018. WWE Backlash.
THIS ONE IS GETTING UGLY.
KNEE RIGHT TO THE FACE.
NAKAMURA WITH A LITTLE PAYBACK.
BOTH MEN DOING ANYTHING THEY CAN NOW AND--
--Oh!
YOU HATE TO SEE THAT!
THEY SAY GREAT MINDS THINK ALIKE, BUT I'M GUESSING THESE TWO WISH THEY COULD THINK AGAIN.
DING DING DING DING
AND THERE'S THE BELL AS THE OFFICIAL HAS MADE HIS DECISION.
AN UNFORTUNATE DOUBLE COUNT OUT.
YOU'RRRE... WELLLLCOME.

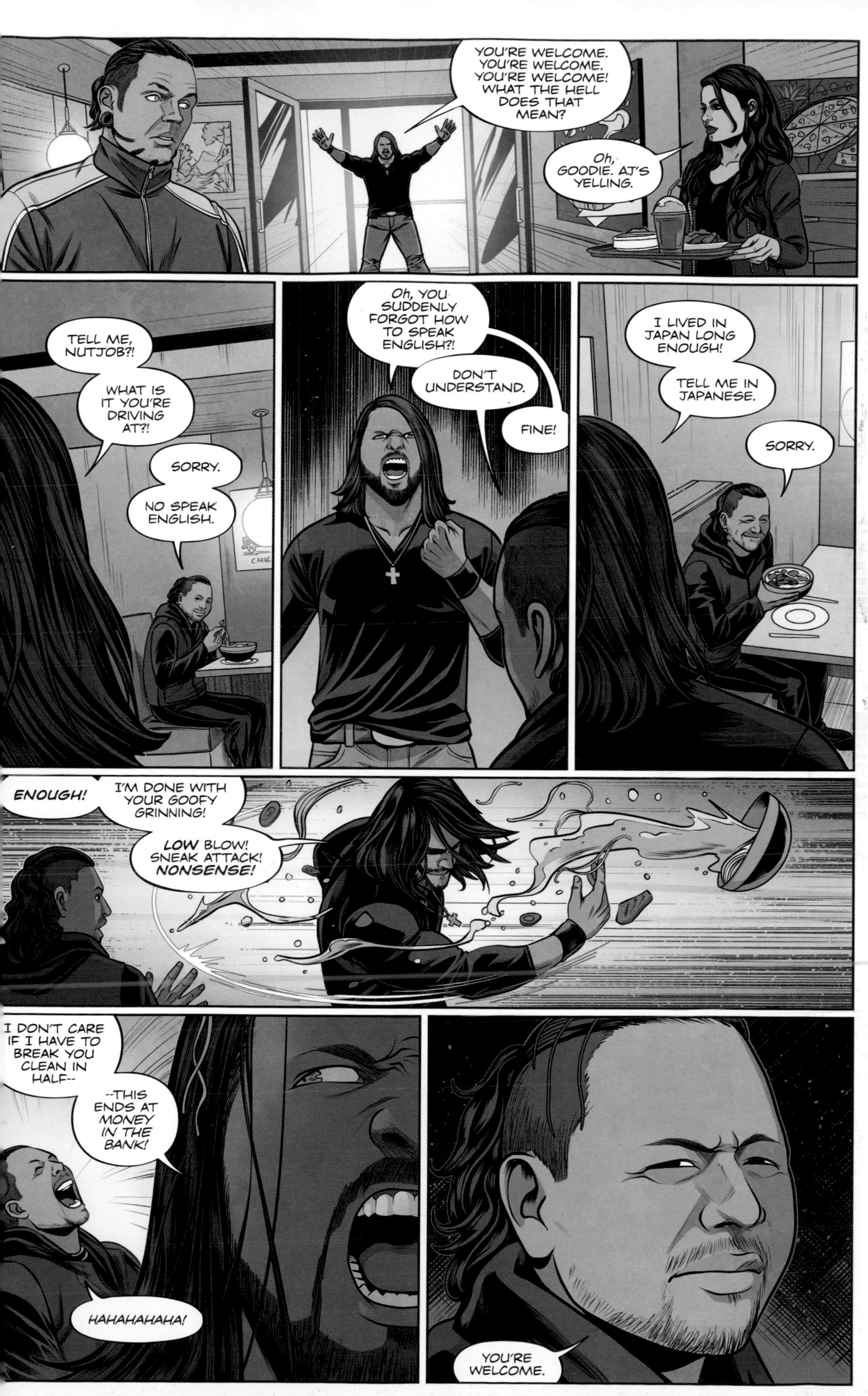
YOU'RE WELCOME. YOU'RE WELCOME. YOU'RE WELCOME! WHAT THE HELL DOES THAT MEAN?
Oh, GOODIE. AJ'S YELLING.
TELL ME, NUTJOB?!
WHAT IS IT YOU'RE DRIVING AT?!
SORRY.
NO SPEAK ENGLISH.
Oh, YOU SUDDENLY FORGOT HOW TO SPEAK ENGLISH?!
DON'T UNDERSTAND.
FINE!
I LIVED IN JAPAN LONG ENOUGH!
TELL ME IN JAPANESE.
SORRY.
ENOUGH!
I'M DONE WITH YOUR GOOFY GRINNING!
LOW BLOW! SNEAK ATTACK! NONSENSE!
I DON'T CARE IF I HAVE TO BREAK YOU CLEAN IN HALF--
--THIS ENDS AT MONEY IN THE BANK!
HAHAHAHAHA!
YOU'RE WELCOME.

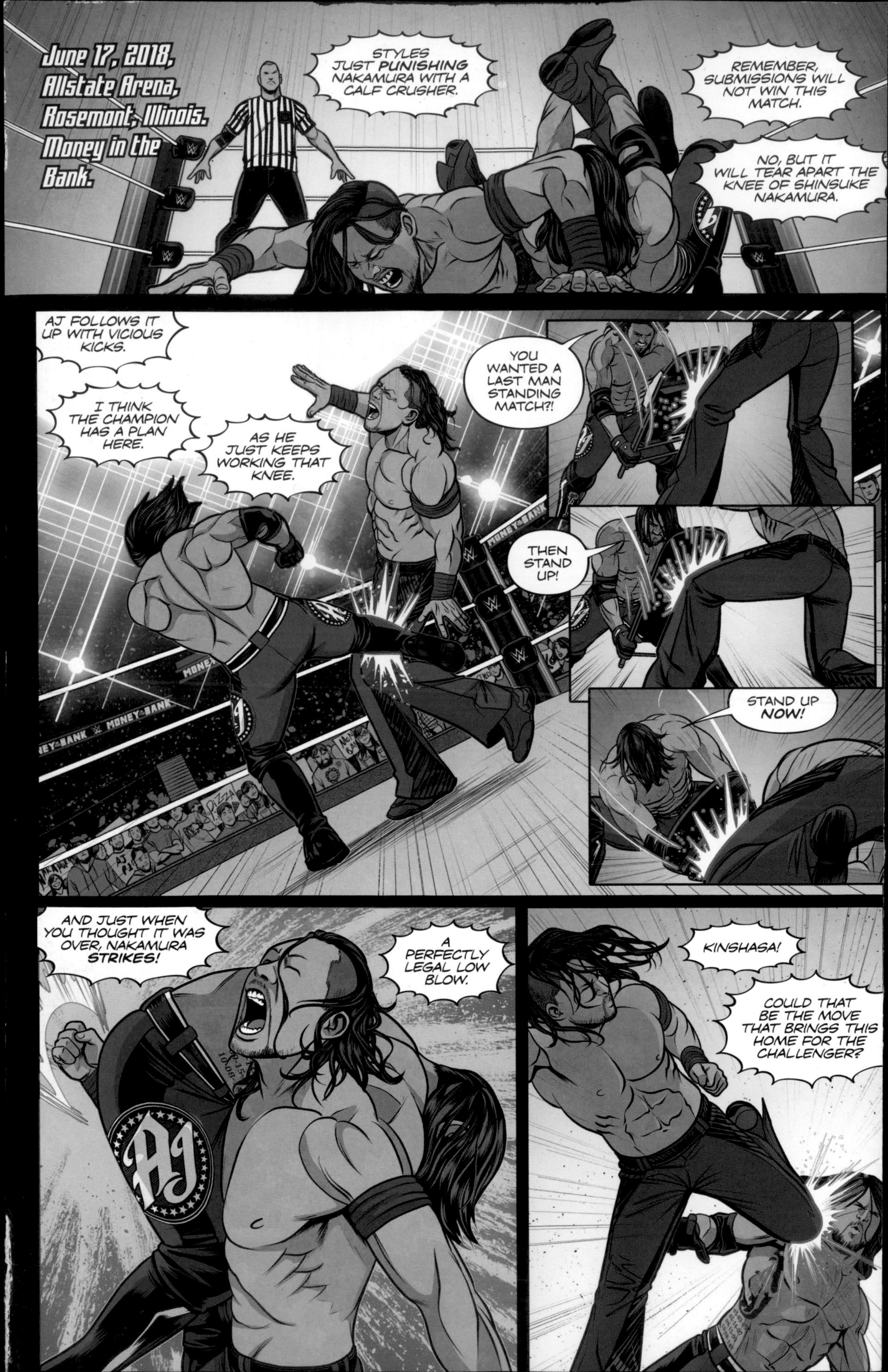
June 17, 2018, Allstate Arena, Rosemont, Illinois. Money in the Bank.
STYLES JUST PUNISHING NAKAMURA WITH A CALF CRUSHER.
REMEMBER, SUBMISSIONS WILL NOT WIN THIS MATCH.
NO, BUT IT WILL TEAR APART THE KNEE OF SHINSUKE NAKAMURA.
AJ FOLLOWS IT UP WITH VICIOUS KICKS.
I THINK THE CHAMPION HAS A PLAN HERE.
AS HE JUST KEEPS WORKING THAT KNEE.
YOU WANTED A LAST MAN STANDING MATCH?!
THEN STAND UP!
STAND UP NOW!
AND JUST WHEN YOU THOUGHT IT WAS OVER, NAKAMURA STRIKES!
A PERFECTLY LEGAL LOW BLOW.
KINSHASA!
COULD THAT BE THE MOVE THAT BRINGS THIS HOME FOR THE CHALLENGER?

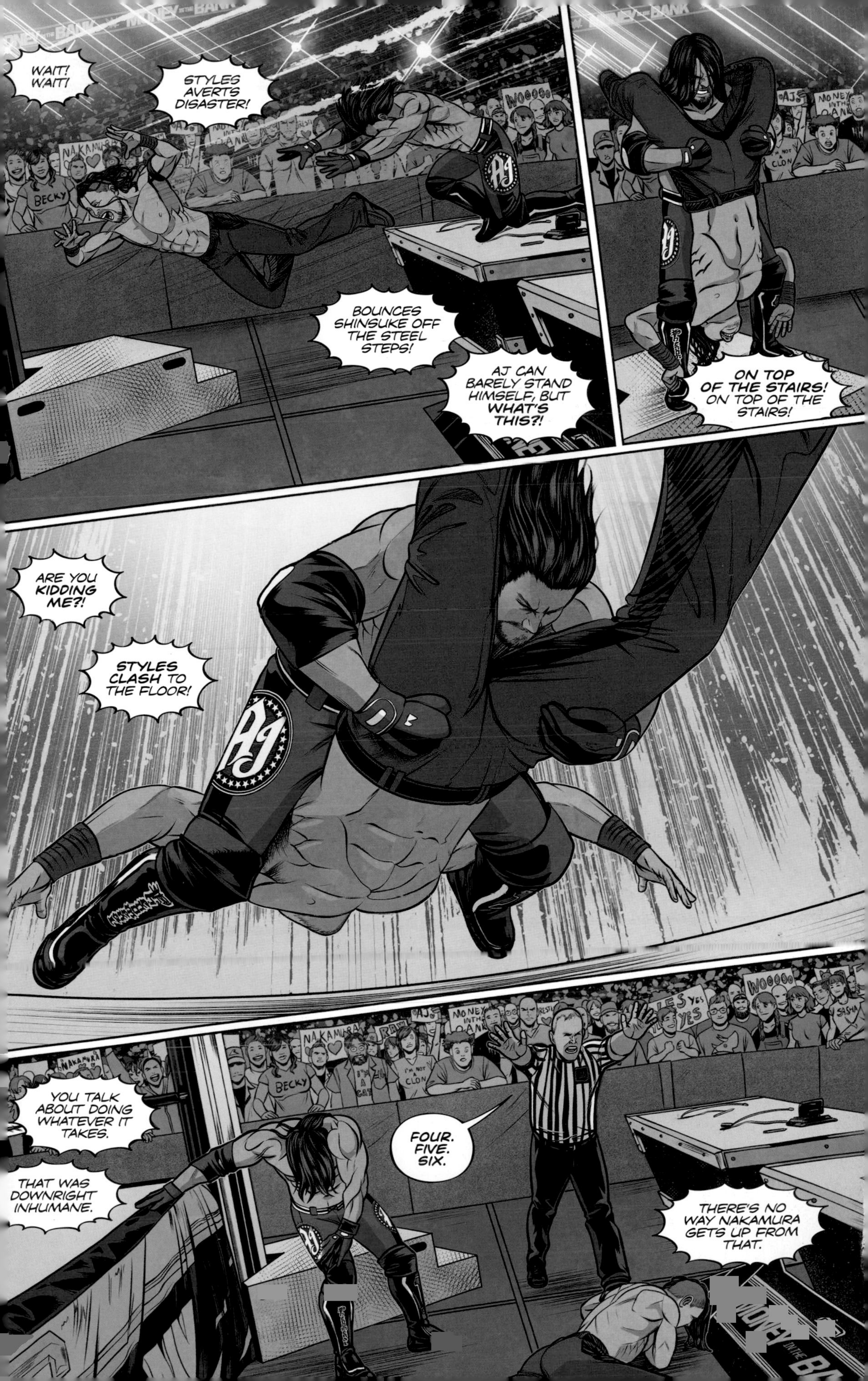
WAIT! WAIT!
STYLES AVERTS DISASTER!
BOUNCES SHINSUKE OFF THE STEEL STEPS!
AJ CAN BARELY STAND HIMSELF, BUT WHAT'S THIS?!
ON TOP OF THE STAIRS! ON TOP OF THE STAIRS!
ARE YOU KIDDING ME?!
STYLES CLASH TO THE FLOOR!
YOU TALK ABOUT DOING WHATEVER IT TAKES.
THAT WAS DOWNRIGHT INHUMANE.
FOUR. FIVE. SIX.
THERE'S NO WAY NAKAMURA GETS UP FROM THAT.

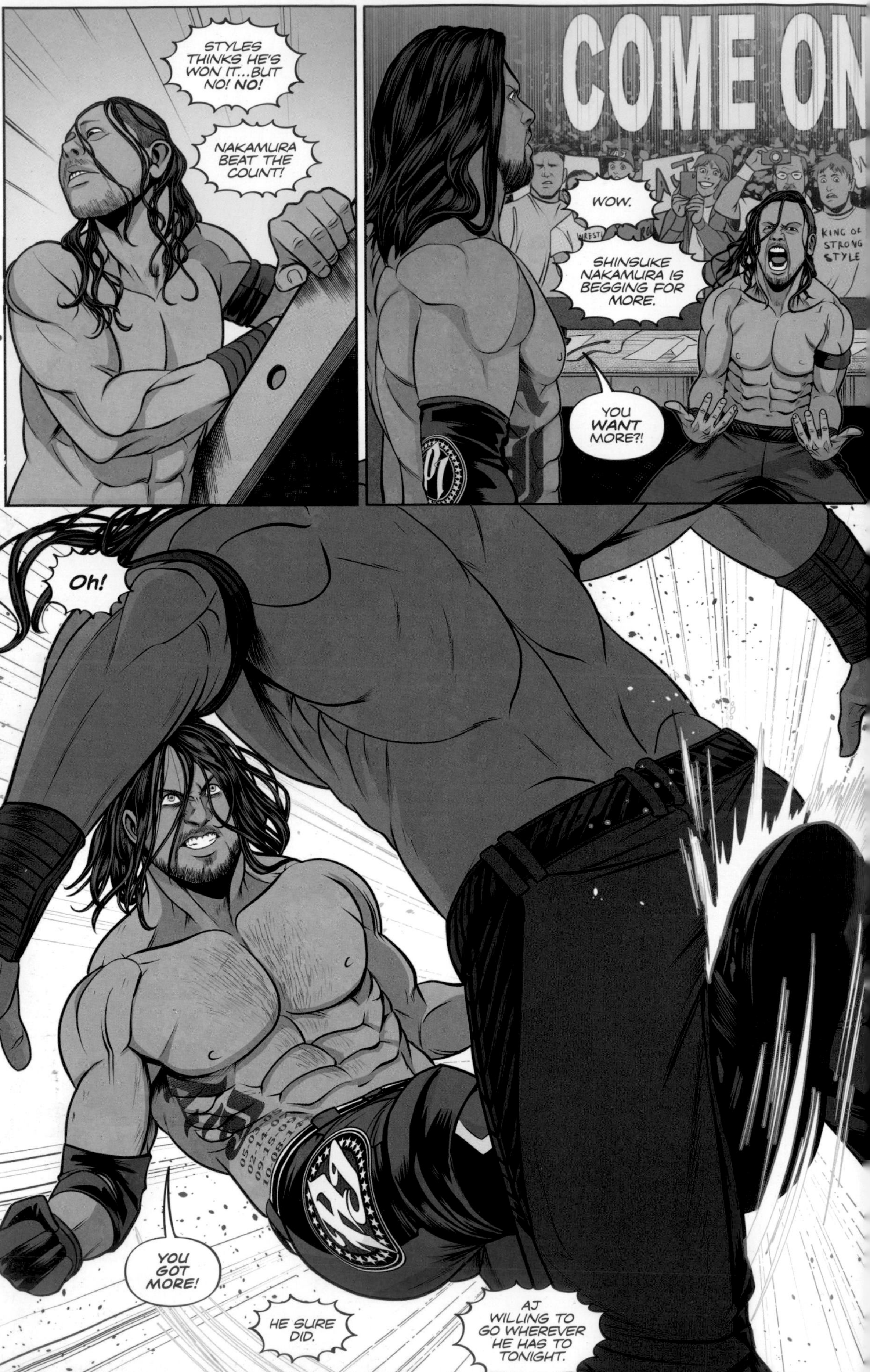
STYLES THINKS HE'S WON IT...BUT NO! NO!
NAKAMURA BEAT THE COUNT!
COME ON
WOW.
KING OF STRONG STYLE
SHINSUKE NAKAMURA IS BEGGING FOR MORE.
YOU WANT MORE?!
Oh!
YOU GOT MORE!
HE SURE DID.
AJ WILLING TO GO WHEREVER HE HAS TO TONIGHT.

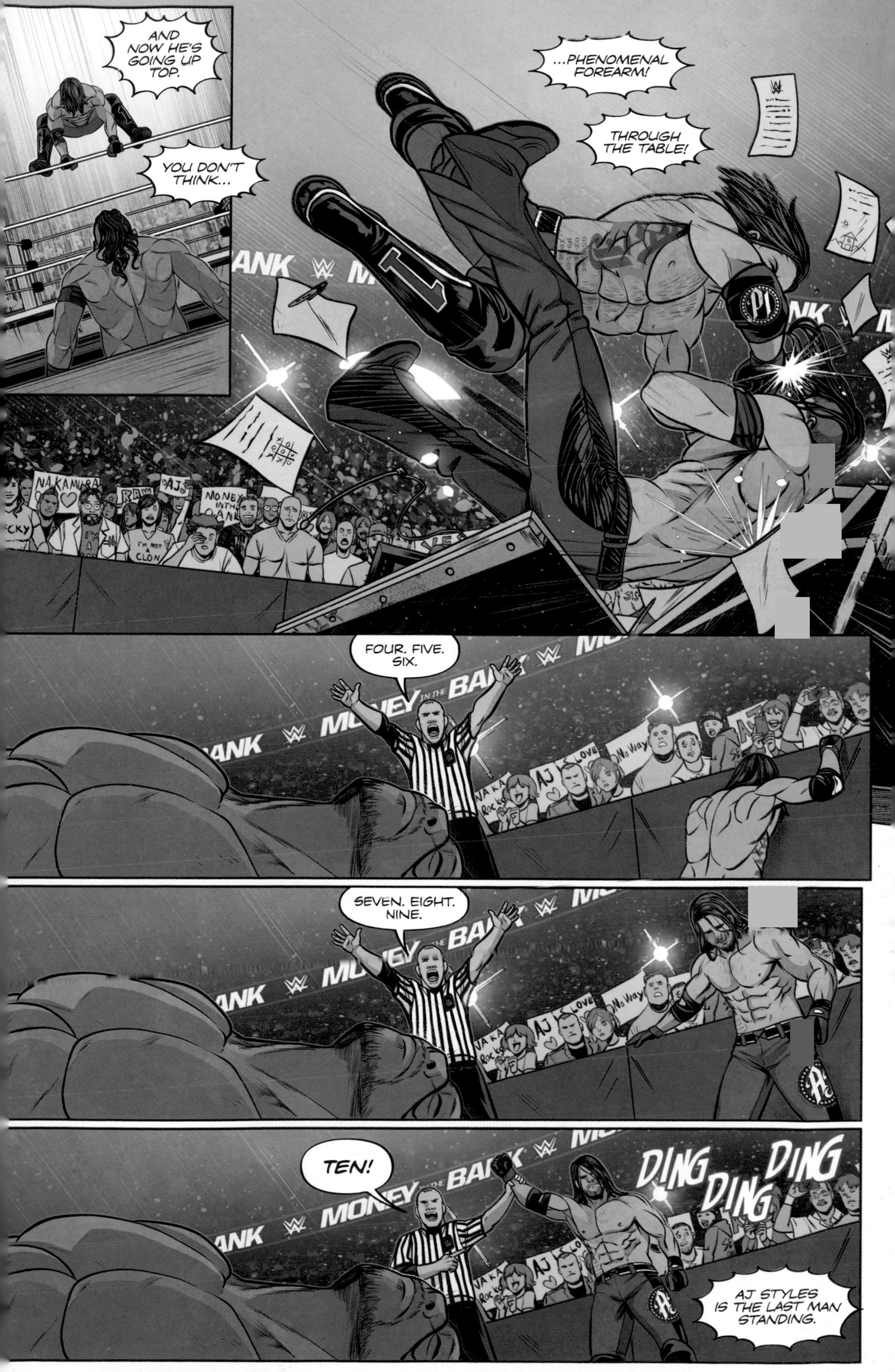

AND NOW HE'S GOING UP TOP.
YOU DON'T THINK...
...PHENOMENAL FOREARM!
THROUGH THE TABLE!
FOUR. FIVE. SIX.
SEVEN. EIGHT. NINE.
TEN!
DING DING DING
AJ STYLES IS THE LAST MAN STANDING.

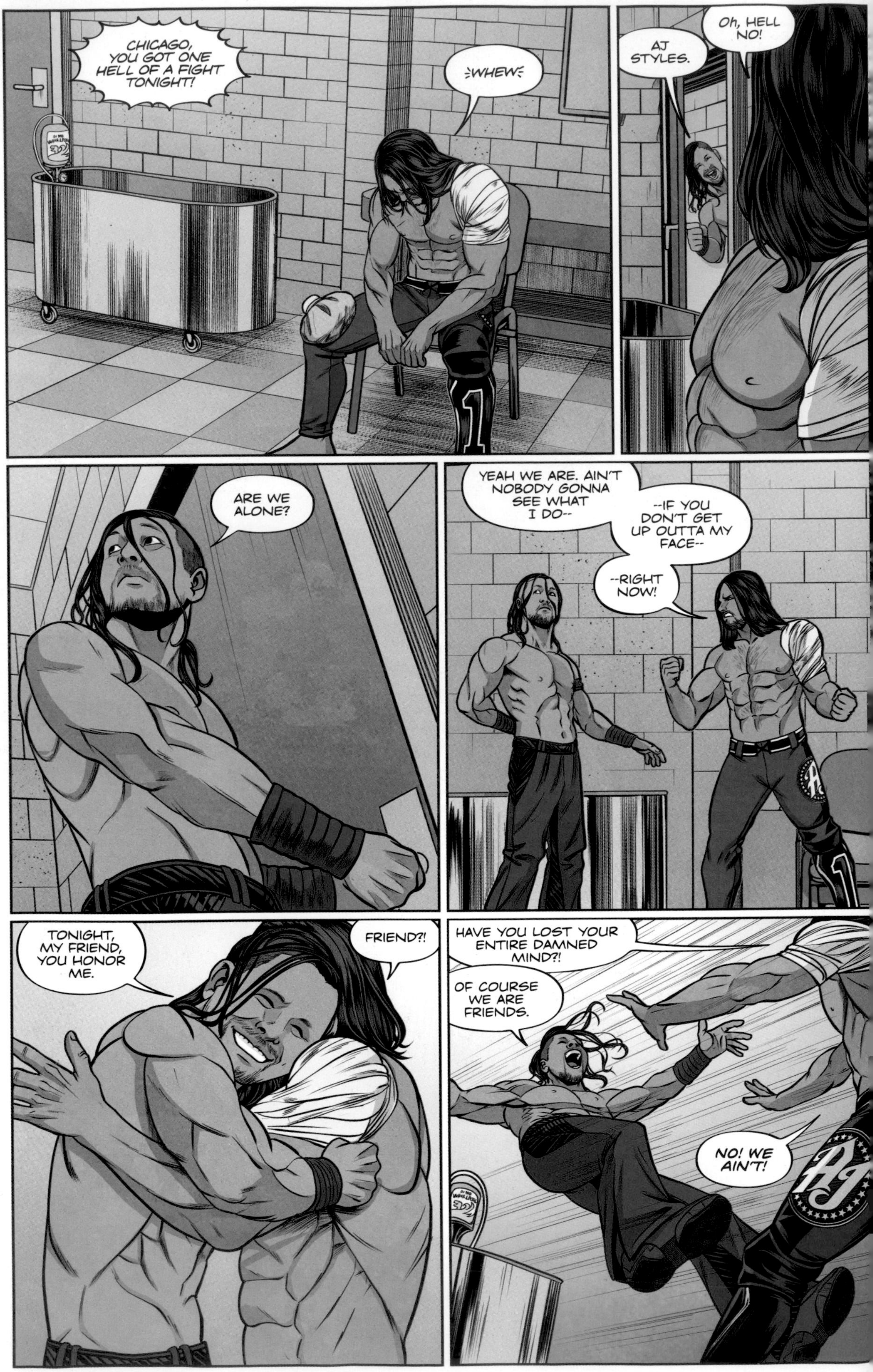
CHICAGO, YOU GOT ONE HELL OF A FIGHT TONIGHT!
WHEW
AJ STYLES.
Oh, HELL NO!
ARE WE ALONE?
YEAH WE ARE. AIN'T NOBODY GONNA SEE WHAT I DO--
--IF YOU DON'T GET UP OUTTA MY FACE--
--RIGHT NOW!
TONIGHT, MY FRIEND, YOU HONOR ME.
FRIEND?!
HAVE YOU LOST YOUR ENTIRE DAMNED MIND?!
OF COURSE WE ARE FRIENDS.
NO! WE AIN'T!

YOU MUST UNDERSTAND, AJ, IT WAS ALL PART OF MY PLAN.

SPLSSH

ALL TO EXTEND THE RIVALRY. ALL LEADING UP TO TONIGHT.

EXTEND THE RIVALRY? WHAT THE HELL ARE YOU ON ABOUT?

TRYING TO TELL ME THIS WAS ALL SOME BIG ACT?

THE FIGHTS, THEY WERE REAL.

EVERY MATCH I WAS OUT TO BEAT YOU. I CAME CLOSE EACH TIME, BUT YOU ARE A SLIPPERY ONE.

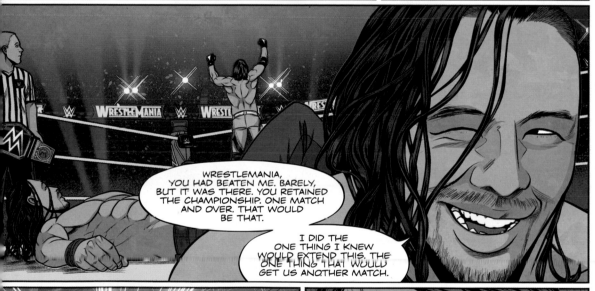

WRESTLEMANIA, YOU HAD BEATEN ME. BARELY, BUT IT WAS THERE. YOU RETAINED THE CHAMPIONSHIP. ONE MATCH AND OVER. THAT WOULD BE THAT.

I DID THE ONE THING I KNEW WOULD EXTEND THIS. THE ONE THING THAT WOULD GET US ANOTHER MATCH.

"THE LOW BLOW."

YOU WANTED TO PISS ME OFF.

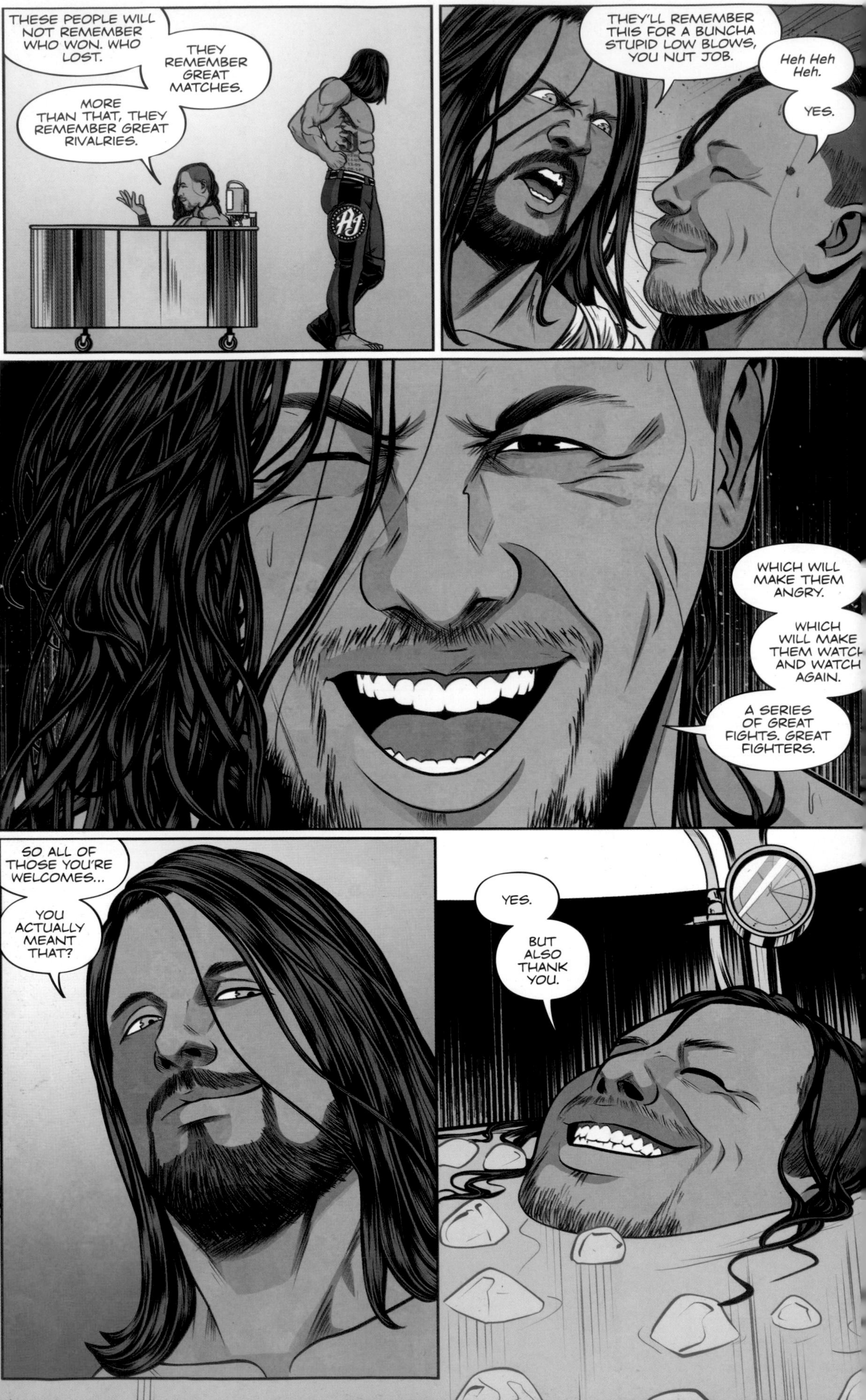

THESE PEOPLE WILL NOT REMEMBER WHO WON. WHO LOST.
THEY REMEMBER GREAT MATCHES.
MORE THAN THAT, THEY REMEMBER GREAT RIVALRIES.
THEY'LL REMEMBER THIS FOR A BUNCHA STUPID LOW BLOWS, YOU NUT JOB.
Heh Heh Heh.
YES.
WHICH WILL MAKE THEM ANGRY.
WHICH WILL MAKE THEM WATCH AND WATCH AGAIN.
A SERIES OF GREAT FIGHTS. GREAT FIGHTERS.
SO ALL OF THOSE YOU'RE WELCOMES...
YOU ACTUALLY MEANT THAT?
YES.
BUT ALSO THANK YOU.

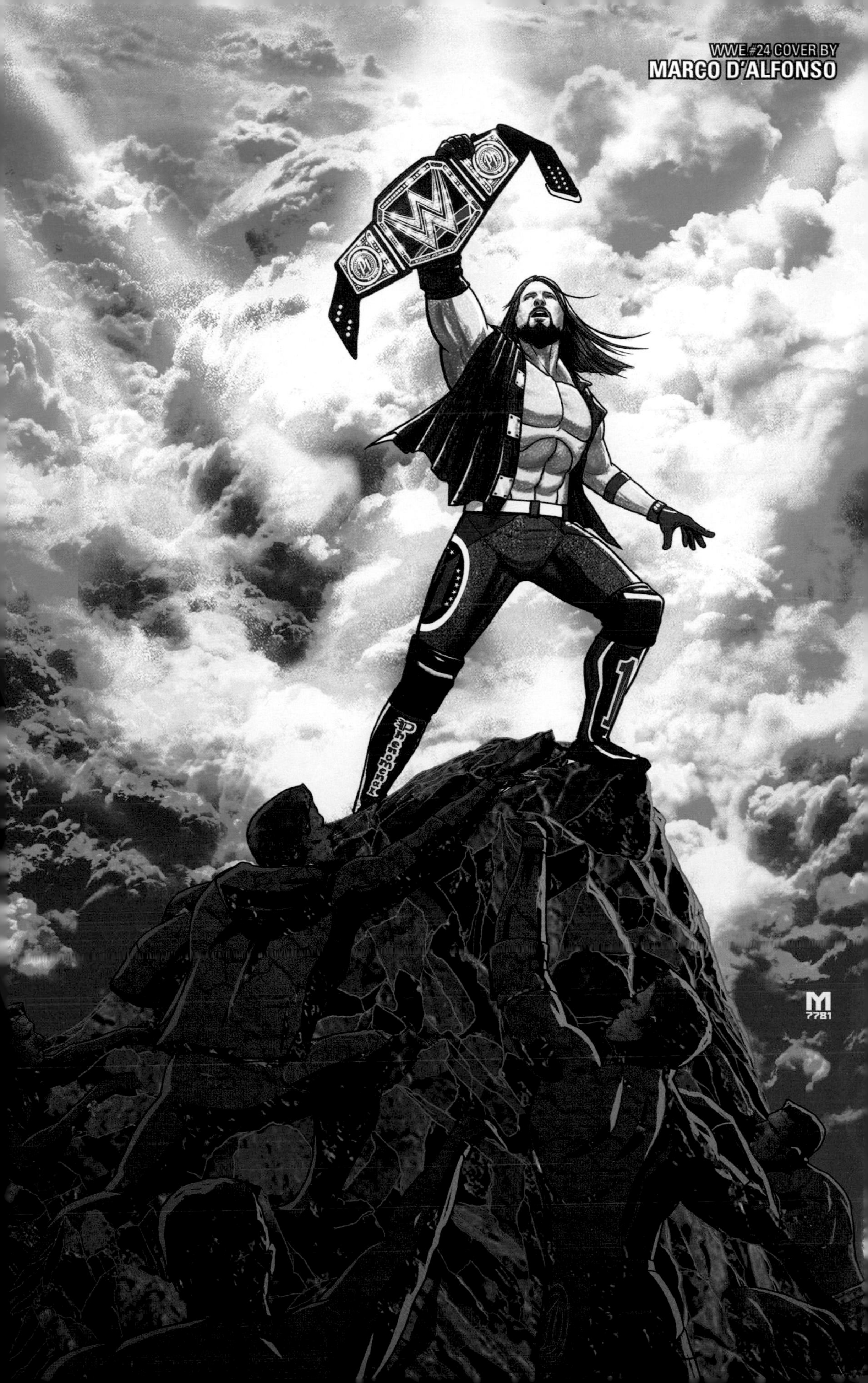

WWE #24 COVER BY
MARCO D'ALFONSO

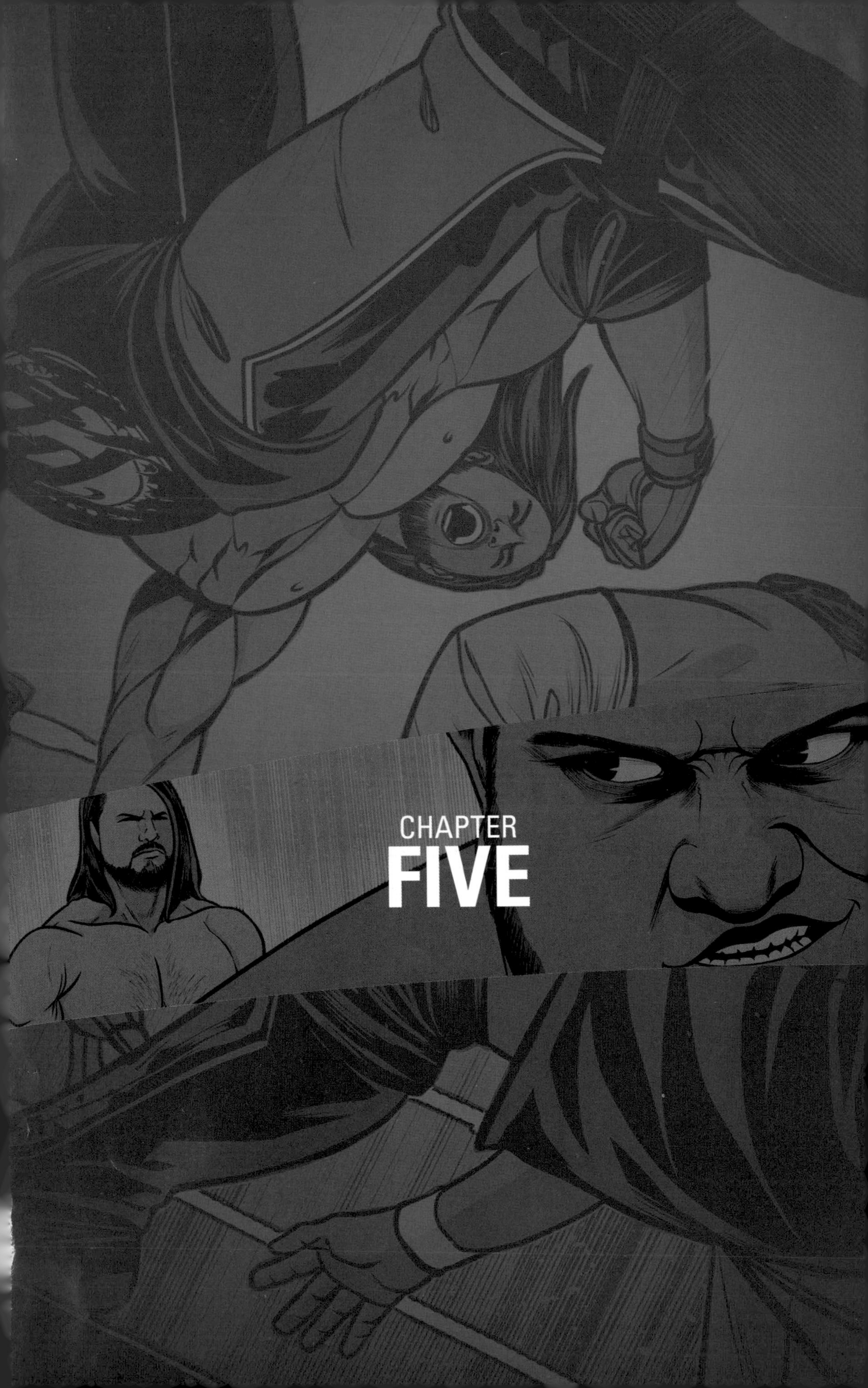

CHAPTER FIVE

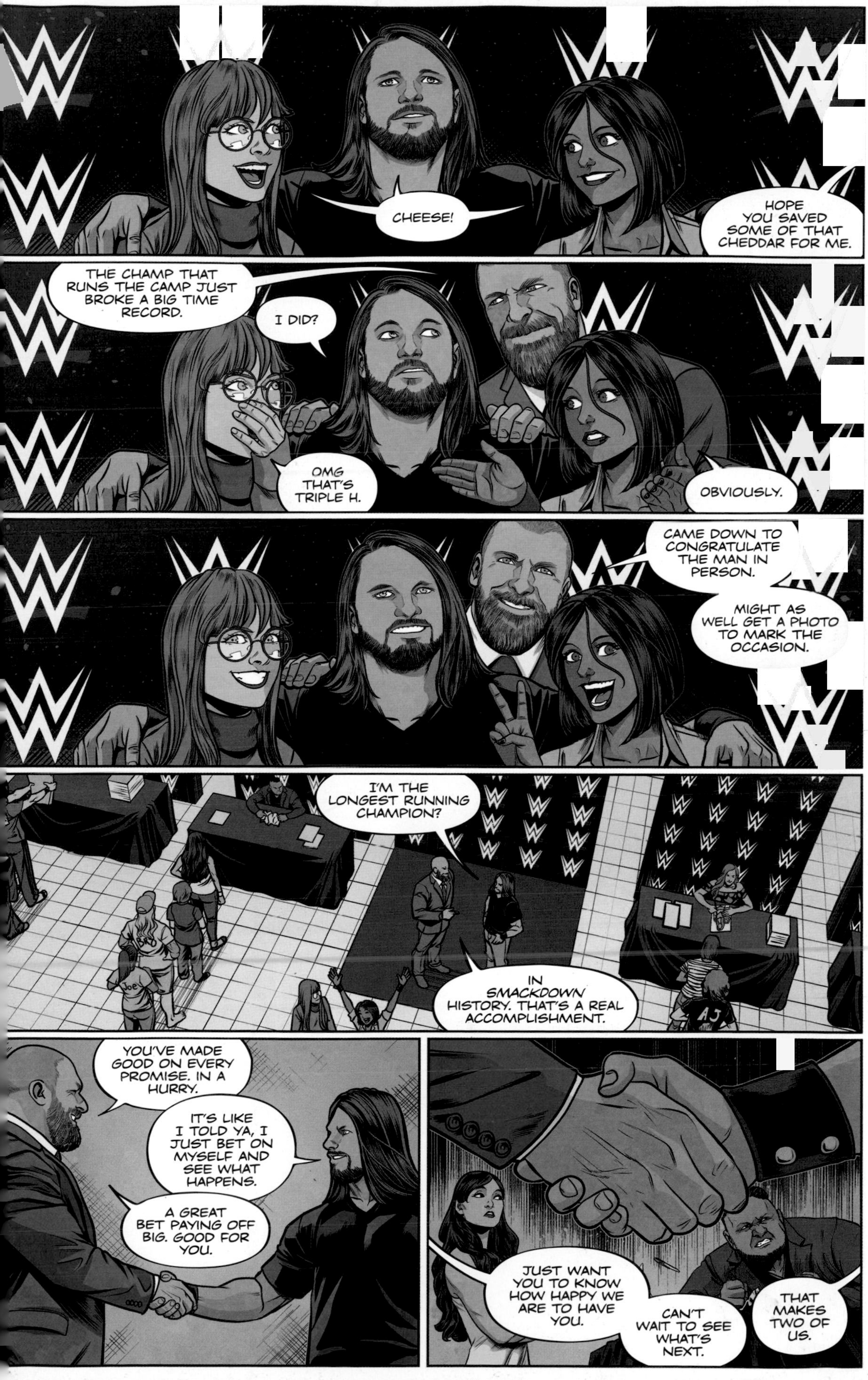
CHEESE!
HOPE YOU SAVED SOME OF THAT CHEDDAR FOR ME.
THE CHAMP THAT RUNS THE CAMP JUST BROKE A BIG TIME RECORD.
I DID?
OMG THAT'S TRIPLE H.
OBVIOUSLY.
CAME DOWN TO CONGRATULATE THE MAN IN PERSON.
MIGHT AS WELL GET A PHOTO TO MARK THE OCCASION.
I'M THE LONGEST RUNNING CHAMPION?
IN SMACKDOWN HISTORY. THAT'S A REAL ACCOMPLISHMENT.
YOU'VE MADE GOOD ON EVERY PROMISE. IN A HURRY.
IT'S LIKE I TOLD YA, I JUST BET ON MYSELF AND SEE WHAT HAPPENS.
A GREAT BET PAYING OFF BIG. GOOD FOR YOU.
JUST WANT YOU TO KNOW HOW HAPPY WE ARE TO HAVE YOU.
CAN'T WAIT TO SEE WHAT'S NEXT.
THAT MAKES TWO OF US.

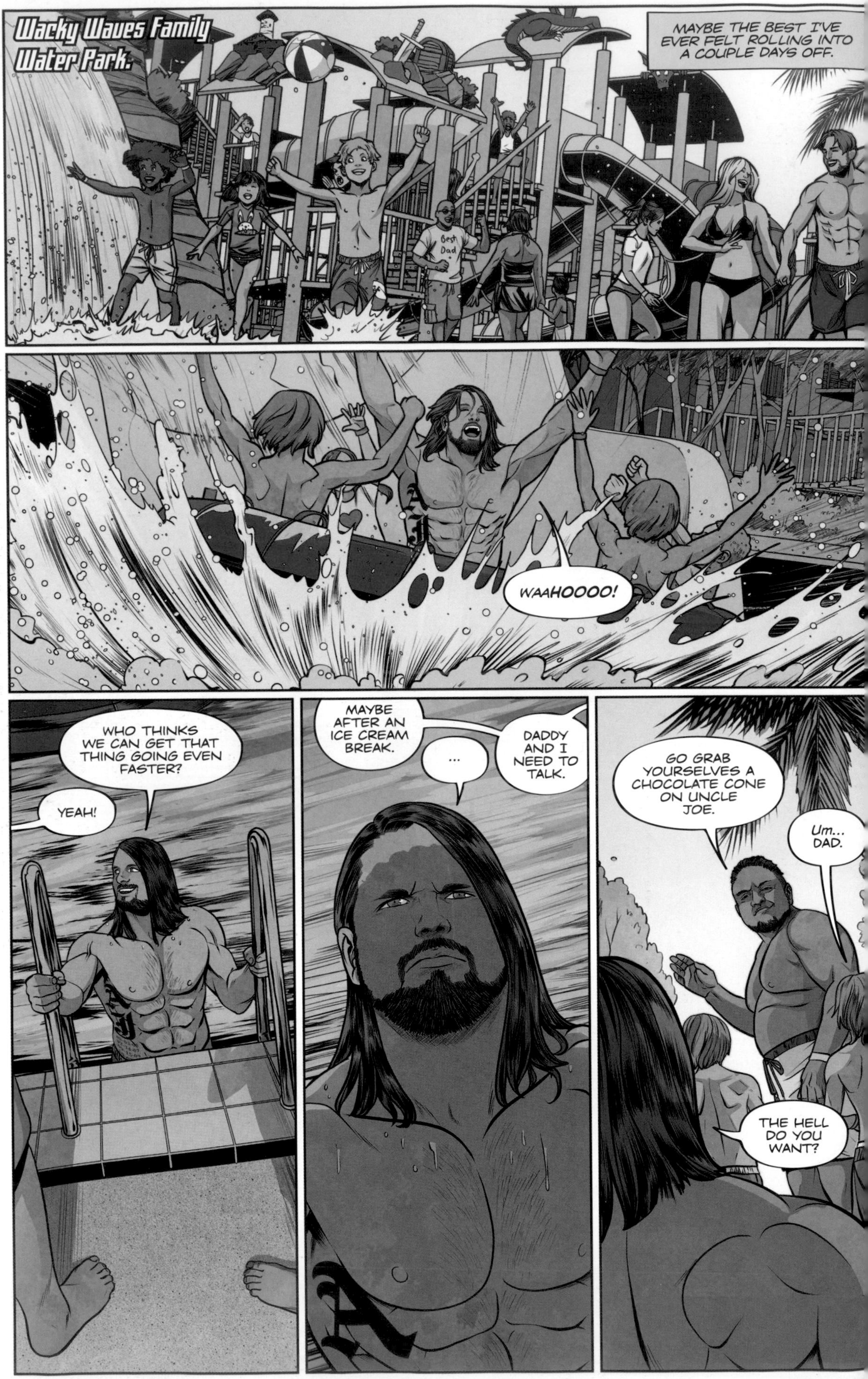
Wacky Waves Family Water Park.
MAYBE THE BEST I'VE EVER FELT ROLLING INTO A COUPLE DAYS OFF.
Best Dad
WAAHOOOO!
WHO THINKS WE CAN GET THAT THING GOING EVEN FASTER?
YEAH!
MAYBE AFTER AN ICE CREAM BREAK.
...
DADDY AND I NEED TO TALK.
GO GRAB YOURSELVES A CHOCOLATE CONE ON UNCLE JOE.
Um... DAD.
THE HELL DO YOU WANT?

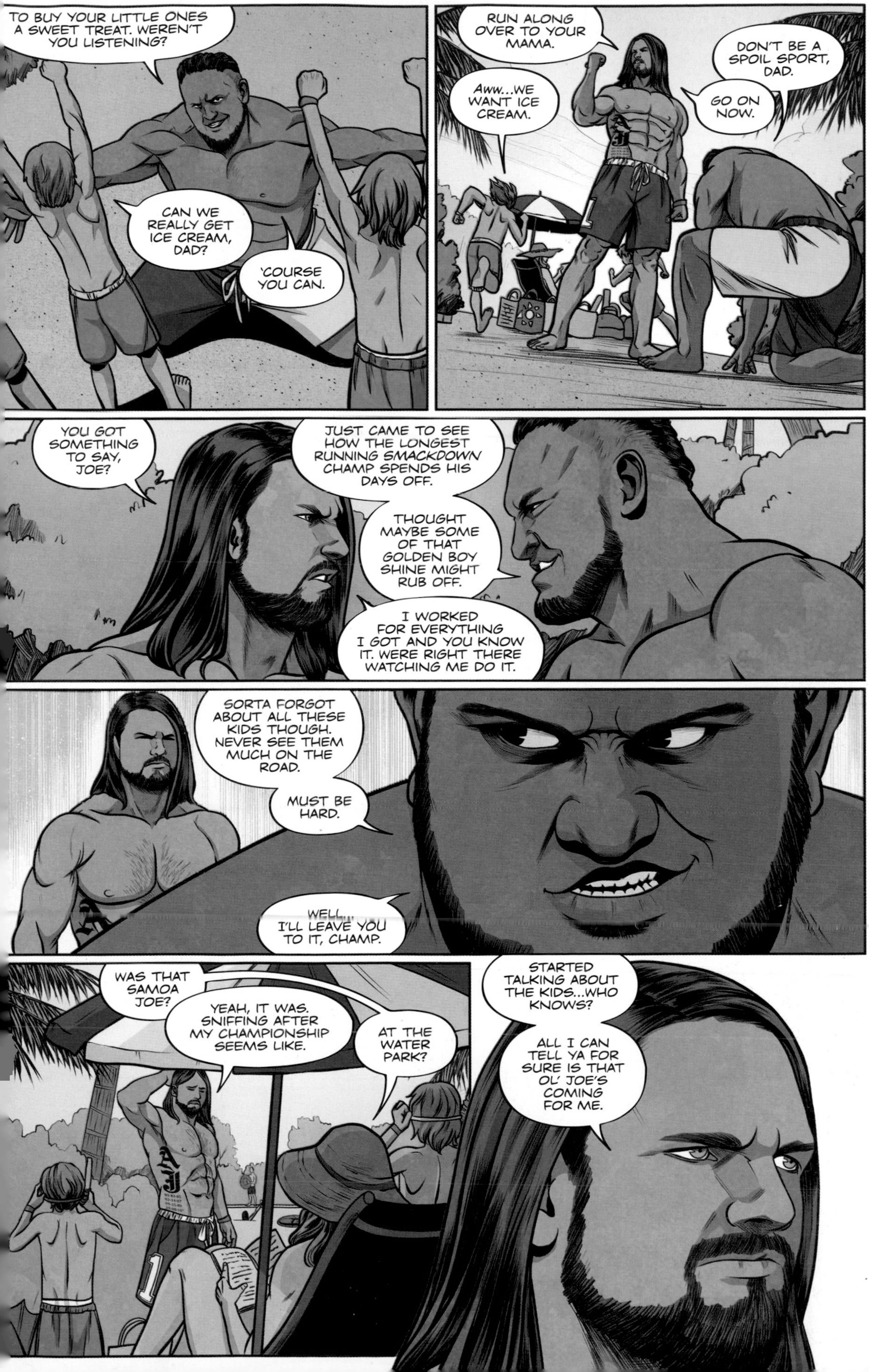

TO BUY YOUR LITTLE ONES A SWEET TREAT. WEREN'T YOU LISTENING?
CAN WE REALLY GET ICE CREAM, DAD?
'COURSE YOU CAN.
RUN ALONG OVER TO YOUR MAMA.
Aww...WE WANT ICE CREAM.
DON'T BE A SPOIL SPORT, DAD.
GO ON NOW.
YOU GOT SOMETHING TO SAY, JOE?
JUST CAME TO SEE HOW THE LONGEST RUNNING SMACKDOWN CHAMP SPENDS HIS DAYS OFF.
THOUGHT MAYBE SOME OF THAT GOLDEN BOY SHINE MIGHT RUB OFF.
I WORKED FOR EVERYTHING I GOT AND YOU KNOW IT. WERE RIGHT THERE WATCHING ME DO IT.
SORTA FORGOT ABOUT ALL THESE KIDS THOUGH. NEVER SEE THEM MUCH ON THE ROAD.
MUST BE HARD.
WELL... I'LL LEAVE YOU TO IT, CHAMP.
WAS THAT SAMOA JOE?
YEAH, IT WAS. SNIFFING AFTER MY CHAMPIONSHIP SEEMS LIKE.
AT THE WATER PARK?
STARTED TALKING ABOUT THE KIDS...WHO KNOWS?
ALL I CAN TELL YA FOR SURE IS THAT OL' JOE'S COMING FOR ME.

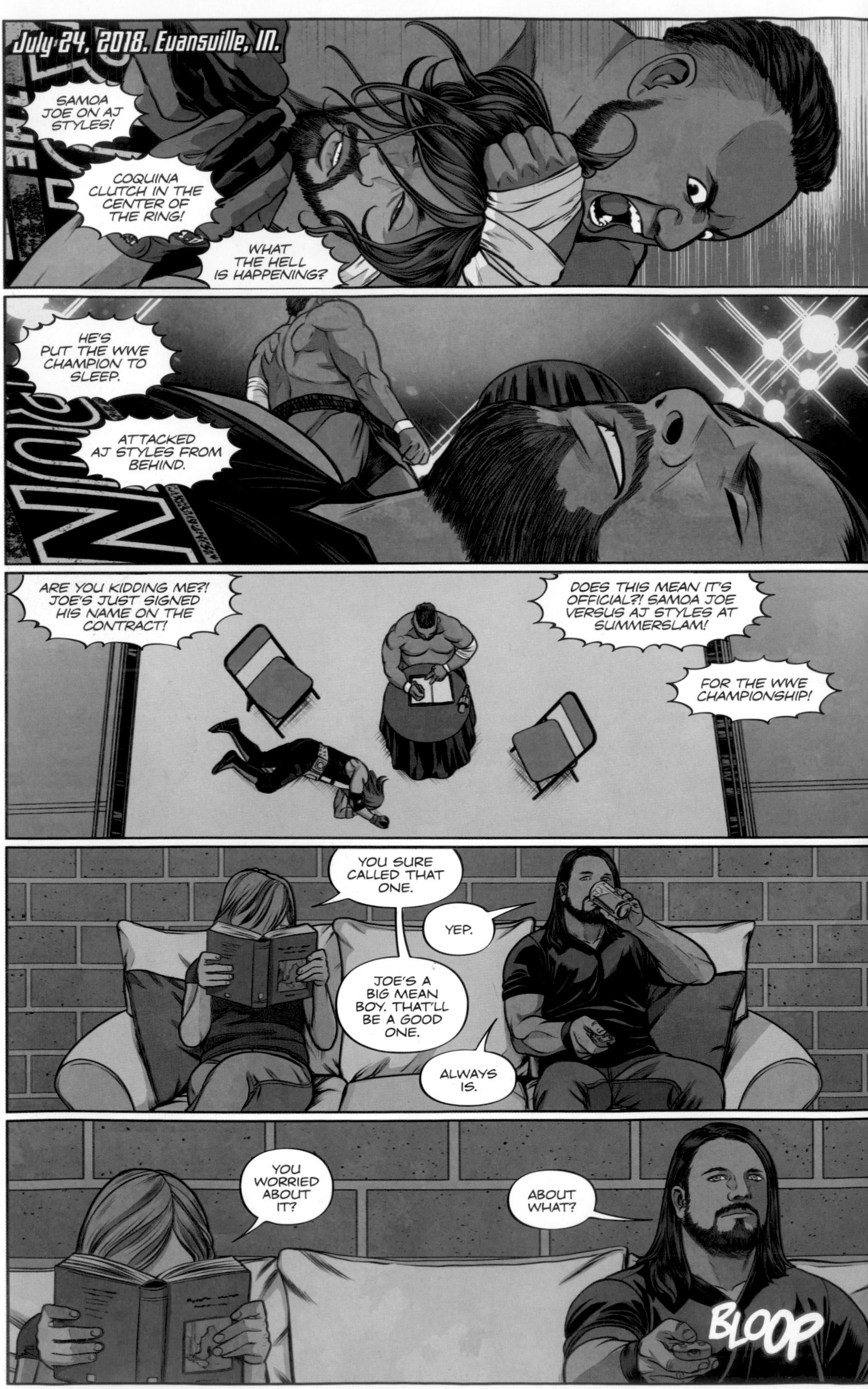
July 24, 2018. Evansville, IN.
SAMOA JOE ON AJ STYLES!
COQUINA CLUTCH IN THE CENTER OF THE RING!
WHAT THE HELL IS HAPPENING?
HE'S PUT THE WWE CHAMPION TO SLEEP.
ATTACKED AJ STYLES FROM BEHIND.
ARE YOU KIDDING ME?! JOE'S JUST SIGNED HIS NAME ON THE CONTRACT!
DOES THIS MEAN IT'S OFFICIAL?! SAMOA JOE VERSUS AJ STYLES AT SUMMERSLAM!
FOR THE WWE CHAMPIONSHIP!
YOU SURE CALLED THAT ONE.
YEP.
JOE'S A BIG MEAN BOY. THAT'LL BE A GOOD ONE.
ALWAYS IS.
YOU WORRIED ABOUT IT?
ABOUT WHAT?
BLOOP

LAST NIGHT, THAT WAS ME SENDING A MESSAGE. AND, AJ, I THINK YOU'RE MORE THAN FAMILIAR WITH MY FAVORITE FORM OF COMMUNICATION.

NO HARD FEELINGS.

TRUTH BE TOLD, I RESPECT YOU.

I RESPECT THE GRIND. I RESPECT THAT TITLE. AND MOST OF ALL, I RESPECT WHAT YOU'VE SACRIFICED TO KEEP IT.

YOU SAY YOU'RE PROUD TO BE ABLE TO LOOK YOUR CHILDREN IN THEIR EYES AND TELL THEM THEY CAN BE ANYTHING. ACCOMPLISH ANYTHING.

BUT WE BOTH KNOW YOU'RE BARELY EVER HOME LONG ENOUGH TO HUG THOSE CHILDREN. LET ALONE TEACH THEM LIFE LESSONS.

YOU'VE ALWAYS BEEN MORE COMFORTABLE ON THE ROAD LIVING OUT OF A SUITCASE. THAN YOU EVER HAVE BEEN AT HOME WITH YOUR FAMILY.

YOU'VE PUT BEING CHAMPION OVER EVERYTHING ELSE.

EVEN IF IT MEANS YOU'RE A FAILURE...AS A HUSBAND. AND A FATHER.

Oh, I'M WATCHING IT.

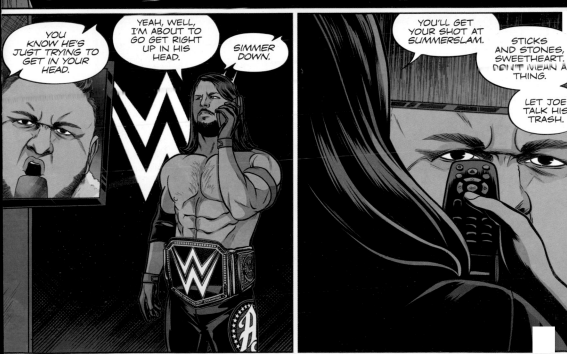

YOU KNOW HE'S JUST TRYING TO GET IN YOUR HEAD.

YEAH, WELL, I'M ABOUT TO GO GET RIGHT UP IN HIS HEAD.

SIMMER DOWN.

YOU'LL GET YOUR SHOT AT SUMMERSLAM.

STICKS AND STONES, SWEETHEART. DON'T MEAN A THING.

LET JOE TALK HIS TRASH.

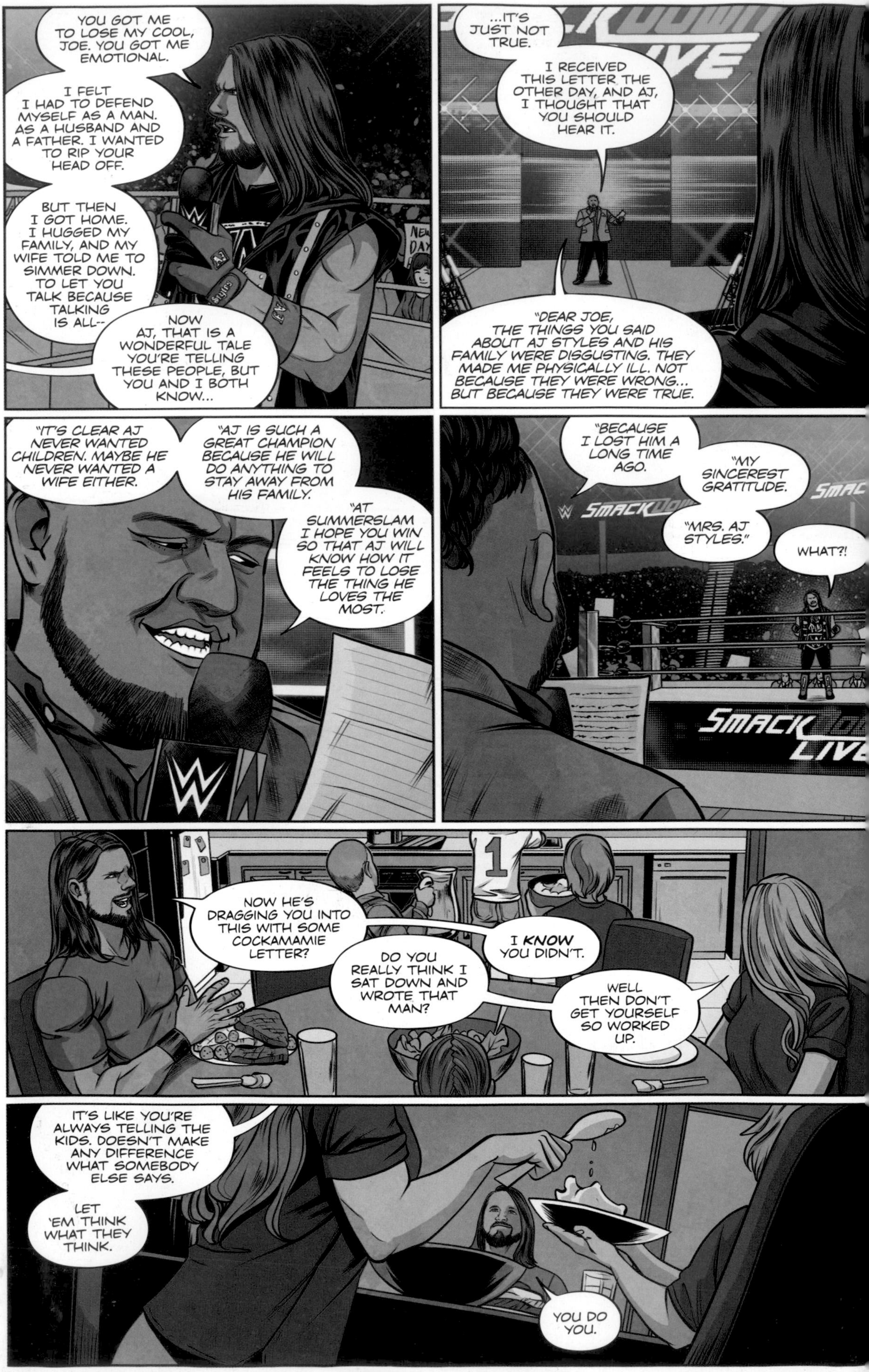
YOU GOT ME TO LOSE MY COOL, JOE. YOU GOT ME EMOTIONAL.
I FELT I HAD TO DEFEND MYSELF AS A MAN. AS A HUSBAND AND A FATHER. I WANTED TO RIP YOUR HEAD OFF.
BUT THEN I GOT HOME. I HUGGED MY FAMILY, AND MY WIFE TOLD ME TO SIMMER DOWN. TO LET YOU TALK BECAUSE TALKING IS ALL--
NOW AJ, THAT IS A WONDERFUL TALE YOU'RE TELLING THESE PEOPLE, BUT YOU AND I BOTH KNOW...
...IT'S JUST NOT TRUE.
I RECEIVED THIS LETTER THE OTHER DAY, AND AJ, I THOUGHT THAT YOU SHOULD HEAR IT.
"DEAR JOE, THE THINGS YOU SAID ABOUT AJ STYLES AND HIS FAMILY WERE DISGUSTING. THEY MADE ME PHYSICALLY ILL. NOT BECAUSE THEY WERE WRONG... BUT BECAUSE THEY WERE TRUE.
"IT'S CLEAR AJ NEVER WANTED CHILDREN. MAYBE HE NEVER WANTED A WIFE EITHER.
"AJ IS SUCH A GREAT CHAMPION BECAUSE HE WILL DO ANYTHING TO STAY AWAY FROM HIS FAMILY.
"AT SUMMERSLAM I HOPE YOU WIN SO THAT AJ WILL KNOW HOW IT FEELS TO LOSE THE THING HE LOVES THE MOST.
"BECAUSE I LOST HIM A LONG TIME AGO.
"MY SINCEREST GRATITUDE.
"MRS. AJ STYLES."
WHAT?!
NOW HE'S DRAGGING YOU INTO THIS WITH SOME COCKAMAMIE LETTER?
I **KNOW** YOU DIDN'T.
DO YOU REALLY THINK I SAT DOWN AND WROTE THAT MAN?
WELL THEN DON'T GET YOURSELF SO WORKED UP.
IT'S LIKE YOU'RE ALWAYS TELLING THE KIDS. DOESN'T MAKE ANY DIFFERENCE WHAT SOMEBODY ELSE SAYS.
LET 'EM THINK WHAT THEY THINK.
YOU DO YOU.

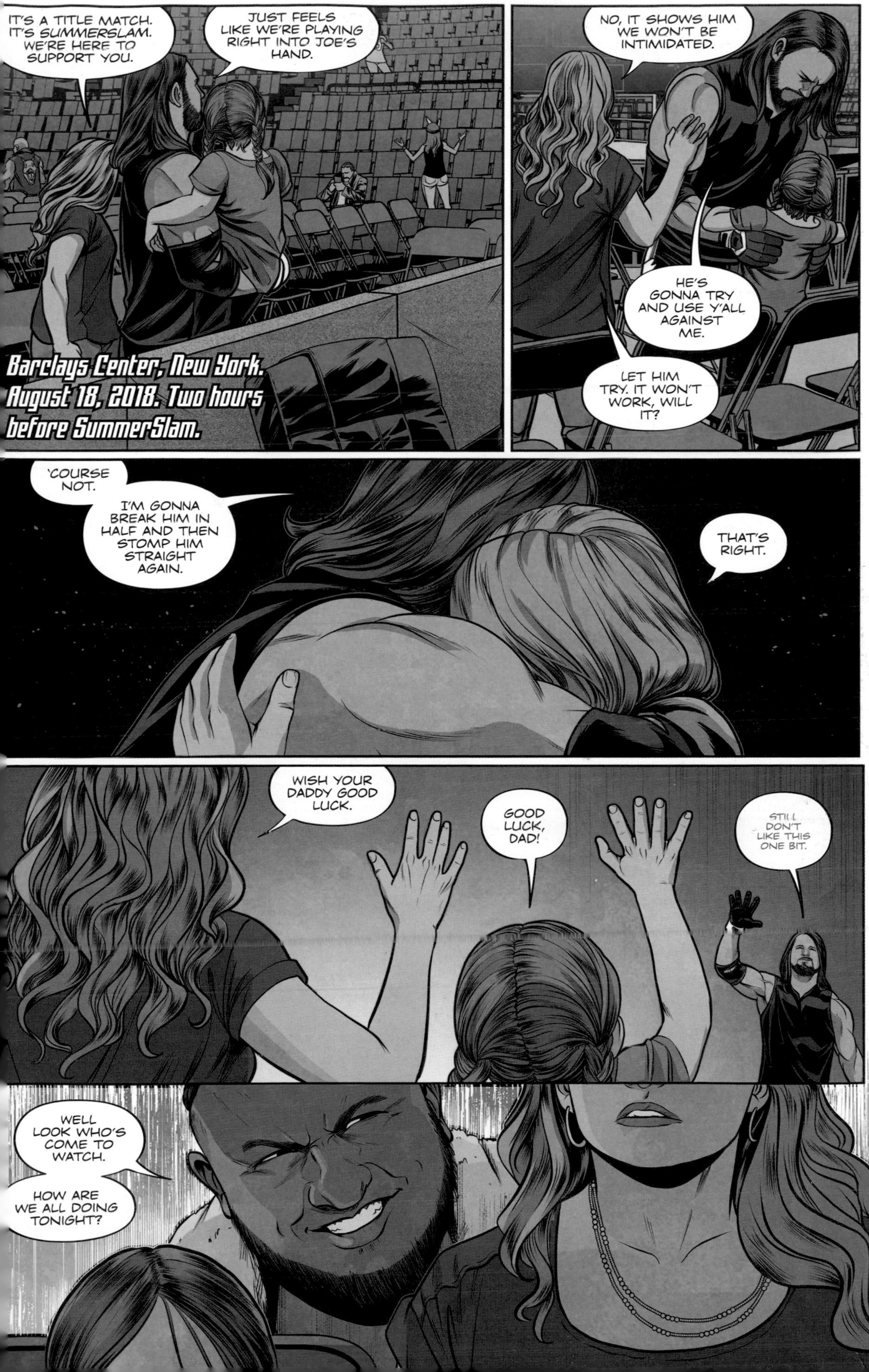
IT'S A TITLE MATCH. IT'S SUMMERSLAM. WE'RE HERE TO SUPPORT YOU.
JUST FEELS LIKE WE'RE PLAYING RIGHT INTO JOE'S HAND.
Barclays Center, New York. August 18, 2018. Two hours before SummerSlam.
NO, IT SHOWS HIM WE WON'T BE INTIMIDATED.
HE'S GONNA TRY AND USE Y'ALL AGAINST ME.
LET HIM TRY. IT WON'T WORK, WILL IT?
'COURSE NOT.
I'M GONNA BREAK HIM IN HALF AND THEN STOMP HIM STRAIGHT AGAIN.
THAT'S RIGHT.
WISH YOUR DADDY GOOD LUCK.
GOOD LUCK, DAD!
STILL DON'T LIKE THIS ONE BIT.
WELL LOOK WHO'S COME TO WATCH.
HOW ARE WE ALL DOING TONIGHT?

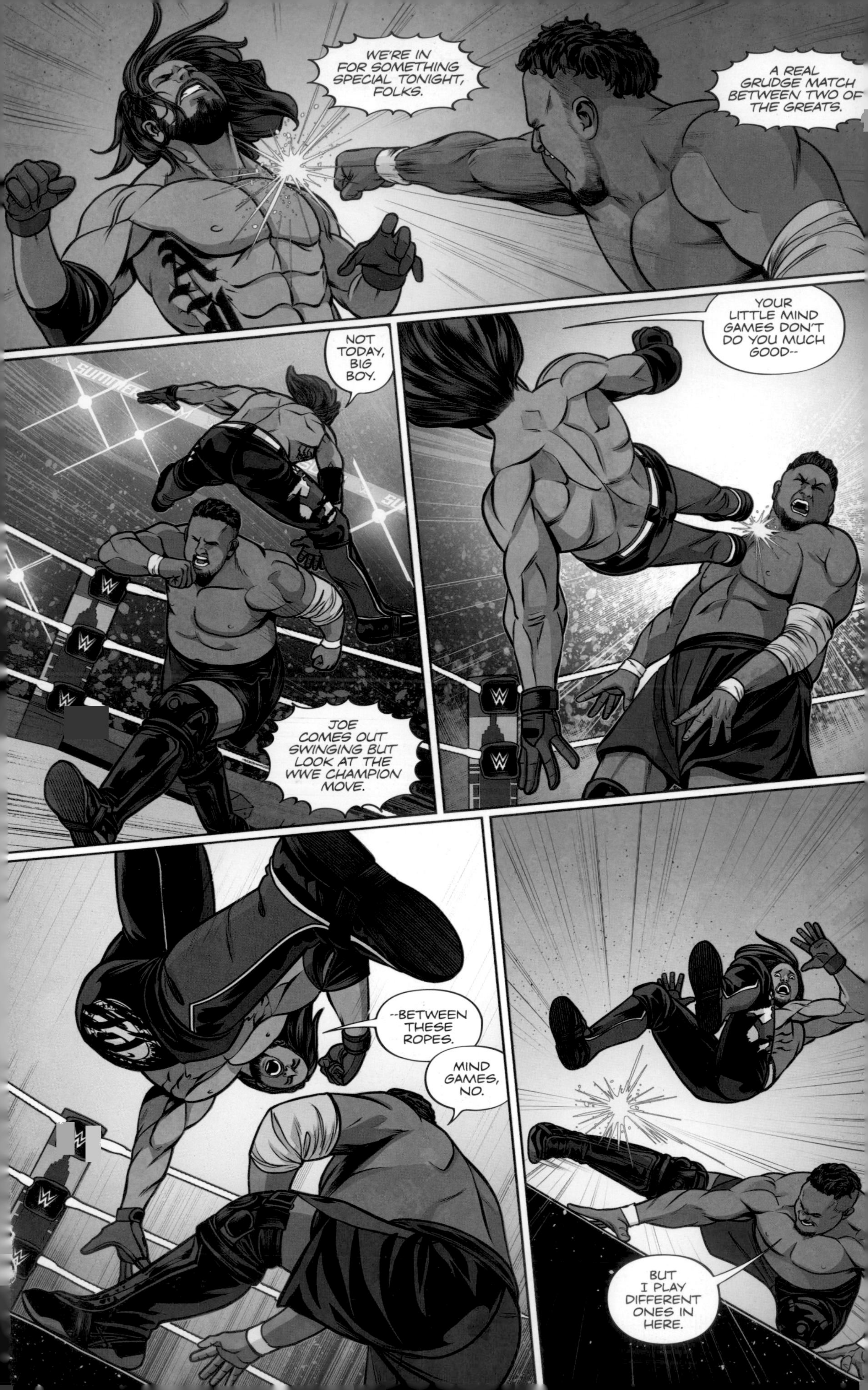
WE'RE IN FOR SOMETHING SPECIAL TONIGHT, FOLKS.
A REAL GRUDGE MATCH BETWEEN TWO OF THE GREATS.
NOT TODAY, BIG BOY.
JOE COMES OUT SWINGING BUT LOOK AT THE WWE CHAMPION MOVE.
YOUR LITTLE MIND GAMES DON'T DO YOU MUCH GOOD--
--BETWEEN THESE ROPES.
MIND GAMES, NO.
BUT I PLAY DIFFERENT ONES IN HERE.

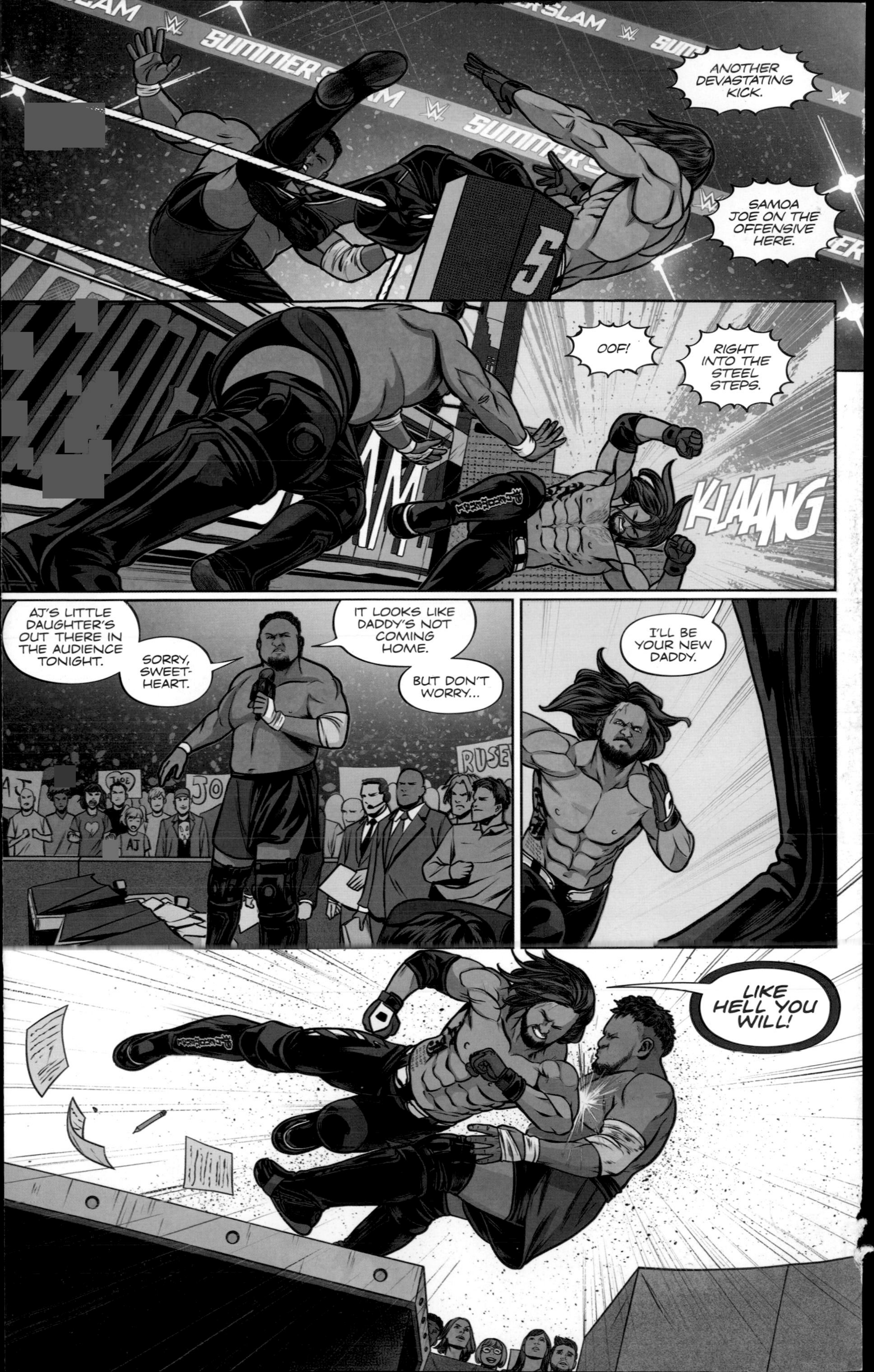
SUMMERSLAM
ANOTHER DEVASTATING KICK.
SAMOA JOE ON THE OFFENSIVE HERE.
OOF!
RIGHT INTO THE STEEL STEPS.
KLAANG
AJ'S LITTLE DAUGHTER'S OUT THERE IN THE AUDIENCE TONIGHT.
SORRY, SWEET-HEART.
IT LOOKS LIKE DADDY'S NOT COMING HOME.
BUT DON'T WORRY...
I'LL BE YOUR NEW DADDY.
LIKE HELL YOU WILL!

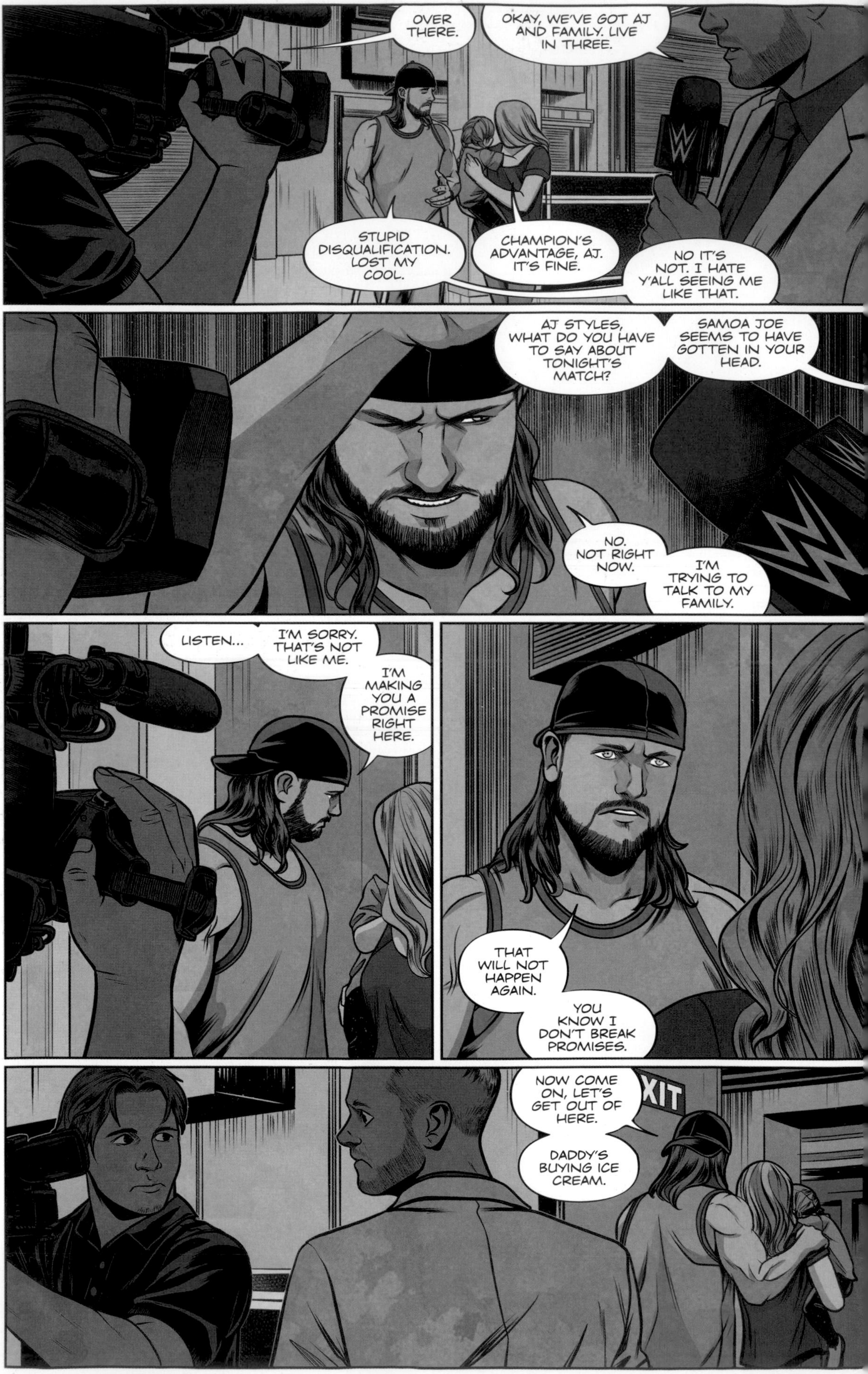
OVER THERE.
OKAY, WE'VE GOT AJ AND FAMILY. LIVE IN THREE.
STUPID DISQUALIFICATION. LOST MY COOL.
CHAMPION'S ADVANTAGE, AJ. IT'S FINE.
NO IT'S NOT. I HATE Y'ALL SEEING ME LIKE THAT.
AJ STYLES, WHAT DO YOU HAVE TO SAY ABOUT TONIGHT'S MATCH?
SAMOA JOE SEEMS TO HAVE GOTTEN IN YOUR HEAD.
NO. NOT RIGHT NOW.
I'M TRYING TO TALK TO MY FAMILY.
LISTEN...
I'M SORRY. THAT'S NOT LIKE ME.
I'M MAKING YOU A PROMISE RIGHT HERE.
THAT WILL NOT HAPPEN AGAIN.
YOU KNOW I DON'T BREAK PROMISES.
NOW COME ON, LET'S GET OUT OF HERE.
DADDY'S BUYING ICE CREAM.
EXIT

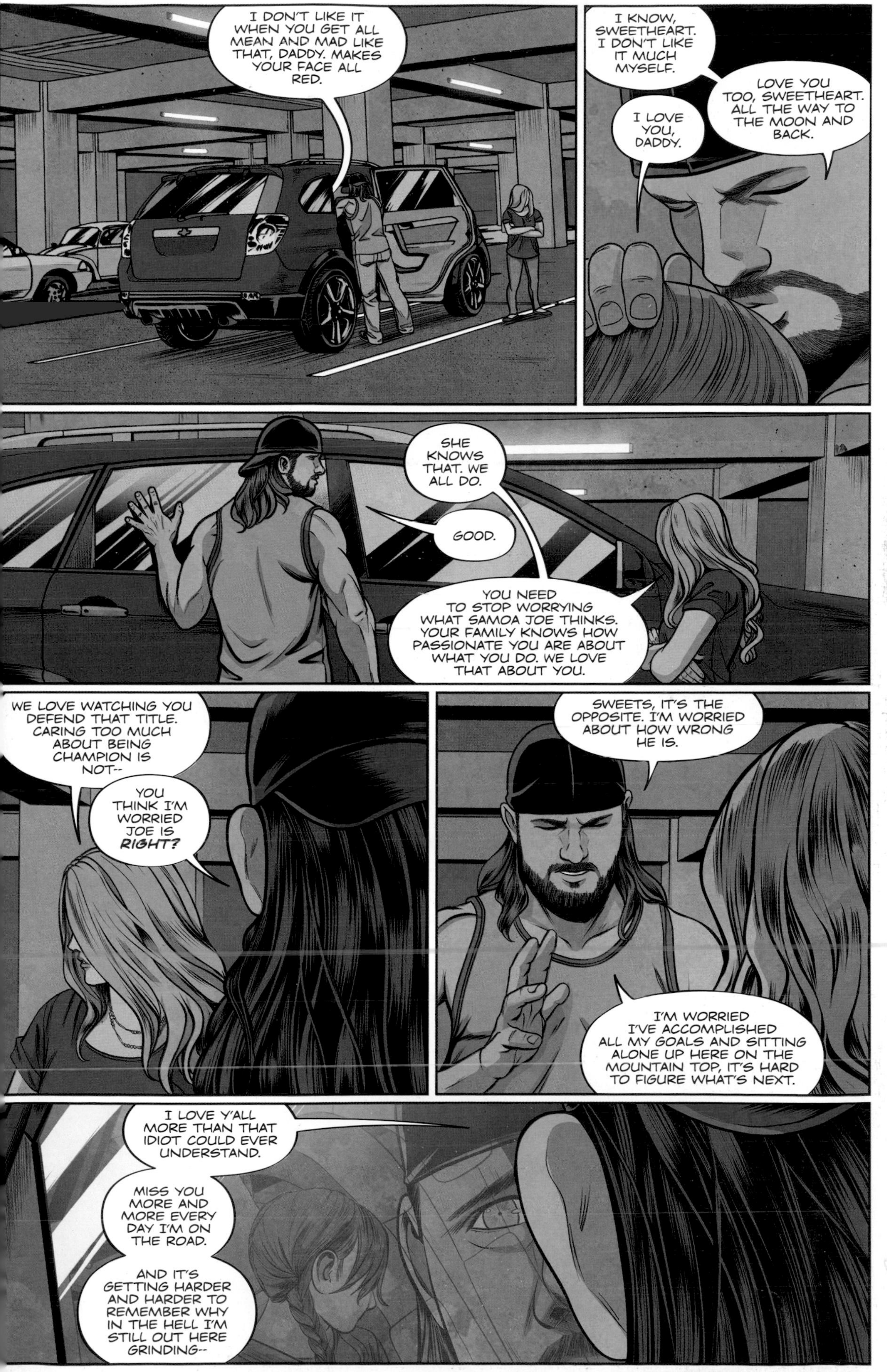
I DON'T LIKE IT WHEN YOU GET ALL MEAN AND MAD LIKE THAT, DADDY. MAKES YOUR FACE ALL RED.
I KNOW, SWEETHEART. I DON'T LIKE IT MUCH MYSELF.
I LOVE YOU, DADDY.
LOVE YOU TOO, SWEETHEART. ALL THE WAY TO THE MOON AND BACK.
SHE KNOWS THAT. WE ALL DO.
GOOD.
YOU NEED TO STOP WORRYING WHAT SAMOA JOE THINKS. YOUR FAMILY KNOWS HOW PASSIONATE YOU ARE ABOUT WHAT YOU DO. WE LOVE THAT ABOUT YOU.
WE LOVE WATCHING YOU DEFEND THAT TITLE. CARING TOO MUCH ABOUT BEING CHAMPION IS NOT--
YOU THINK I'M WORRIED JOE IS *RIGHT?*
SWEETS, IT'S THE OPPOSITE. I'M WORRIED ABOUT HOW WRONG HE IS.
I'M WORRIED I'VE ACCOMPLISHED ALL MY GOALS AND SITTING ALONE UP HERE ON THE MOUNTAIN TOP, IT'S HARD TO FIGURE WHAT'S NEXT.
I LOVE Y'ALL MORE THAN THAT IDIOT COULD EVER UNDERSTAND.
MISS YOU MORE AND MORE EVERY DAY I'M ON THE ROAD.
AND IT'S GETTING HARDER AND HARDER TO REMEMBER WHY IN THE HELL I'M STILL OUT HERE GRINDING--

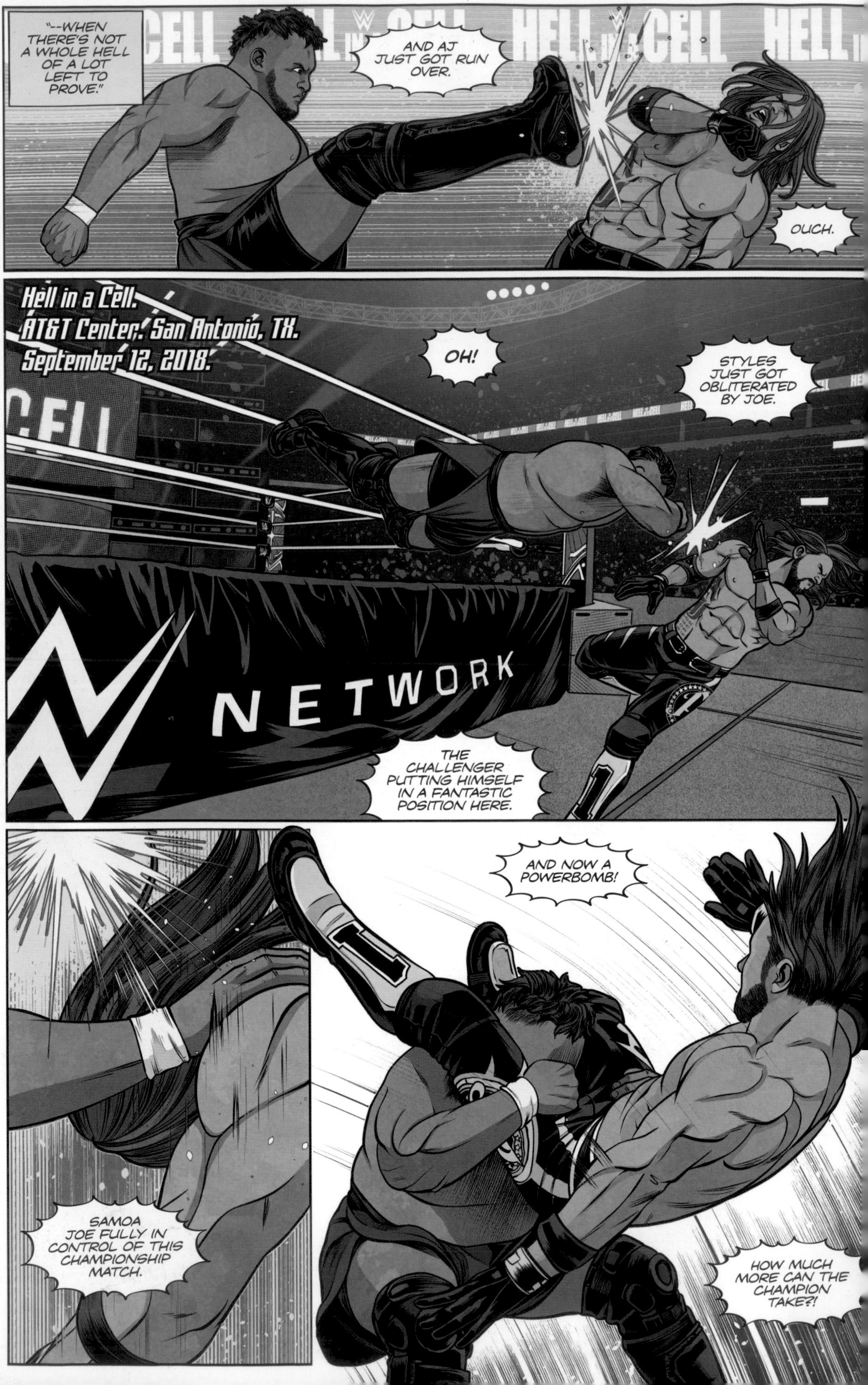
"--WHEN THERE'S NOT A WHOLE HELL OF A LOT LEFT TO PROVE."
AND AJ JUST GOT RUN OVER.
OUCH.
Hell in a Cell.
AT&T Center, San Antonio, TX.
September 12, 2018.
OH!
STYLES JUST GOT OBLITERATED BY JOE.
NETWORK
THE CHALLENGER PUTTING HIMSELF IN A FANTASTIC POSITION HERE.
AND NOW A POWERBOMB!
SAMOA JOE FULLY IN CONTROL OF THIS CHAMPIONSHIP MATCH.
HOW MUCH MORE CAN THE CHAMPION TAKE?!

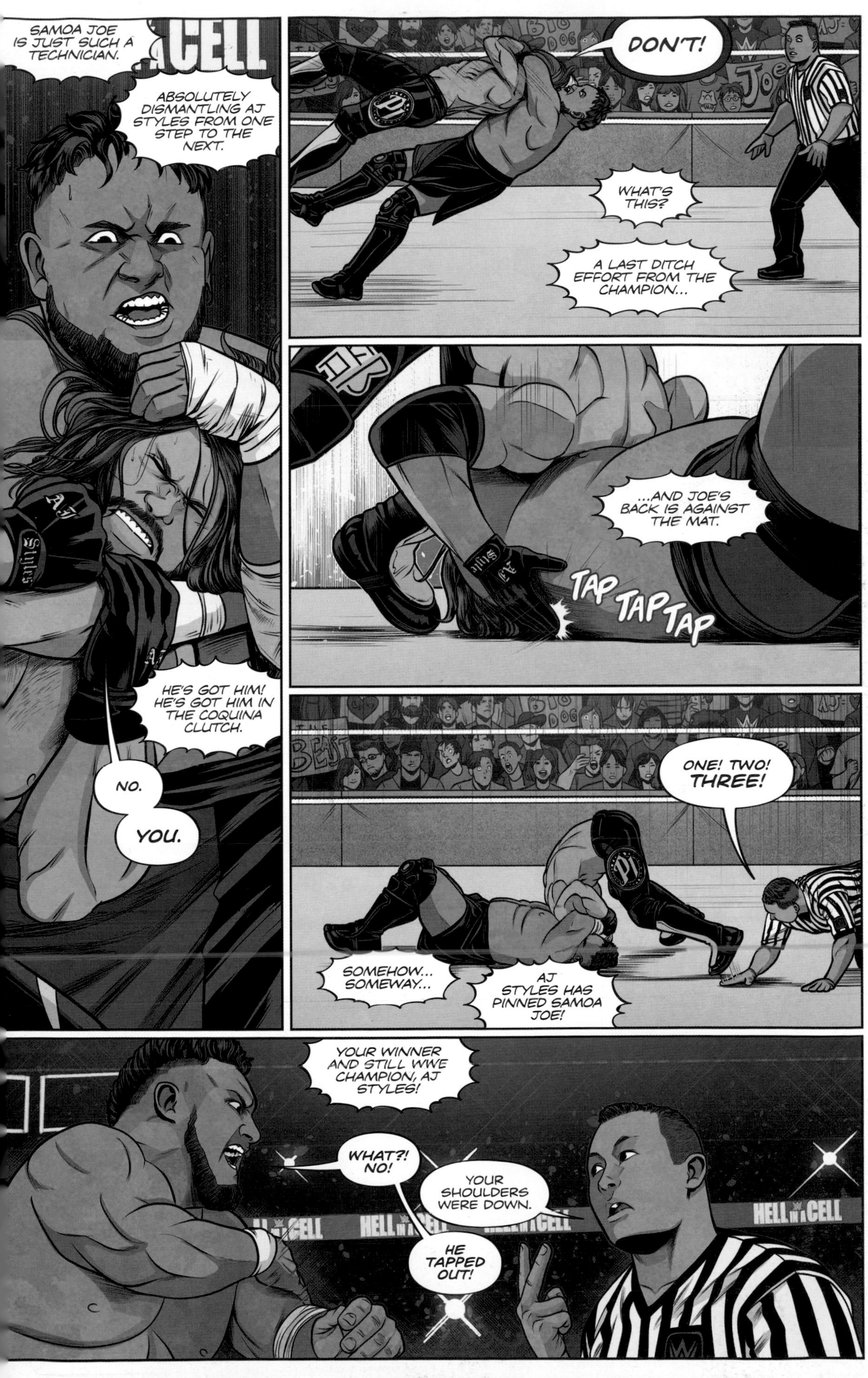
SAMOA JOE IS JUST SUCH A TECHNICIAN.
ABSOLUTELY DISMANTLING AJ STYLES FROM ONE STEP TO THE NEXT.
HE'S GOT HIM! HE'S GOT HIM IN THE COQUINA CLUTCH.
NO.
YOU.
DON'T!
WHAT'S THIS?
A LAST DITCH EFFORT FROM THE CHAMPION...
...AND JOE'S BACK IS AGAINST THE MAT.
TAP TAP TAP
ONE! TWO! THREE!
SOMEHOW... SOMEWAY...
AJ STYLES HAS PINNED SAMOA JOE!
YOUR WINNER AND STILL WWE CHAMPION, AJ STYLES!
WHAT?! NO!
YOUR SHOULDERS WERE DOWN.
HE TAPPED OUT!
HELL IN A CELL

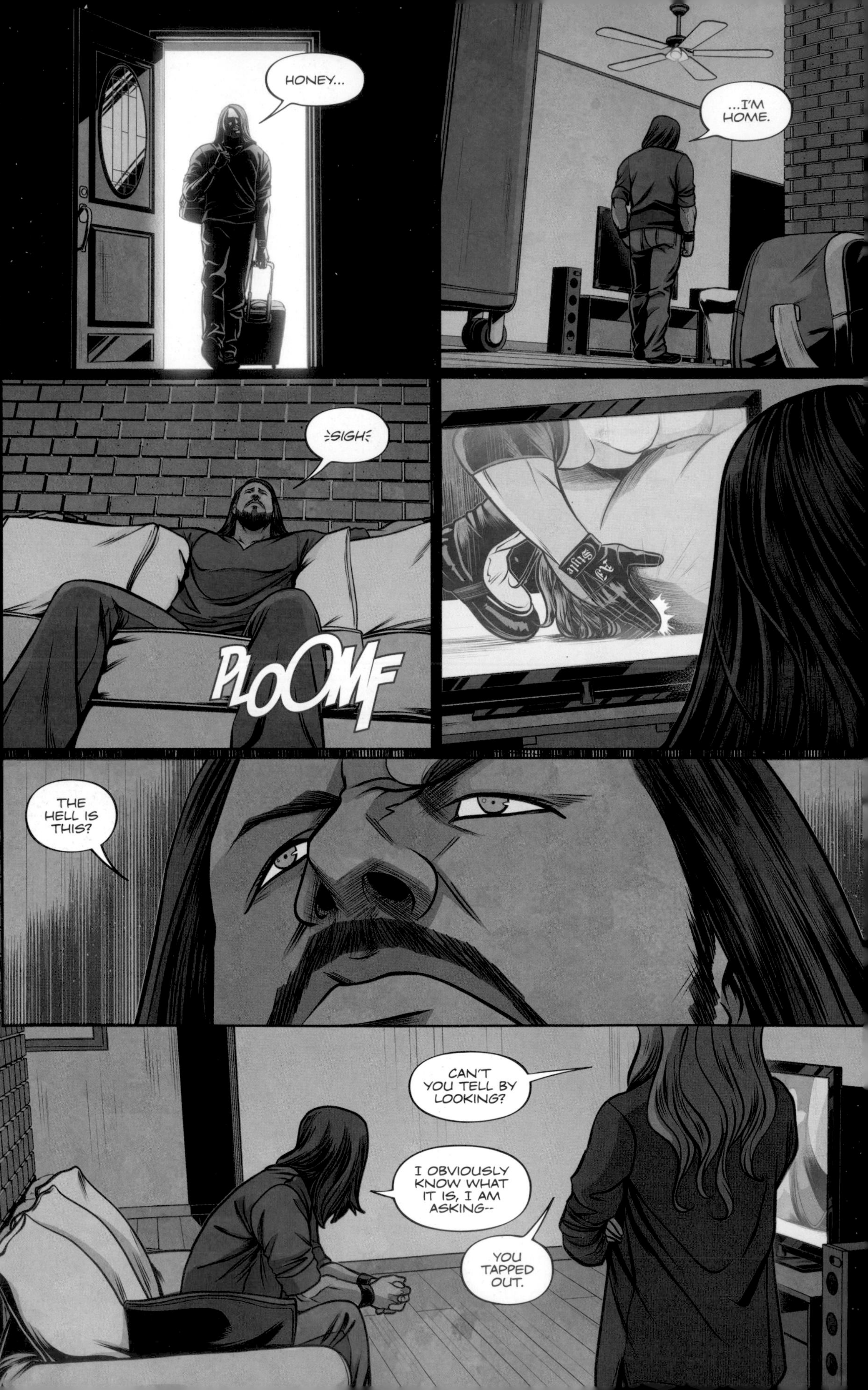
HONEY...
...I'M HOME.
SIGH
PLOOMF
THE HELL IS THIS?
CAN'T YOU TELL BY LOOKING?
I OBVIOUSLY KNOW WHAT IT IS, I AM ASKING--
YOU TAPPED OUT.

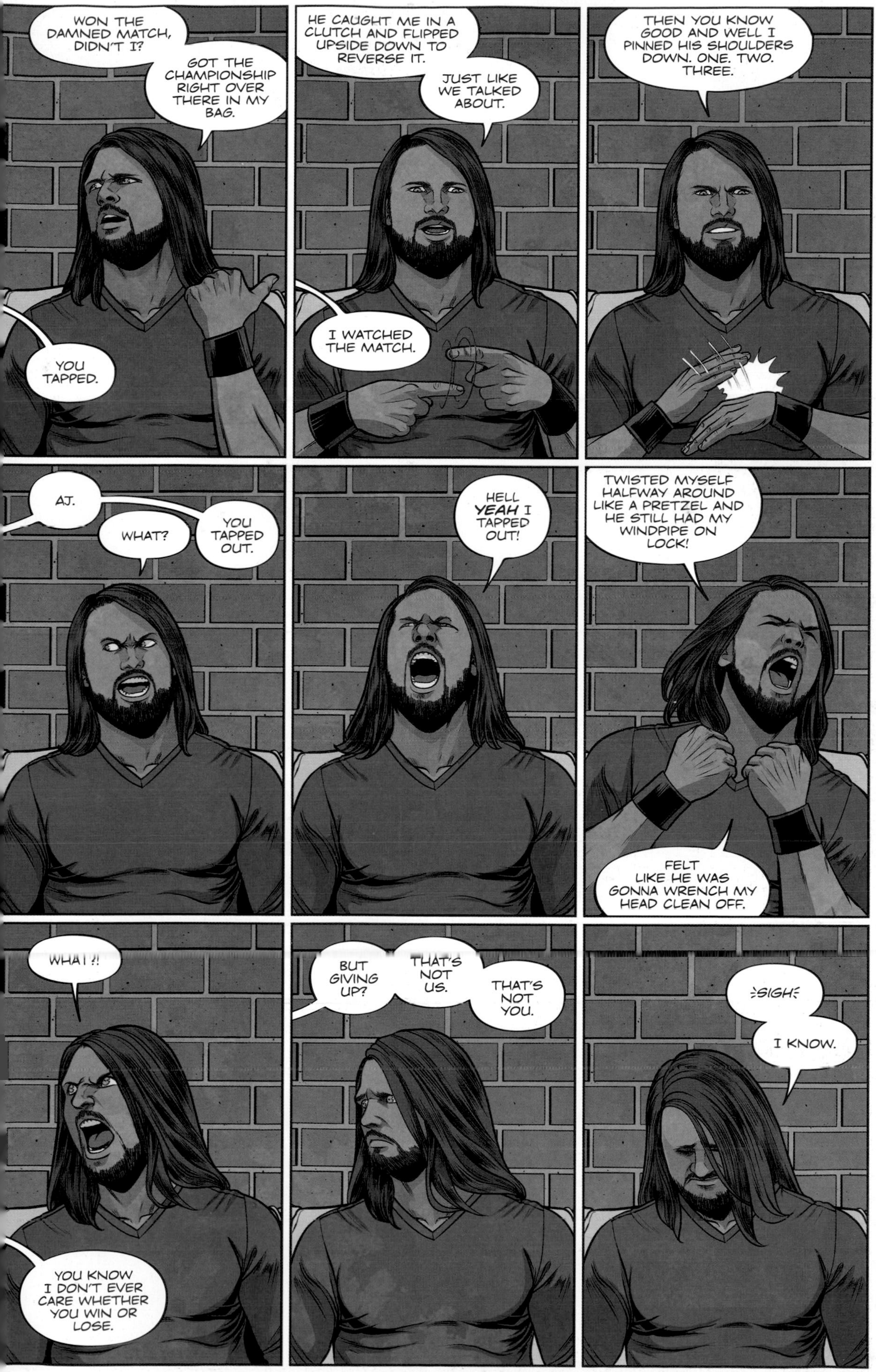
WON THE DAMNED MATCH, DIDN'T I?
GOT THE CHAMPIONSHIP RIGHT OVER THERE IN MY BAG.
YOU TAPPED.
HE CAUGHT ME IN A CLUTCH AND FLIPPED UPSIDE DOWN TO REVERSE IT.
JUST LIKE WE TALKED ABOUT.
I WATCHED THE MATCH.
THEN YOU KNOW GOOD AND WELL I PINNED HIS SHOULDERS DOWN. ONE. TWO. THREE.
AJ.
WHAT?
YOU TAPPED OUT.
HELL YEAH I TAPPED OUT!
TWISTED MYSELF HALFWAY AROUND LIKE A PRETZEL AND HE STILL HAD MY WINDPIPE ON LOCK!
FELT LIKE HE WAS GONNA WRENCH MY HEAD CLEAN OFF.
WHAT?!
YOU KNOW I DON'T EVER CARE WHETHER YOU WIN OR LOSE.
BUT GIVING UP?
THAT'S NOT US.
THAT'S NOT YOU.
SIGH
I KNOW.

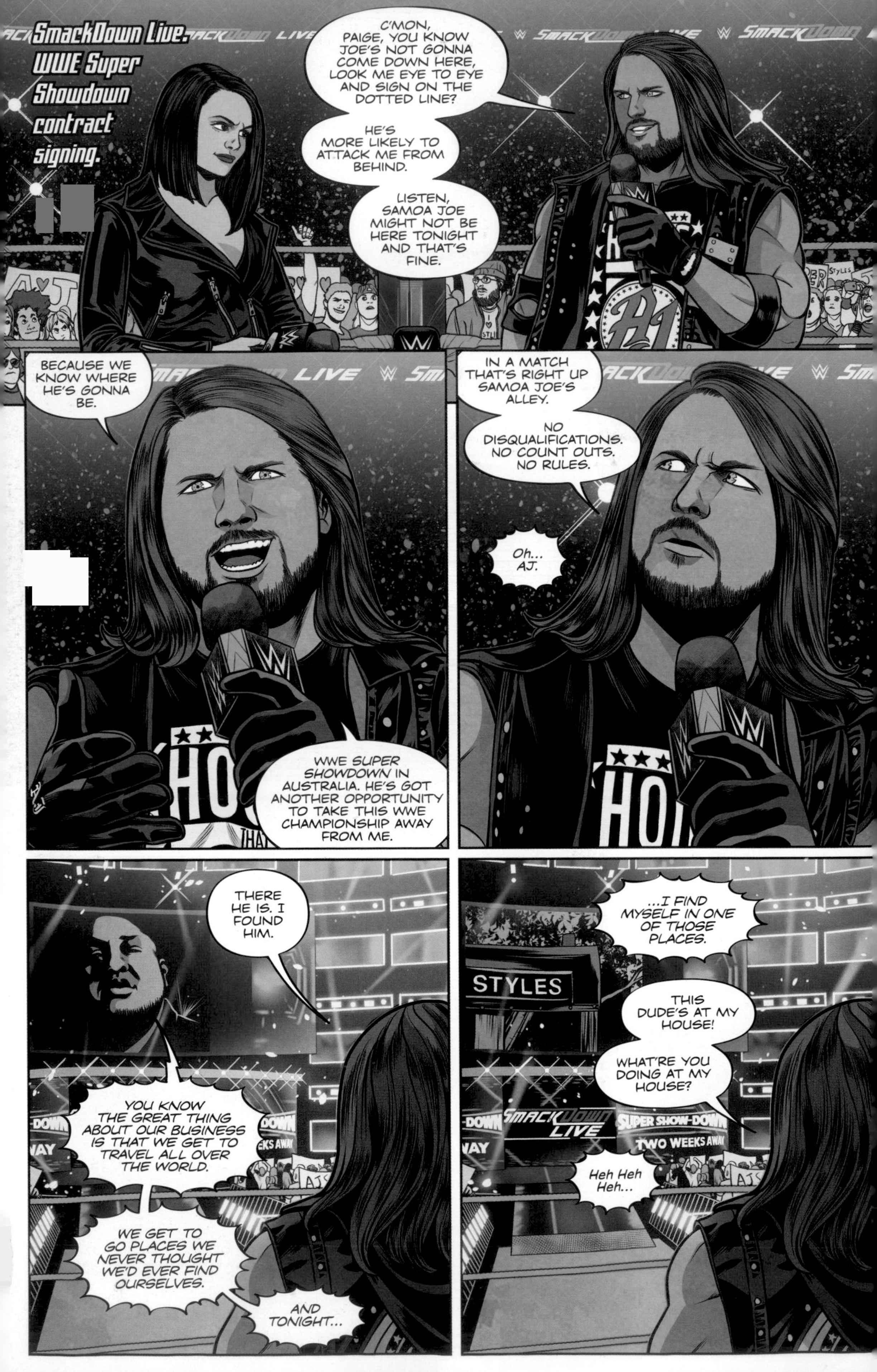

SmackDown Live. WWE Super Showdown contract signing.
C'MON, PAIGE, YOU KNOW JOE'S NOT GONNA COME DOWN HERE, LOOK ME EYE TO EYE AND SIGN ON THE DOTTED LINE?
HE'S MORE LIKELY TO ATTACK ME FROM BEHIND.
LISTEN, SAMOA JOE MIGHT NOT BE HERE TONIGHT AND THAT'S FINE.
BECAUSE WE KNOW WHERE HE'S GONNA BE.
WWE SUPER SHOWDOWN IN AUSTRALIA. HE'S GOT ANOTHER OPPORTUNITY TO TAKE THIS WWE CHAMPIONSHIP AWAY FROM ME.
IN A MATCH THAT'S RIGHT UP SAMOA JOE'S ALLEY.
NO DISQUALIFICATIONS. NO COUNT OUTS. NO RULES.
Oh... AJ.
THERE HE IS. I FOUND HIM.
YOU KNOW THE GREAT THING ABOUT OUR BUSINESS IS THAT WE GET TO TRAVEL ALL OVER THE WORLD.
WE GET TO GO PLACES WE NEVER THOUGHT WE'D EVER FIND OURSELVES.
AND TONIGHT...
...I FIND MYSELF IN ONE OF THOSE PLACES.
THIS DUDE'S AT MY HOUSE!
WHAT'RE YOU DOING AT MY HOUSE?
Heh Heh Heh...
STYLES
SUPER SHOW-DOWN
TWO WEEKS AWAY

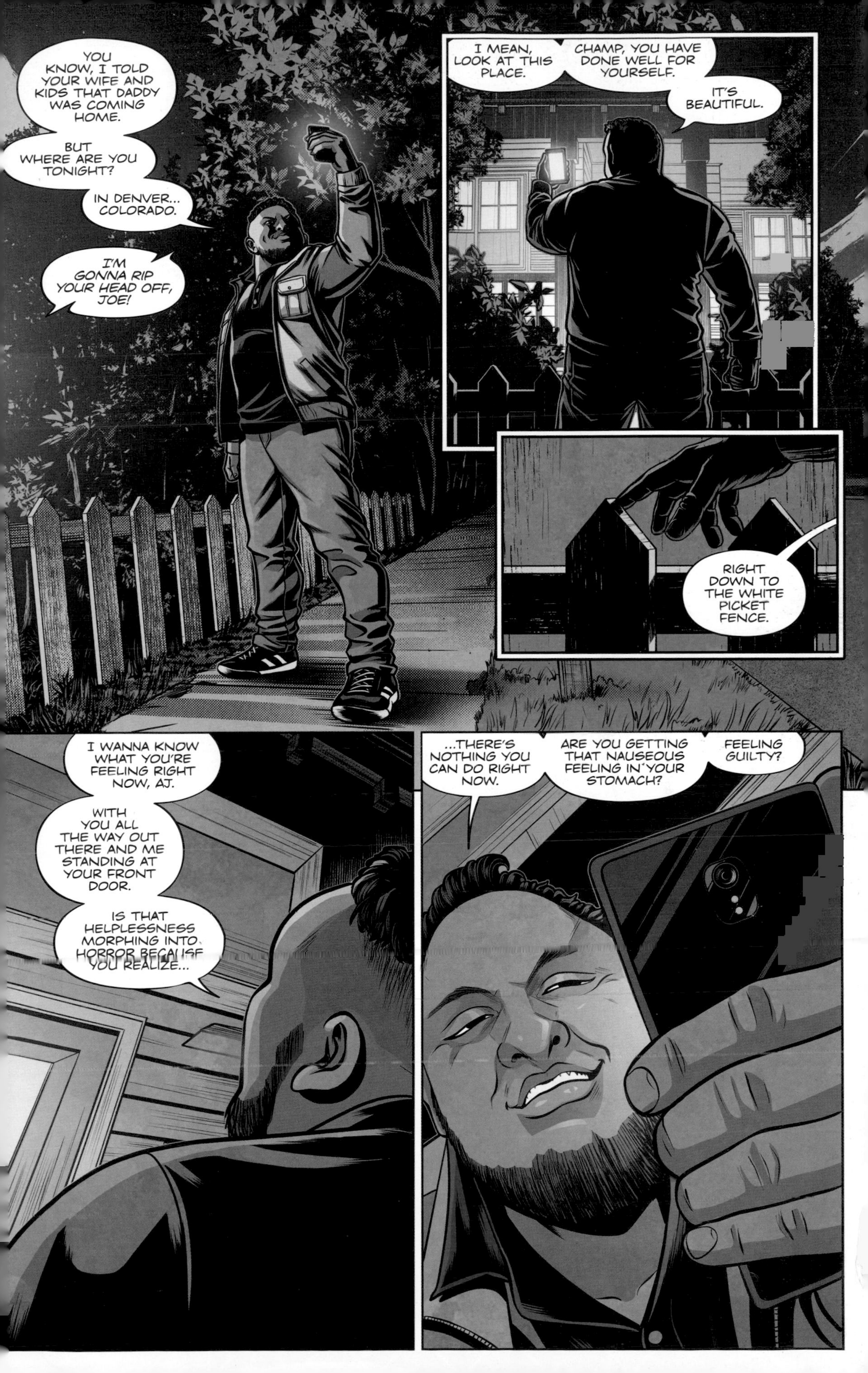
YOU KNOW, I TOLD YOUR WIFE AND KIDS THAT DADDY WAS COMING HOME.
BUT WHERE ARE YOU TONIGHT?
IN DENVER... COLORADO.
I'M GONNA RIP YOUR HEAD OFF, JOE!
I MEAN, LOOK AT THIS PLACE.
CHAMP, YOU HAVE DONE WELL FOR YOURSELF.
IT'S BEAUTIFUL.
RIGHT DOWN TO THE WHITE PICKET FENCE.
I WANNA KNOW WHAT YOU'RE FEELING RIGHT NOW, AJ.
WITH YOU ALL THE WAY OUT THERE AND ME STANDING AT YOUR FRONT DOOR.
IS THAT HELPLESSNESS MORPHING INTO HORROR BECAUSE YOU REALIZE...
...THERE'S NOTHING YOU CAN DO RIGHT NOW.
ARE YOU GETTING THAT NAUSEOUS FEELING IN YOUR STOMACH?
FEELING GUILTY?

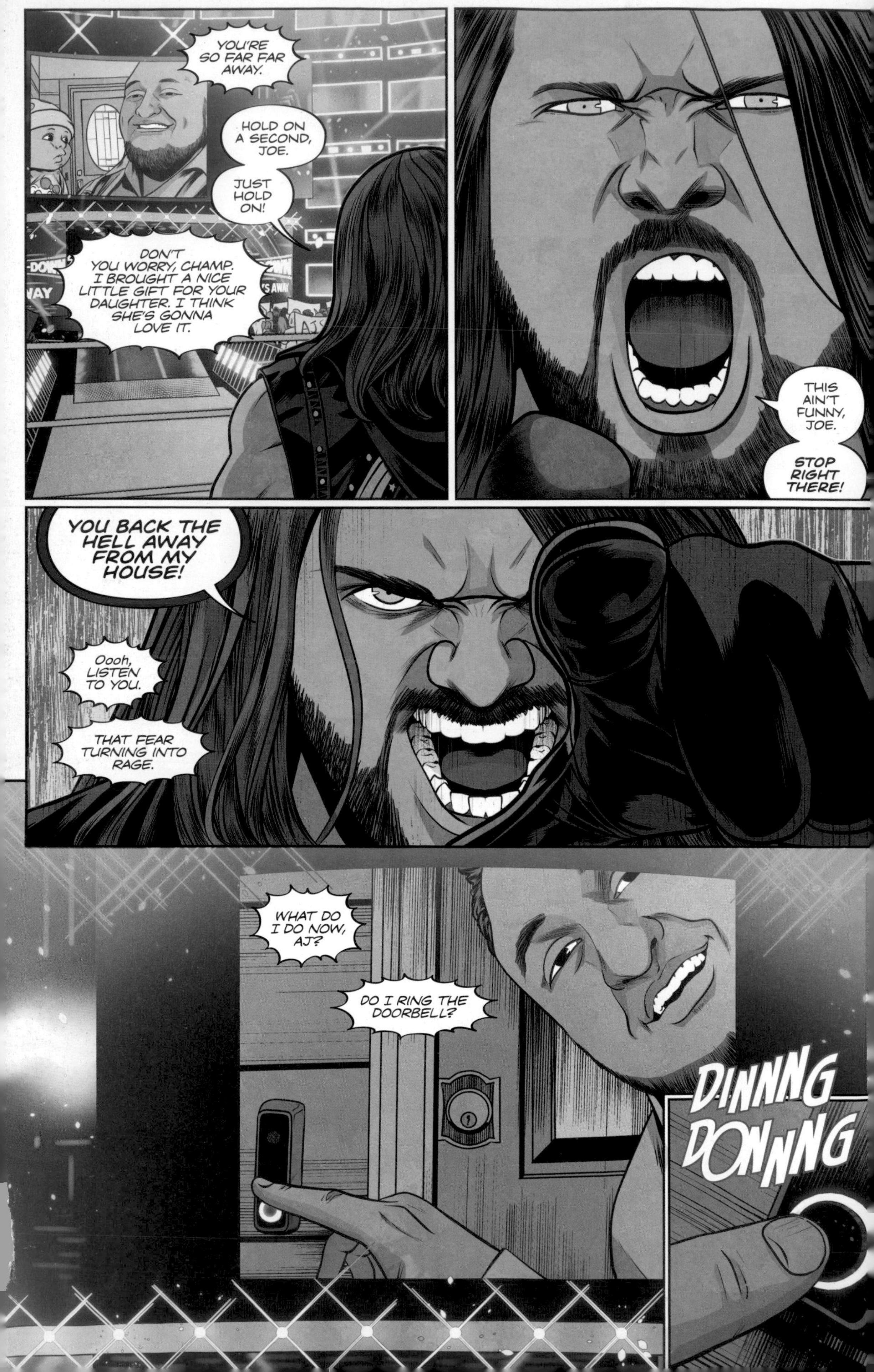
YOU'RE SO FAR FAR AWAY.
HOLD ON A SECOND, JOE.
JUST HOLD ON!
DON'T YOU WORRY, CHAMP. I BROUGHT A NICE LITTLE GIFT FOR YOUR DAUGHTER. I THINK SHE'S GONNA LOVE IT.
THIS AIN'T FUNNY, JOE.
STOP RIGHT THERE!
YOU BACK THE HELL AWAY FROM MY HOUSE!
Oooh, LISTEN TO YOU.
THAT FEAR TURNING INTO RAGE.
WHAT DO I DO NOW, AJ?
DO I RING THE DOORBELL?
DINNNG DONNNG

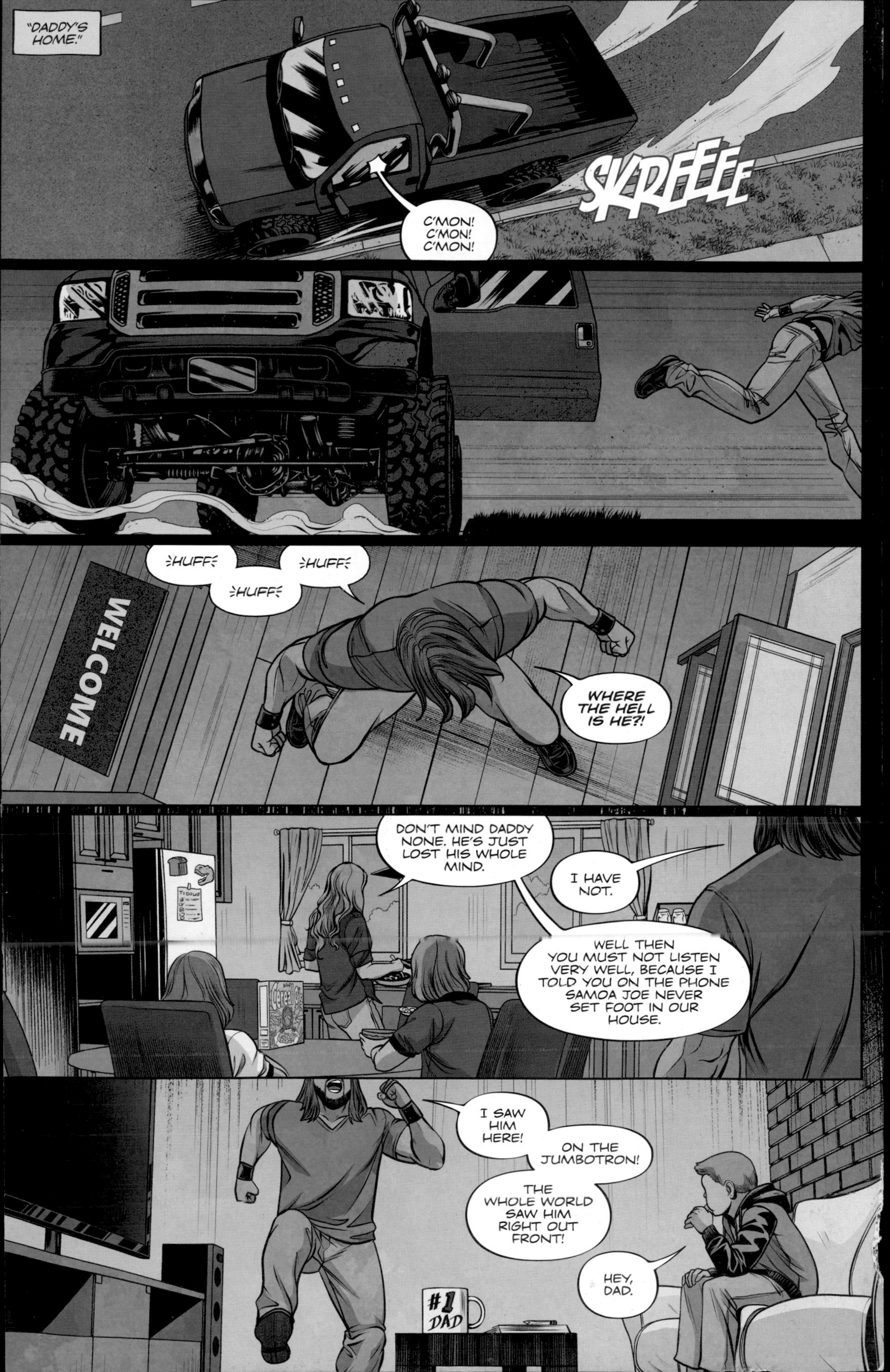
"DADDY'S HOME."
C'MON! C'MON! C'MON!
SKRFEEEE
HUFF
HUFF
HUFF
WELCOME
WHERE THE HELL IS HE?!
DON'T MIND DADDY NONE. HE'S JUST LOST HIS WHOLE MIND.
I HAVE NOT.
WELL THEN YOU MUST NOT LISTEN VERY WELL, BECAUSE I TOLD YOU ON THE PHONE SAMOA JOE NEVER SET FOOT IN OUR HOUSE.
I SAW HIM HERE!
ON THE JUMBOTRON!
THE WHOLE WORLD SAW HIM RIGHT OUT FRONT!
HEY, DAD.
#1 DAD

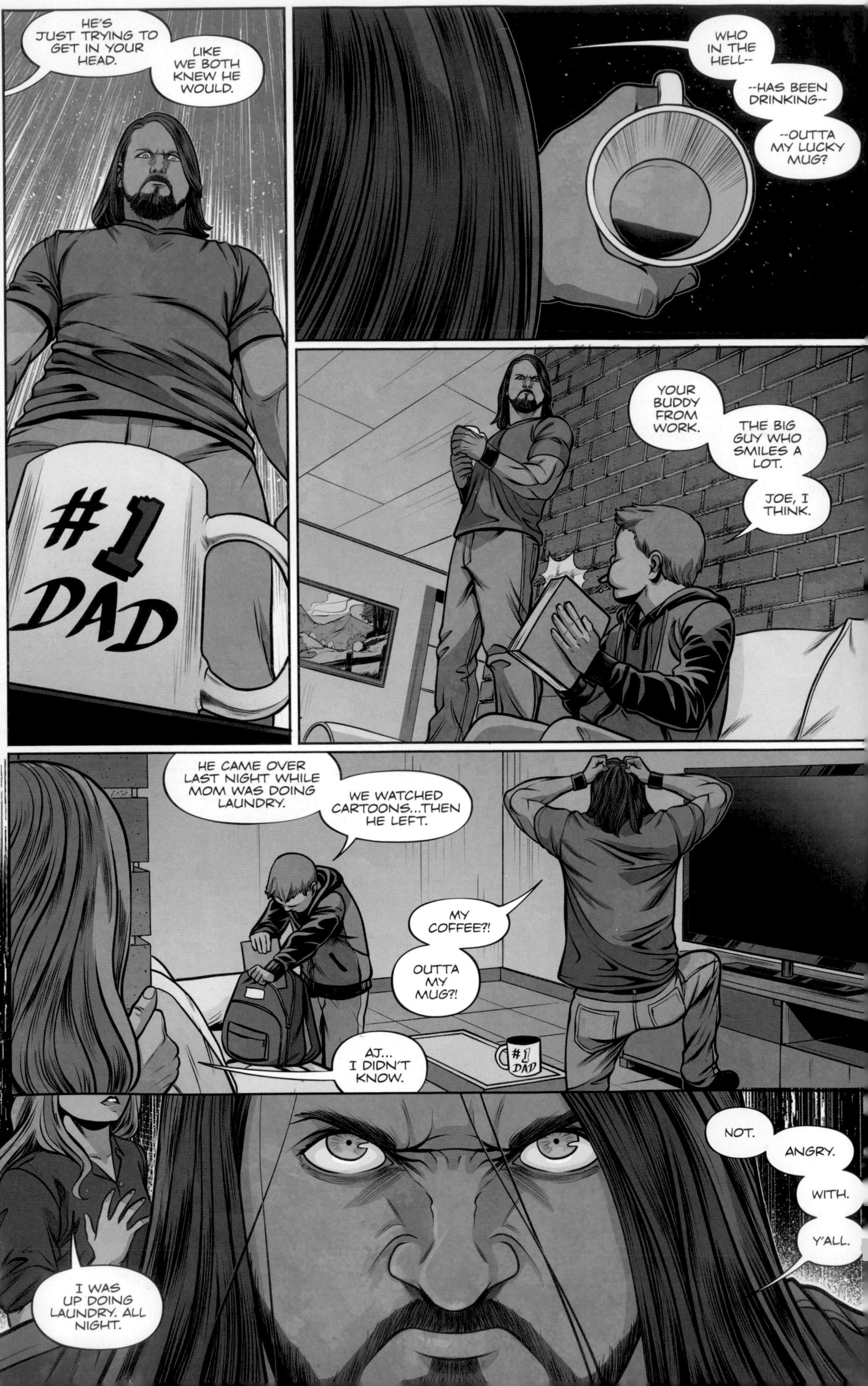
HE'S JUST TRYING TO GET IN YOUR HEAD.
LIKE WE BOTH KNEW HE WOULD.
#1 DAD
WHO IN THE HELL--
--HAS BEEN DRINKING--
--OUTTA MY LUCKY MUG?
YOUR BUDDY FROM WORK.
THE BIG GUY WHO SMILES A LOT.
JOE, I THINK.
HE CAME OVER LAST NIGHT WHILE MOM WAS DOING LAUNDRY.
WE WATCHED CARTOONS...THEN HE LEFT.
MY COFFEE?!
OUTTA MY MUG?!
AJ... I DIDN'T KNOW.
#1 DAD
I WAS UP DOING LAUNDRY. ALL NIGHT.
NOT.
ANGRY.
WITH.
Y'ALL.

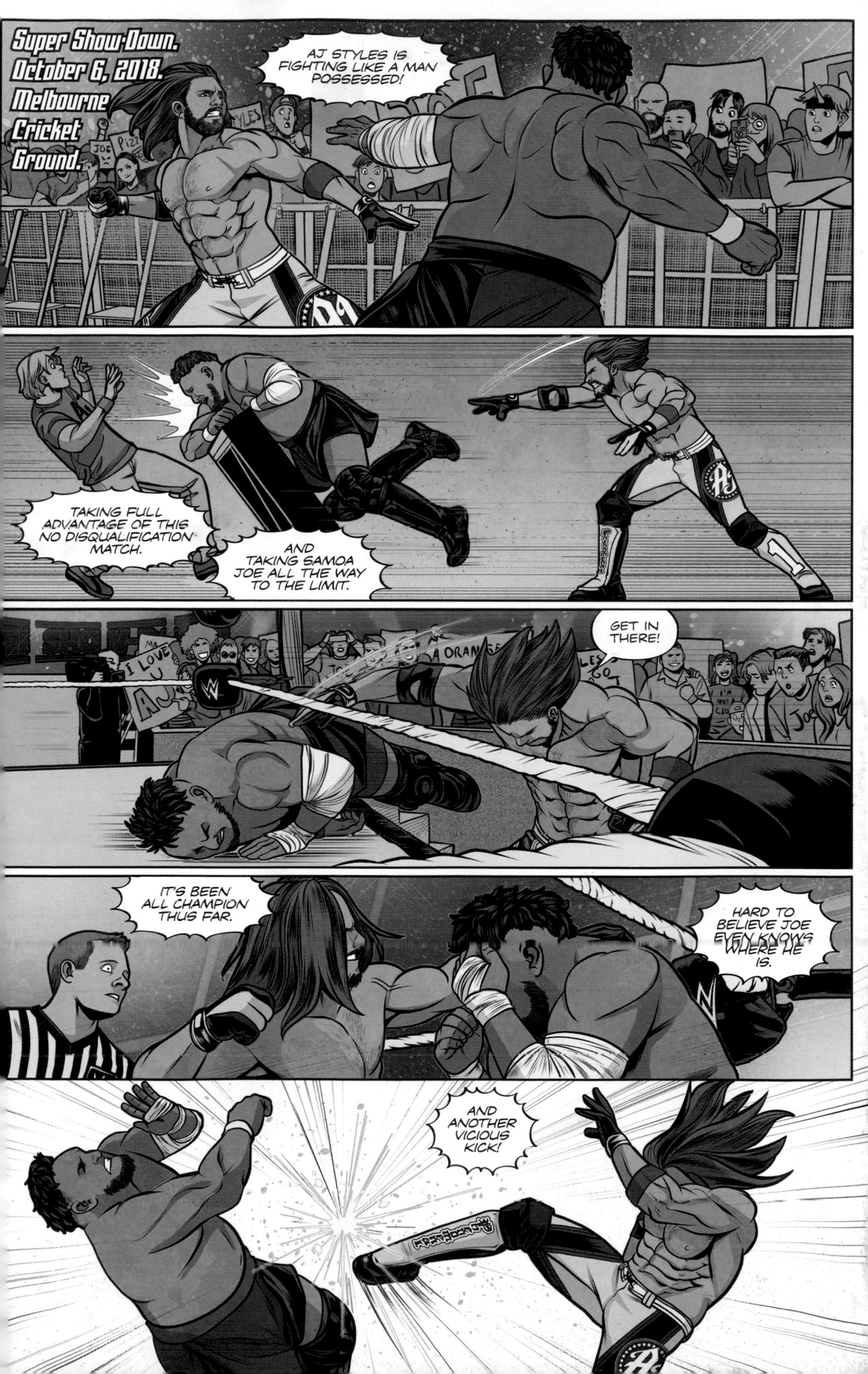
Super Show-Down. October 6, 2018. Melbourne Cricket Ground.
AJ STYLES IS FIGHTING LIKE A MAN POSSESSED!
TAKING FULL ADVANTAGE OF THIS NO DISQUALIFICATION MATCH.
AND TAKING SAMOA JOE ALL THE WAY TO THE LIMIT.
GET IN THERE!
I LOVE U AJ
IT'S BEEN ALL CHAMPION THUS FAR.
HARD TO BELIEVE JOE EVEN KNOWS WHERE HE IS.
AND ANOTHER VICIOUS KICK!

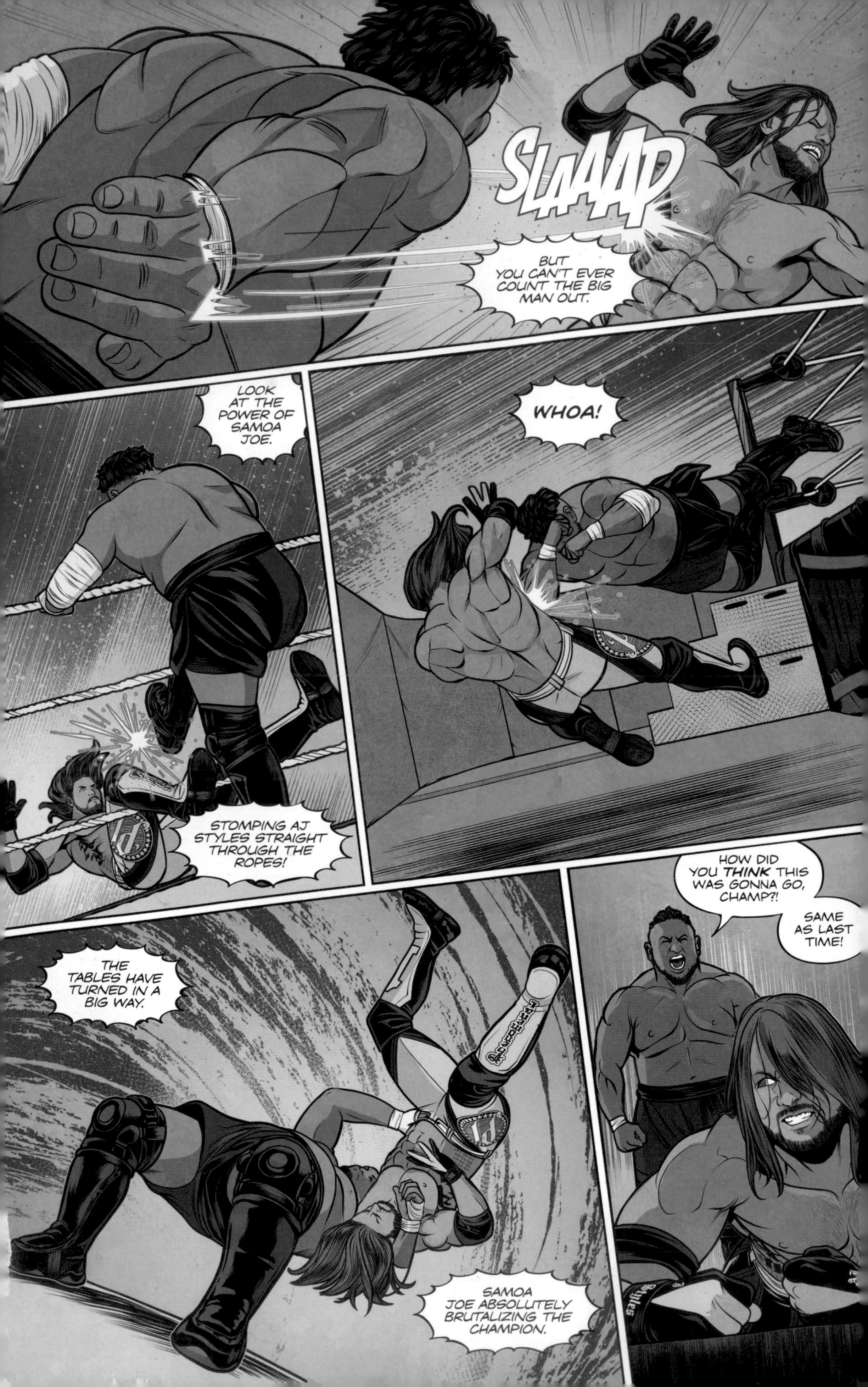
SLAAAP
BUT YOU CAN'T EVER COUNT THE BIG MAN OUT.
LOOK AT THE POWER OF SAMOA JOE.
STOMPING AJ STYLES STRAIGHT THROUGH THE ROPES!
WHOA!
THE TABLES HAVE TURNED IN A BIG WAY.
SAMOA JOE ABSOLUTELY BRUTALIZING THE CHAMPION.
HOW DID YOU THINK THIS WAS GONNA GO, CHAMP?!
SAME AS LAST TIME!

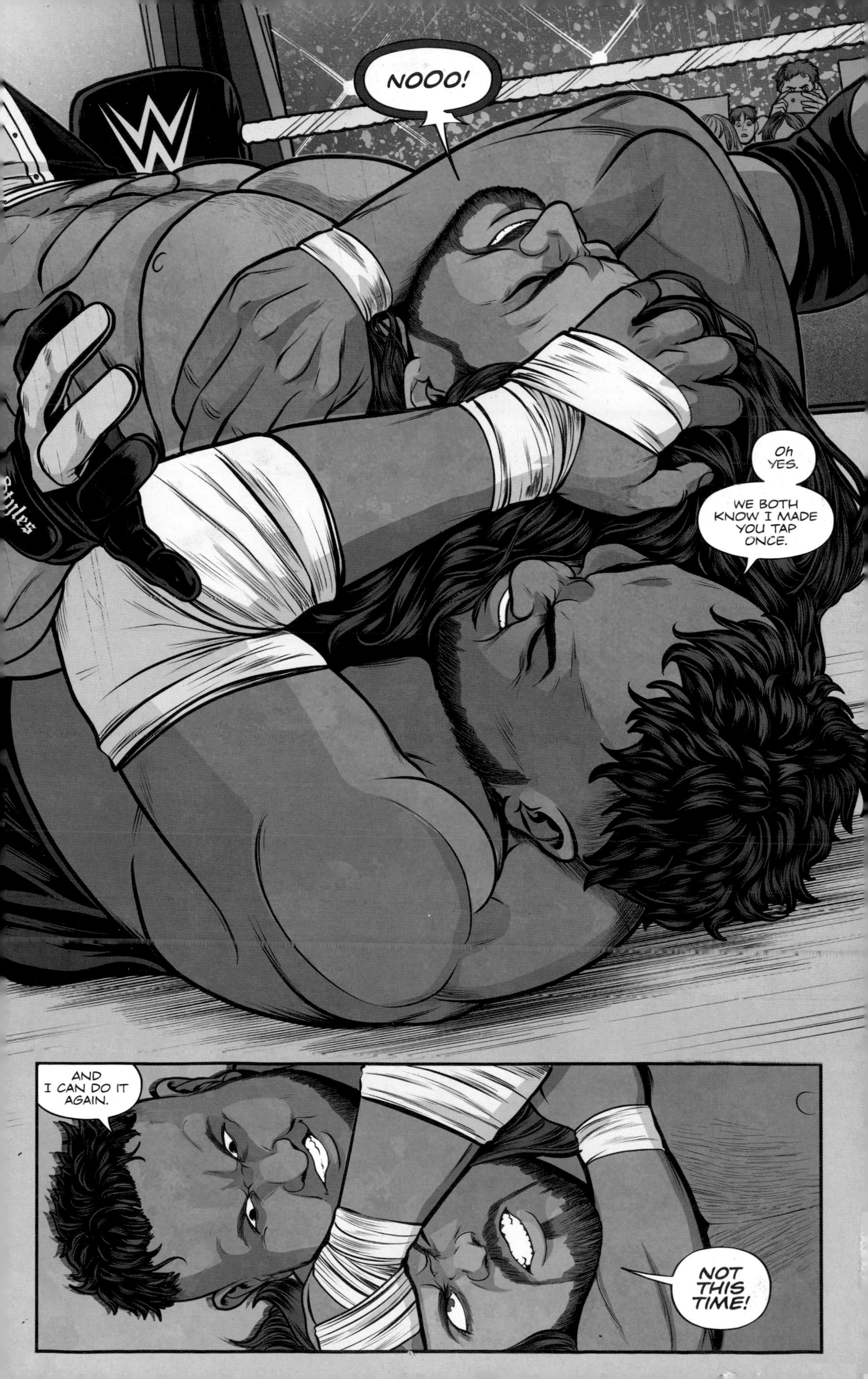
NOOO!
Oh YES.
WE BOTH KNOW I MADE YOU TAP ONCE.
AND I CAN DO IT AGAIN.
NOT THIS TIME!

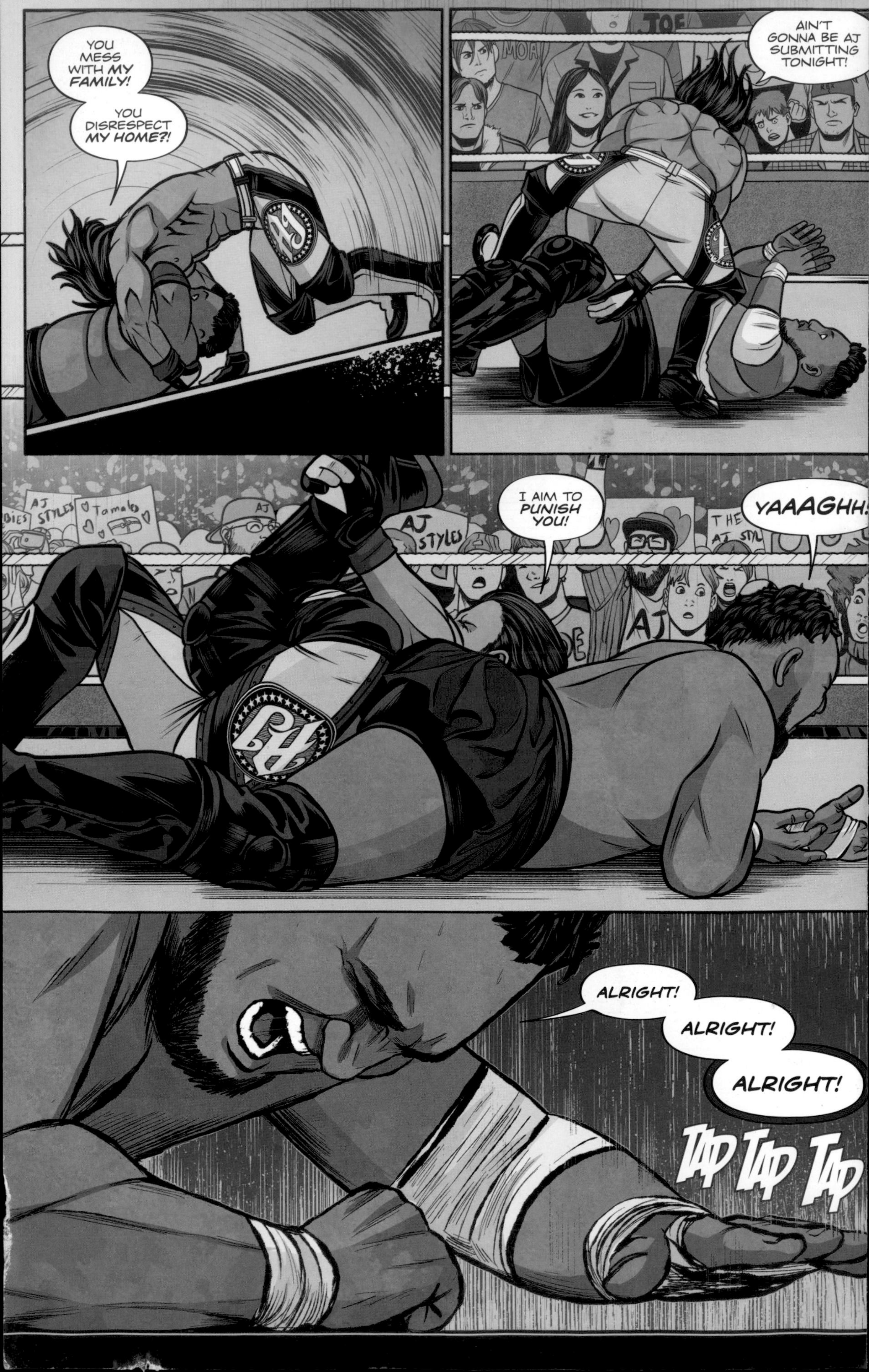
YOU MESS WITH MY FAMILY!
YOU DISRESPECT MY HOME?!
AIN'T GONNA BE AJ SUBMITTING TONIGHT!
AJ STYLES
Tamales
AJ STYLES
I AIM TO PUNISH YOU!
YAAAGHH!
ALRIGHT!
ALRIGHT!
ALRIGHT!
TAP TAP TAP

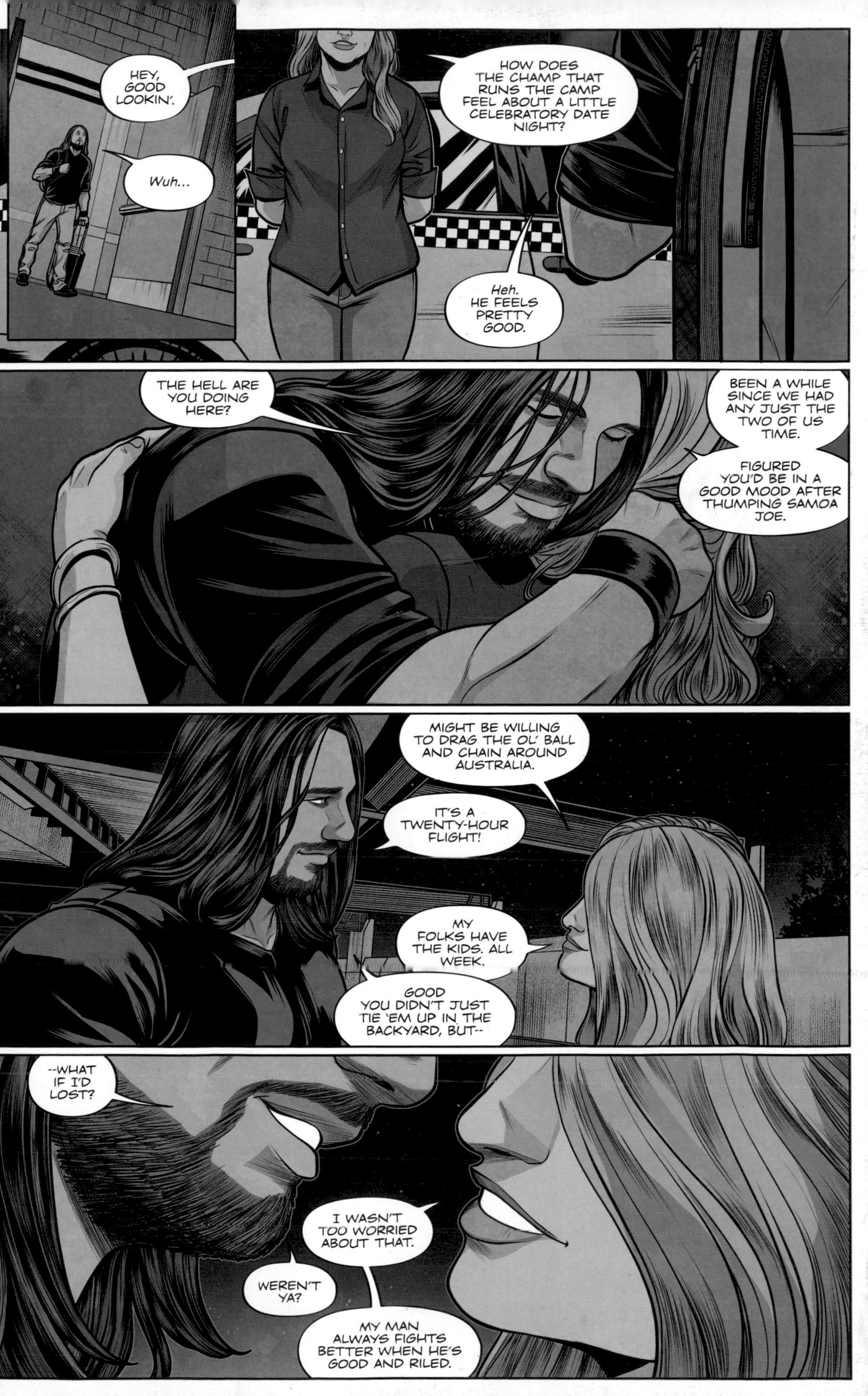
HEY, GOOD LOOKIN'.
Wuh...
HOW DOES THE CHAMP THAT RUNS THE CAMP FEEL ABOUT A LITTLE CELEBRATORY DATE NIGHT?
Heh. HE FEELS PRETTY GOOD.
THE HELL ARE YOU DOING HERE?
BEEN A WHILE SINCE WE HAD ANY JUST THE TWO OF US TIME.
FIGURED YOU'D BE IN A GOOD MOOD AFTER THUMPING SAMOA JOE.
MIGHT BE WILLING TO DRAG THE OL' BALL AND CHAIN AROUND AUSTRALIA.
IT'S A TWENTY-HOUR FLIGHT!
MY FOLKS HAVE THE KIDS. ALL WEEK.
GOOD YOU DIDN'T JUST TIE 'EM UP IN THE BACKYARD, BUT--
--WHAT IF I'D LOST?
I WASN'T TOO WORRIED ABOUT THAT.
WEREN'T YA?
MY MAN ALWAYS FIGHTS BETTER WHEN HE'S GOOD AND RILED.

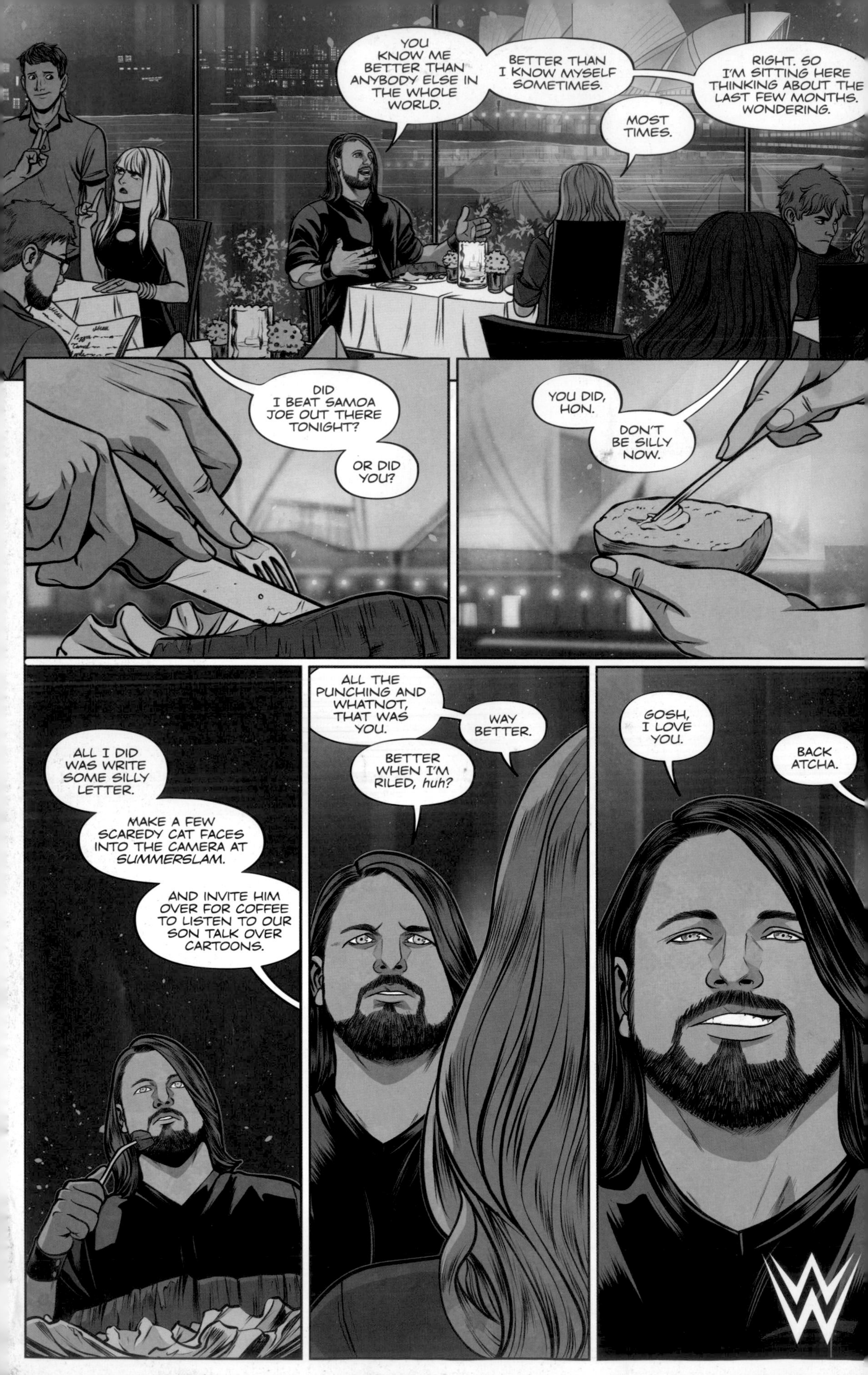
YOU KNOW ME BETTER THAN ANYBODY ELSE IN THE WHOLE WORLD.
BETTER THAN I KNOW MYSELF SOMETIMES.
MOST TIMES.
RIGHT. SO I'M SITTING HERE THINKING ABOUT THE LAST FEW MONTHS. WONDERING.
DID I BEAT SAMOA JOE OUT THERE TONIGHT?
OR DID YOU?
YOU DID, HON.
DON'T BE SILLY NOW.
ALL I DID WAS WRITE SOME SILLY LETTER.
MAKE A FEW SCAREDY CAT FACES INTO THE CAMERA AT SUMMERSLAM.
AND INVITE HIM OVER FOR COFFEE TO LISTEN TO OUR SON TALK OVER CARTOONS.
ALL THE PUNCHING AND WHATNOT, THAT WAS YOU.
WAY BETTER.
BETTER WHEN I'M RILED, *huh?*
GOSH, I LOVE YOU.
BACK ATCHA.

WWE #21 BRAUN STROWMAN COVER AND #25 COVER BY
MARCO D'ALFONSO

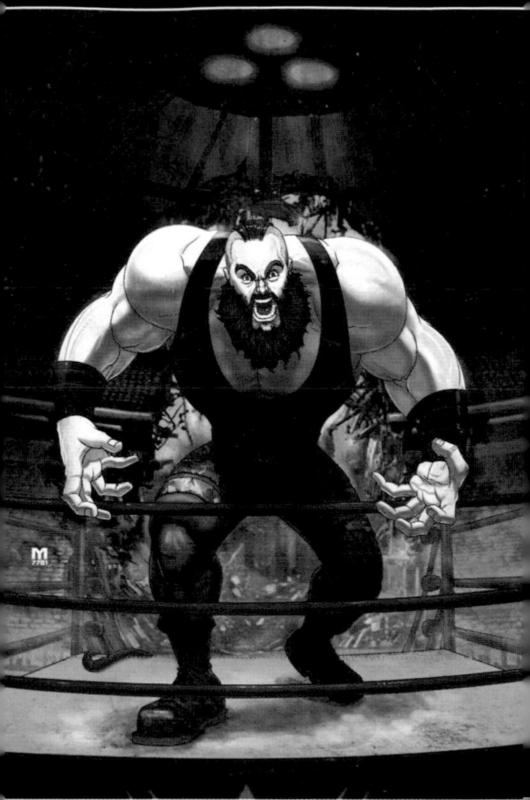

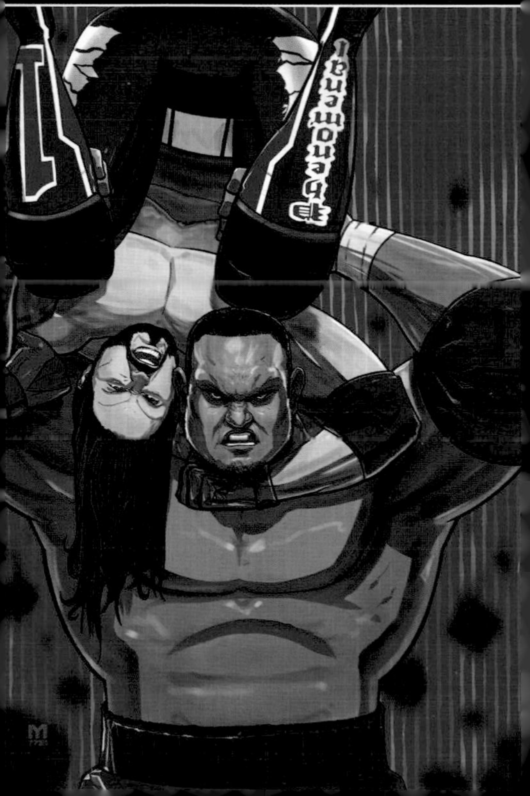
Phenomenal

WWE #22
THE IRON SHEIK COVER BY
RAHZZAH

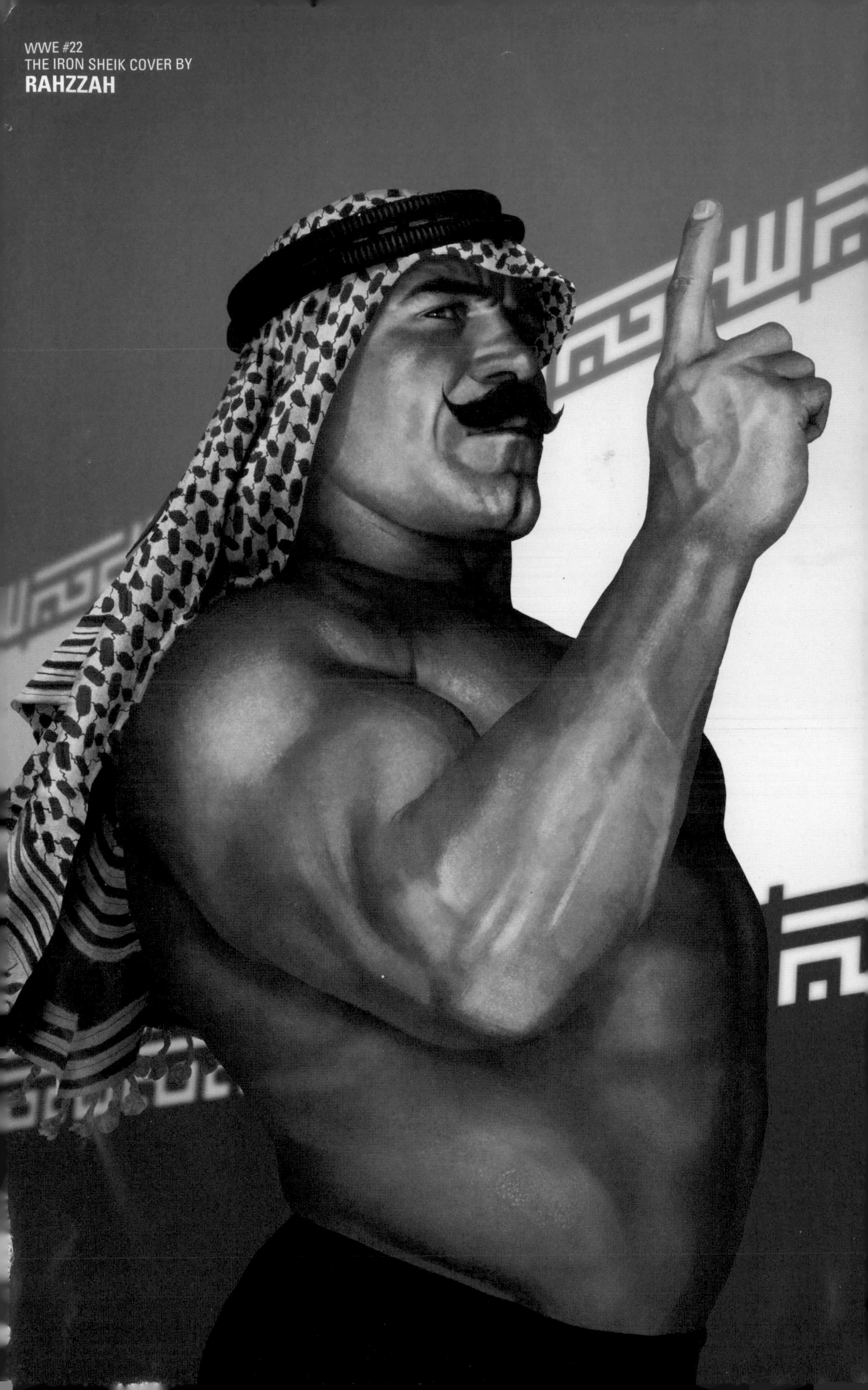

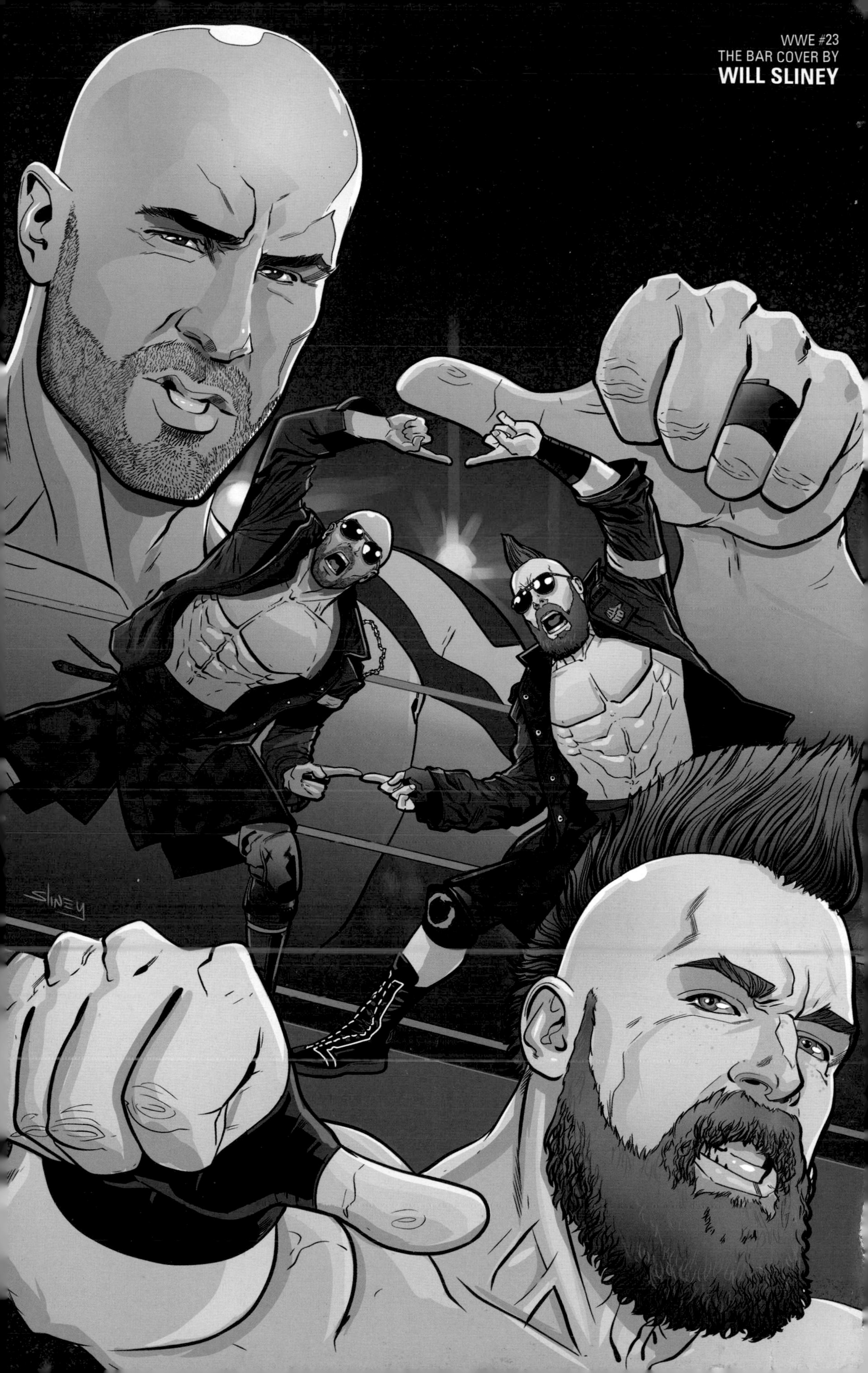
SLINEY

WWE #23
THE BAR COVER BY
WILL SLINEY

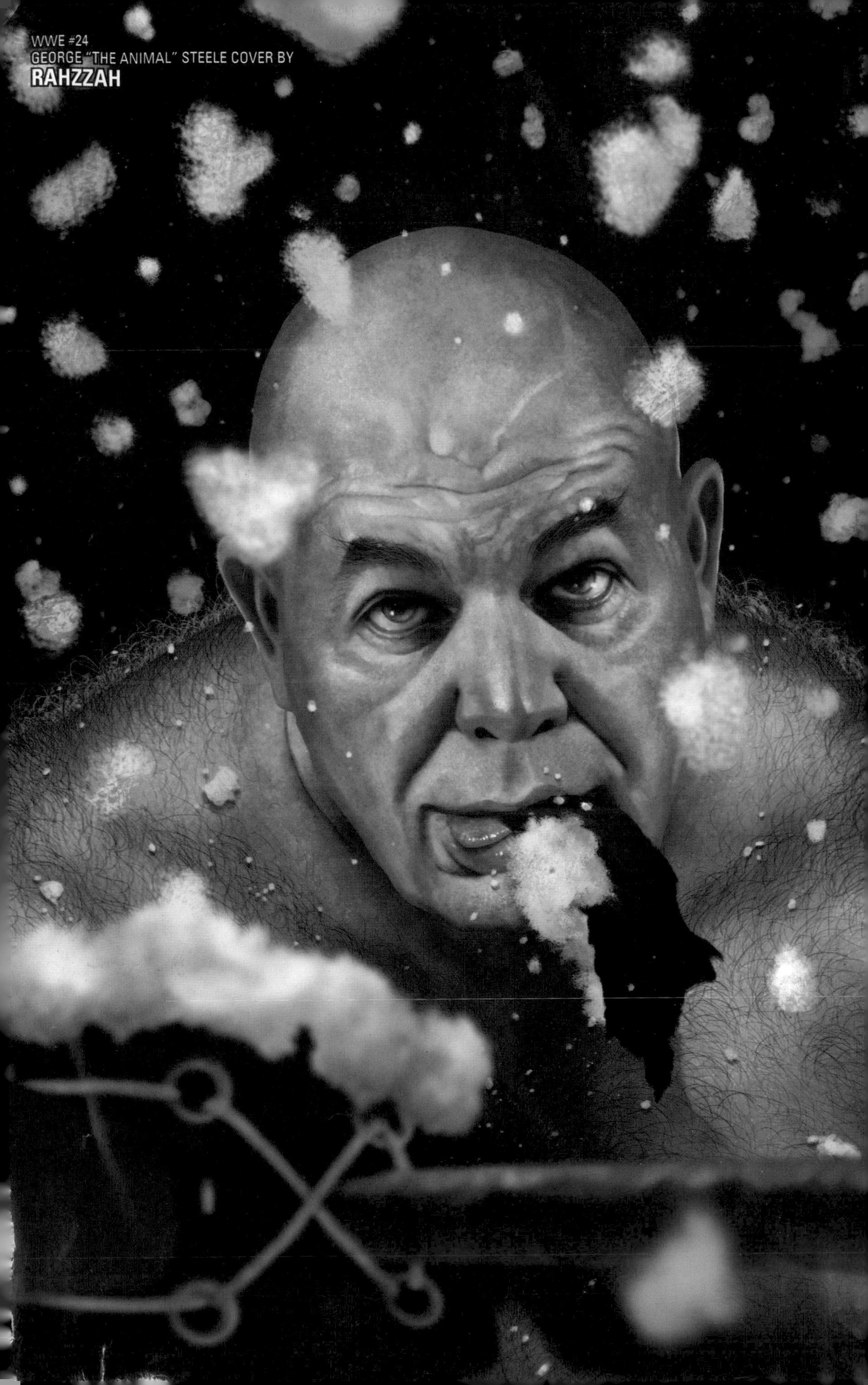

WWE #24
GEORGE "THE ANIMAL" STEELE COVER BY
RAHZZAH

WWE #25
NIA JAX COVER BY
XERMÁNICO

WWE #25
SHINSUKE NAKAMURA COVER BY
ERIC GARZA

ACTION FIGURE COVERS BY
ADAM RICHES

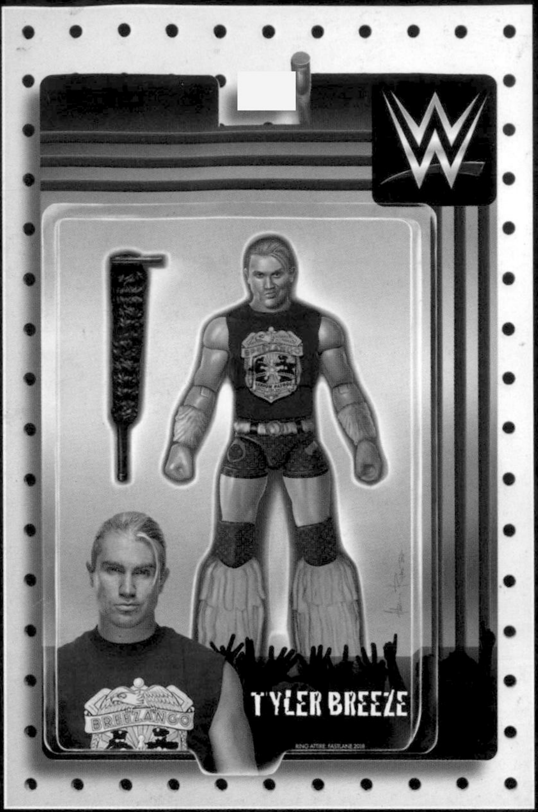
BREEZANGO
TYLER BREEZE

WWE #21
TYLER BREEZE

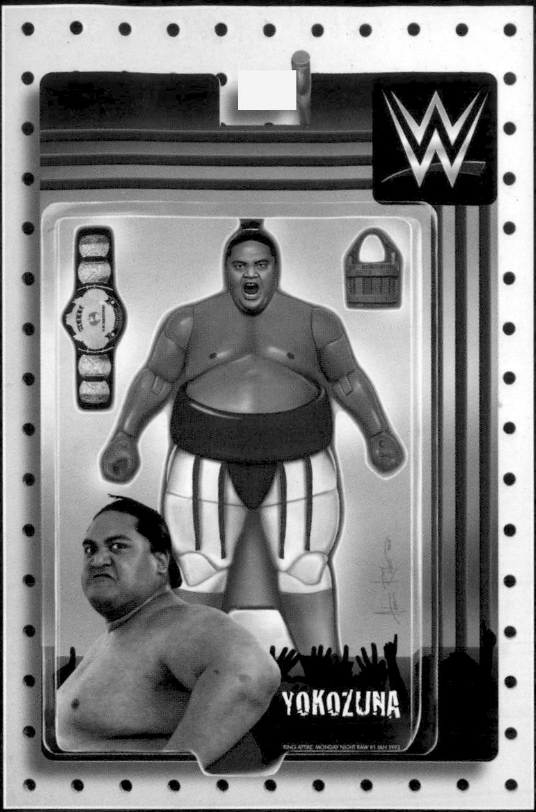
YOKOZUNA

WWE #22
YOKOZUNA

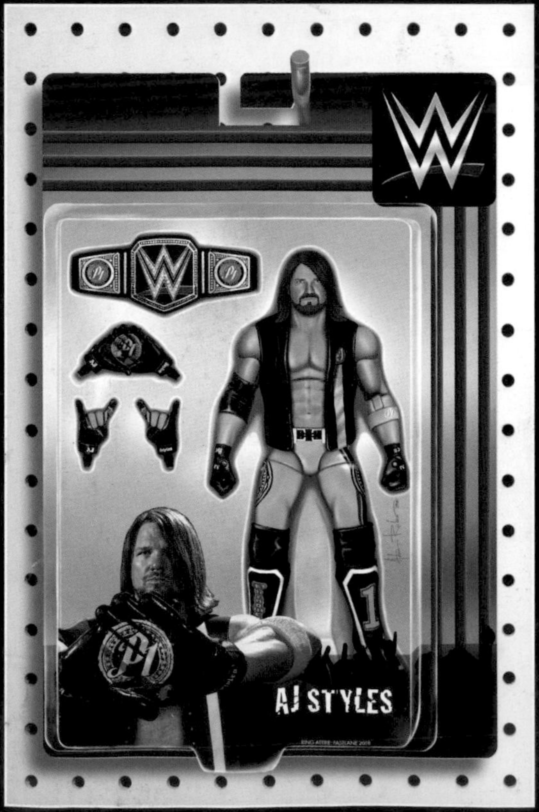
AJ STYLES

WWE #23
AJ STYLES

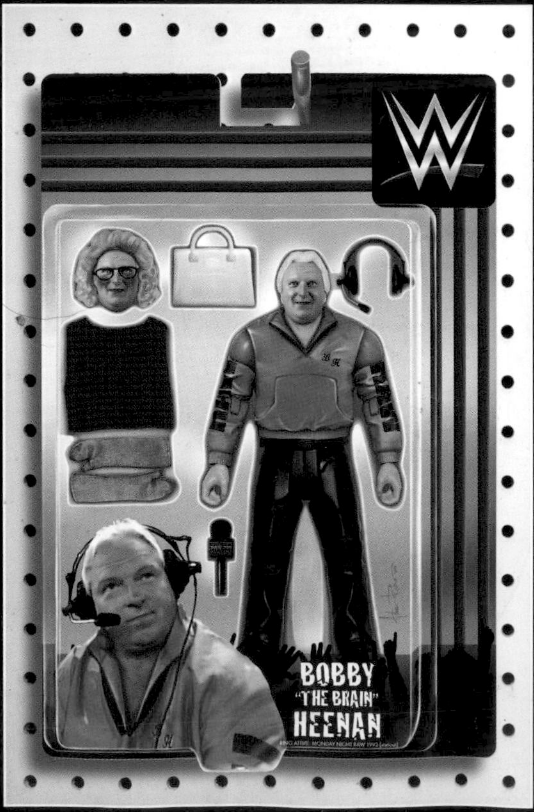
BOBBY
"THE BRAIN"
HEENAN

WWE #24
BOBBY "THE BRAIN" HEENAN